Culture/Clinic 1

APPLIED LACANIAN PSYCHOANALYSIS

"WE'RE ALL MAD HERE"

Culture/Clinic **1**
APPLIED LACANIAN PSYCHOANALYSIS
Jacques-Alain Miller and Maire Jaanus, *Editors*

Culture/Clinic is a series of books published by the University of Minnesota Press that brings the findings of Lacanian cultural studies and clinical practice to bear on one another. The series applies the methods of analysis to culture, isolating the new and present forms of the discontents of civilization and drawing on the strengths of the university and the clinic.

Culture/Clinic 1

APPLIED LACANIAN PSYCHOANALYSIS

Jacques-Alain Miller

Maire Jaanus

Editors

"WE'RE ALL MAD HERE"

MINNESOTA

University of Minnesota Press
Minneapolis • London

Published here for the first time in English, three articles by Jacques Lacan were published previously in the original French. "There Are Four Discourses" was published in *Ornicar?* 17/18 (1979): 278; "Yale University: Lecture on the Body" was published in *Scilicet* 6/7 (1976): 38–41; "Columbia University: Lecture on the Symptom" was published in *Scilicet*: 6/7 (1976): 42–52.

Published by the University of Minnesota Press
111 Third Avenue South, Suite 290
Minneapolis, MN 55401-2520
http://www.upress.umn.edu

Culture/Clinic is available online through JSTOR's Current Scholarship Program at http://jstor.org.

ISSN 2168-0981
eISSN 2168-099X
ISBN 978-0-8166-8319-2 (pbk. : alk. paper)

Printed in the United States of America on acid-free paper

20 19 18 17 16 15 14 13 10 9 8 7 6 5 4 3 2 1

Culture/Clinic **1**

The Analytic Experience

Cultural Fictions

Speaker's Corner

Editors' Introduction

MARIE-HÉLÈNE BROUSSE AND MAIRE JAANUS

Culture/Clinic: Two Different Fields but a Single Orientation

C/C THE SLASH IN *Culture/Clinic (C/C)* underlines the difference but also the proximity between these two entities. Both in France and the United States, psychoanalysis in the Lacanian orientation has developed in two directions: psychoanalysis applied to mental suffering and psychoanalysis applied to culture. *C/C* will be the site of a debate freed from what often becomes a paralyzing opposition between the individual and the social. Two cornerstones of Jacques Lacan's thought—"The unconscious is structured like a language" and "The social bond is a discourse"—allow a movement beyond this impasse. Lacan's reduction of the psychical apparatus to language, speech, and discourse renders this opposition untenable and enables culture and clinic, with their differing emphases, to focus on what is common to them both, the real of the symptom.

On June 16, 1971, in Seminar XVIII, Lacan underlined that the notion of "symptom," as defined in the nineteenth century by Freud and Marx, produced "an operation of subversion" in traditional knowledge (2006a, 164). This first properly psychoanalytic (rather than medical, philosophical, religious, or psychological) definition of the symptom turned the world of knowledge applied to human practices and affairs upside down. Symptoms disturb the plane of reality in the subject and the social world. They have contact with the real, from which alone change and new realities emerge. For the late Lacan, real history is made by those subjects who have found a way to handle and use their symptoms. Their discourse, "entwined around the void," as Lacan says, comes closest to not being a semblance. By contrast, the discourse of knowledge is a semblance, a "dupery," or terror, covering or negating the symptoms both on the subjective and historical planes.

Lacan's concept of "discourse" enables these two directions of the clinic and culture to overlap. In the four discourses, the symptom circulates with its effects on the body and on thought, creating resonances and soundings that seek both readdress and address. The analytic and hysteric discourses reveal how the analyst and analysand in the clinic may face and experience new symptoms, new desires, and new forms of *jouissance*, whereas the master and university discourses expose how other cultural writers and theorists may relate to developments in cultural, social, political, economic, and scientific fields. For the two directions within the Lacanian orientation, a series of original approaches to new formations in the subject, in society, politics, and the sciences have opened up from the symptomatic, unconscious knowledge born from analytic experience and research and their case histories. In Europe and particularly in France, this research was almost exclusively confined to the clinical and analytical world; in the United States, conversely, Lacanian psychoanalysis thrived largely, though not exclusively, in the academic environment of cultural studies. It seemed necessary to create a space in which American and European traditions would come into contact, encounter each other, where clinical experience and civilization—considered as a symptom—could exchange views. Universities are such places. *C/C* is therefore an academic journal for psychoanalysis in the Lacanian orientation, designed to welcome, as Lacan said, "the whorl into which [this] era draws [us] in the ongoing enterprise of Babel." We shall strive to be "interpreters in the strife of languages" (2006b, 264).

Therefore the slash in *C/C* means "with." But how are they articulated?

We hold that the analytic discourse cannot exist without the experience of the couch. It is its absolute condition, just as experimentation and calculation are the absolute conditions of experimental sciences. The couch is psychoanalysis's laboratory. Yet cultural productions teach analysts just as much as the texts produced by the free associations of analysands during the analytic treatment. In his "Hommage fait à Marguerite Duras" (2001), Lacan too acknowledged this when he wrote: we must "remember with Freud that in his domain the artist always precedes (the analyst) and that the analyst should not behave as a psychologist where the artist is paving the way. This is precisely what I recognize in the *Ravissement de Lol V. Stein*, in which it turns out that Marguerite Duras knows without me what I am teaching" (192–93). When we look at artworks or other creative and inventive practices, it is always in this spirit and according to the analytic method, the two poles of which are the signifying chain on the one hand, and the mode of jouissance on the other. These are the two, knotted forces of contradiction and truth that make the modern subject the paradoxical being that Shakespeare so preeminently dramatized. Jacques-Alain Miller, referring to Lacan's last teaching, names them the "unconscious of deciphering" and the "real unconscious." This is also the spirit in which we will apprehend the signifying elements organizing the current discourse of the master.

In interpreting the slash in *C/C*, we take inspiration from the matheme of the discourses: the slash (/) is the trait that separates S_1, the master-signifier, from *a*, the object that organizes modes of jouissance. *C/C* is therefore, as many of Lacan's logical cuts were, a space of conjunction and disjunction, a space simultaneously of cuts and knots. *C/C* is to be read as follows:

$$\frac{\text{Culture}}{\text{Clinic}} \qquad \frac{\text{master-signifier}}{\text{object } a} \qquad \text{and} \qquad \frac{\text{object } a}{\text{knowledge}} \qquad \frac{\text{Clinic}}{\text{Culture}}$$

If psychoanalysis is being taught by being receptive to the inventions and creations of analysands and artists (among others), what does it have to offer over and beyond the contributions of cultural studies? Lacan's contribution to the formation of analysts was to assert that analysts were not "taught and trained" by other analysts. Rather, analysts are trained (or not) by their own analyses. Such a self-authorization can be demonstrated through the procedure of the Pass. We can illustrate these points through the example of the TV series. What interests us in series is not to analyze them but the fact that they analyze us. First, they analyze the place of the analyst in our society (in *The Sopranos*, for example); second, they analyze the symptoms of the hypermodern subject (as in *Dexter*); third, they analyze the changing relation to language and codes (as in *The Wire*). The creators of the best TV series are outstanding clinicians, staging fragments of subjective discourses.

Last, the deliberately heterogeneous nature of contributions to *C/C* aims to oppose the formation of a standardized discourse on Lacanian psychoanalysis. *C/C*, inspired by Lacan's rejection of hierarchies within psychoanalytic institutions, will not discriminate between authors on the basis of their perceived competence. The journal is not driven by pedagogy but by the transmission of desire and its enigmas.

■ C/C ANATOMY

C/C is divided into four sections.

I. The Theme: "We're All Mad Here"

Every issue of *C/C* will focus on a central theme. For our first issue, we chose to discuss the proposition that "we are all mad here." At the age of global mental health and the *DSM (Diagnostic and Statistical Manual of Mental Disorders)*, when our ideal of universal normalcy is destroyed on a regular basis by the sheer reality of world events, psychoanalysis is with Lewis Carroll. Tim Burton made this very clear recently, with a brilliant clinical demonstration (in his film *Alice in Wonderland*, 2010). The articles collected here are nothing but realistic. They do not praise folly but state a plain fact: there is no such thing as mental health. There are only symptoms that fit more or less well with the different discourses that surround us as speaking beings.

Among these articles are three fundamental documents: three unpublished translations of interventions by Jacques Lacan. The first short text, initially published in *Ornicar?* in 1979, was written by Lacan as a defense of the presence of psychoanalysis in universities given that the analytic discourse cannot be taught. The context is that of the transfer from Vincennes to Saint-Denis for Paris VIII University, which hosted the first department of psychoanalysis in France. In this text Lacan counterpoises the analytic discourse to the university discourse and returns to the Freudian thesis according to which everyone is mad, that is, delusional. It sets the tone for the theme we have chosen for this first issue: "We're all mad here." The next text, "Lecture on the Body," is the first in Lacan's North American Universities conference series, delivered in 1975 at Yale University. Here, Lacan explores the status of the body as a "bubble of air, a bag of skin," an imaginary figure dealing with real material. Lacan brings in Borromean topology to address the question of what knots the heterogeneous dimensions at play for man, dimensions attested to in the analytic experience. Freud's id is the real; the symbolic has to do with the hole; the body is imagined. The fourth element has to do with the symptom. In "Lecture on the Symptom," delivered at Columbia University, Lacan returns to the idea of truth starting from the place of the analytic discourse as a *dit-mension*—"the place where *un dit*, a saying, resides." He develops the idea that an act of saying is an act of saying the truth. Truth has the structure of fiction, and it is because truth has the structure of fiction that the whole truth cannot be said. Lacan proposes "speaking being" as an appropriate name for the unconscious, which has nothing to do with instinct and everything to do with the signifier, a term that privileges the sound of the word over its sense.

In 2007–8, Jacques-Alain Miller delivered, as he does every year, his public research seminar, *L'Orientation lacanienne,* which he calls his *Cours.* The text published here makes up the last two sessions. It is in these sessions that he finds, retrospectively, by returning to Lacan's 1979 proposition according to which everyone is mad, that is, delusional, the title for his own teaching of that year: "Everyone Is Mad." Miller presents this proposition as a compass for reading Lacan's late work, and for today's clinical practice: this sentence signals that we live and practice in a time no longer ordered by the Name-of-the-Father. He then engages in a line-by-line commentary of the short text in which Lacan utters such a proposition and draws a number of theoretical consequences with regard to knowledge and truth, jouissance and being, the universal and the not-all.

Maire Jaanus's "Happiness and Madness" explores the difference between happiness, master-signifier of our culture, and desire, the structure of which unfolds in analysis. Through a reading of the key references of Western civilization on satisfaction, ethics, enjoyment, and madness—St. Augustine, Aristotle, Plato, Cervantes, Hofmannsthal, Erasmus, and so on—Jaanus exposes the enduring stupidity of enjoying substance beyond the grimacing mask of happiness best represented by the smiley icon of our times. She concludes with a useful distinction between insanity and madness: that we are all mad does not mean that we are all insane.

Pierre-Gilles Guéguen's "Who Is Mad and Who Is Not? On Differential Diagnosis in Psychoanalysis" points out that traditional psychiatric nosography is rapidly disappearing because of the *DSM,* soon to undermine even further the constructs that constituted a common ground for psychoanalysts and psychiatrists in the nineteenth and twentieth centuries. In Lacanian psychoanalysis the issue of diagnosis has always played an important part. The classical period of Lacan's teaching primarily focused on neurosis. Psychosis was studied starting from the theory of neurosis. By contrast, Lacan's late teaching took into consideration the large spectrum of different psychoses and set neurosis apart as one of a kind: it recognizes the Name-of-the-Father as a *sinthome.* Many forms of psychosis will never trigger because they are based on another form of sinthome invented by the subject. We call them "ordinary psychoses." And extraordinary psychoses, which include loss of reality and severe delusions, are to be reconsidered in this light. This article explains why.

In "Treating the Wolf Man as a Case of Ordinary Psychosis," Russell Grigg argues that there are indications in Ruth Mack Brunswick's account of her analysis of the Wolf Man that sometime after the analysis with

Freud an underlying psychosis, undetected by Freud, had been triggered. The discreet nature of both this onset and the accompanying psychotic phenomena becomes comprehensible if we regard the Wolf Man as a case of ordinary psychosis, as elaborated by J.-A. Miller on the basis of Lacan's final contributions to the study of psychosis. Mack Brunswick's analysis also raises some questions about the handling of the transference. She is, Grigg argues, enmeshed in rivalry with the Wolf Man in relation to Freud, and this leads to an interpretation in the imaginary, with serious consequences.

In "And, as in uffish thought he stood," Sophie Marret-Maleval proposes that for Lacan the import of Lewis Carroll's work arises from the conjunction of the position of the poet with that of the mathematician. The *Alice* books are a product of the scientific era. They celebrate it through fiction and question it both. Carroll's language mathematizes itself; neologisms are letters that break with the author's conception of language. Nonsense is part of the scientific era, anticipating the Saussurian definition of language as a differential sign system, going further than the author's conservative Aristotelian position on logic. The unconscious knowledge in Carroll's texts bears upon the real. "Carroll illustrates and even proves all sorts of truths, truths which are certain although not obvious" ([1966] 2002, 9). These truths have to do with the truth of the unconscious, which cannot be known by means of science. Carroll's mathematicized fictions point to the residue of language and the subjective division.

Finally, in "*Memento:* Elementary Phenomena and the Delusion of Interpretation," Jonathan D. Redmond uses Lacan's theory of psychosis to construct a reading of the film *Memento* (2000). The Lacanian concepts of psychotic structure, elementary phenomena, and the construction of a delusion are central to understanding the behavior and actions of the film's protagonist, Leonard. By theorizing *Memento* in terms of psychotic phenomena, as opposed to repetitive memory loss, the viewer is better equipped to understand the significance of Leonard's self-reported neurological "condition." Specifically, psychotic elementary phenomena, meaningless signifiers that are imposed on the subject producing perplexity and confusion, are exemplified in Leonard's self-tattooing. Moreover, his certainty that the tattoos provide clues for tracking down his wife's killer demonstrates how delusional thinking is an interpretative mechanism that is continuous with, and that emerges from, psychotic elementary phenomena.

II. The Analytic Experience

This section will be a permanent feature of all subsequent *C/C* issues. Psychoanalysis is first and foremost a subjective experience. However, the difficulty lies in the conditions under which this unique, intimate, and singular experience is to be transmitted, given that, ethically speaking, the anonymity of patients has to be safeguarded. In psychoanalysis, the personal analysis is part of the training. A field of analytic knowledge to be developed lies in personal testimonies. The analytic experience characterizes psychoanalysis and singles out the knowledge that results from it. This section, which some of our first readers called "awful pieces," will bring the knowledge derived from the analytic experience to the fore. Psychoanalysis is a lived experience, an exercise in improvisation that counterpoises the *tuchè,* the unexpected, the encounter, to the *automaton* of the unconscious's signifying logic and the repetition that makes it a chain. Because it is an intimate experience, and because psychoanalysis protects privacy and secrecy, the authors of the cases published here are the patients themselves. All three testimonies deal with the way each analysand entered the analytic experience. They teach us about the place of the object in the emergence of transference. They testify to their gains in knowledge, to the tailored therapeutic solutions they came up with, and to how a subject can change in the analytic experience. They practice the difficult art of transmission, and in so doing they demonstrate how a subject can be "perfectly calculable." They are pieces of the unconscious, however "awful" that may be.

Heather Chamberlain's "Entering Analysis" explores the nature of the transference that allowed her to enter and continue analysis with two different analysts after she was given a cancer diagnosis. She looks back on the fantasy that she had something to give her analysts as what enabled her to speak to an other and shows how she was able to recognize her own symptomatic position. David Hafner's "The Art of Skipping Sessions and the Gift of Anxiety" narrates the symptom of hypersomnia, a "feigned autistic coma" that brought him to analysis in the first place. He shows how an interpretation from the analyst produced an effect of awakening but highlights what is at stake in his analysis: to sustain his desire long enough to not fall asleep again. France Jaigu's "Two Layers of Time: Experiencing the First Session" examines the relationship among psychoanalysis, storytelling, and chronological time. She evokes, dwelling on her own experience, how she discovered the poetry of free association that links past and present and defeats what Holden Caulfield, the hero of Salinger's *The Catcher in the Rye,* aptly pins down as "all that David Copperfield kind of crap."

III. Cultural Fictions

The third section engages with our culture and our times through its many languages but also the accumulation of contemporary objects that crystallize jouissance. As Lacan put it in his "Hommage à Marguerite Duras" (2001), "the artist is always one step ahead of the analyst," (192) clearing the way. This is key to the Lacanian orientation in applied psychoanalysis. Psychoanalysis, since Freud the discipline of interpretative practice, has a profound kinship with the arts: literature, cinema, theater, television, painting, visual arts, architecture, ballet . . . all are different ways of extracting the place of the object that causes desire. But also, they are different discourses elaborated to circumscribe the changes in the modes of jouissance that drive human interactions, the foundations of any economy and politics.

In its first issue, *C/C* broaches the global phenomenon of TV series, a form of contemporary fiction that has taken the world by storm. Focusing on *The Wire,* the most sophisticated of all series, Gérard Wajcman and Laurent Goumarre in their articles argue that these fictions now constitute our reality and that they have modified our narrative forms. We know that fiction is one of the faces of truth, and we know that there are as many languages as there are series. This time, if we were to speak the *Wire*-rap, the title of the section would be "All in the Game, Yo!" Couch or sofa? Go figure.

In "Three Notes to Introduce the Form of the Series," Gérard Wajcman argues that the series, especially the American TV series, is the narrative form of hypermodernity, as opposed to the Freudian narratives, which were narratives of subjects. By contrast to the Freudian romance, the form "series" is characterized by the triumph of the object, of the fragment and of the city, and by the defeat of psychology. In "Quit Laughing! A Sofa Gets Tossed Out!" Laurent Goumarre offers a retrospective reading of the successful TV series of the past two decades *(Friends, Married . . . with Children, The Nanny, Who's the Boss?).* Goumarre uncovers the relationship between canned laughter and the position the TV audience is placed in. The motif of the sofa thus emerges as a metaphor of the subversive nature of the HBO series *The Wire.*

We have conceived of *C/C* itself as such a series, the form which in hypermodernity replaces narrative and demonstration.

IV. Speaker's Corner

This is our wild card section. *C/C* gives the floor to original and rigorous research carried out in the psychoanalytic field. The editors want a voice to be heard: the voice of a researcher who, at the time of standardization, retains its singularity in order to bring forth new ideas. Because "we are all mad" in this first issue, the first article to be published in this section is Laura's Sokolowsky's "The First Center for Psychoanalytic Consultation." In her study of the Berlin Policlinic, the first institution to attempt to cure "the masses" with psychoanalysis, Sokolowsky points out that in September 1918, Freud affirmed the necessity of creating free psychoanalytic centers to treat people who couldn't afford to pay. His discourse influenced the action of European psychoanalysts during the Weimar Republic, and the first psychoanalytic Policlinic opened in Berlin in 1920. It was soon to be followed by a training institute for analysts. Principles for a standard treatment and for the formation of analysts were progressively developed in what was a world center for psychoanalysis in the 1920s. Yet it was also there that the formation of analysts was standardized, something that Lacan was critical of.

The issue concludes with an interview with Ethan Watters, the author of *Crazy Like Us: The Globalization of the American Psyche (2010). Crazy Like Us* is a journalistic account of symptoms [such as anorexia, post-traumatic stress disorder (PTSD), schizophrenia, and clinical depression] and their treatments in Hong Kong, Sri Lanka, Zanzibar, and Japan, respectively, inspired by anthropological methods. Through four case studies Watters demonstrates the inadequacy of the *DSM* in treating mental illnesses it had no part in constructing culturally. In this interview he answers a series of epistemological questions from the editors of *Culture/Clinic* as to his working hypotheses: his conception of the symptom, its relation to the social bond, the status of science. Watters's answers privilege the importance of culture on shaping mental illnesses over biological determinism and challenge the "universal" status of scientific knowledge. We believe that his work resonates with our first theme, in that it challenges the supposed scientific neutrality of the mental health diagnoses currently in use in the United States, and by extension throughout the world, by demonstrating how culturally embedded symptoms are.

Dear readers, please keep in mind that this journal also welcomes your contributions, reactions, and opinions. Inspired by Jacques Lacan's passion for the real, we designed it so that it would be a place for debate and controversy. Please join us in our striving to be "interpreters in the strife of languages" in "the whorl into which [this] era draws [us] in the ongoing enterprise of Babel." C/C

BIBLIOGRAPHY

Lacan, Jacques. 2001. *Autres Écrits*. Paris: Seuil.

———. 2006a. *D'un discours qui ne serait pas du semblant, Le Séminaire Livre XVIII*. Paris: Seuil.

———. 2006b. *Écrits: The First Complete Edition in English*. New York: Norton.

Watters, Ethan. 2010. *Crazy Like Us: The Globalization of the American Psyche*. New York: Free Press.

"WE'RE ALL MAD HERE"

JACQUES LACAN

There Are Four Discourses

TRANSFER TO SAINT DENIS? LACAN IS FOR VINCENNES!

THERE ARE FOUR DISCOURSES. Each one thinks it is the truth. The only exception is the analytic discourse. We would be better off if it did dominate, people will conclude, but in point of fact this discourse excludes domination; in other words it teaches nothing. There is nothing universal about it, which is precisely why it cannot be taught.

How does one go about teaching what cannot be taught? This is something Freud ventured into. He thought that all is but a dream and that everyone (if one can say such a thing), that everyone is mad, that is, delusional.

This is indeed what the very first step in the direction of teaching demonstrates.

But it does still need to be demonstrated: for this any old object will do, it always presents itself poorly. That is, it needs to be rectified.

Mathematics is for that: rectifying the object. It is a fact that mathematics rectifies and that what it rectifies is the object itself.

Hence my reduction of psychoanalysis to set theory.

Might the antipathy between the university and analytic discourses be overcome at Vincennes? Certainly not. It is being put to work there; at least it has been for the four years I have been observing. It is apparent there that, by coming up against its own impossibility, teaching is refreshed.

Let me set out what these four years have produced in the Department of Psychoanalysis:

- A journal, *Ornicar?*, that debates what is being published everywhere in the name of psychoanalysis
- A postgraduate program in the so-called Freudian Field, in which it behooves psychoanalysis to rectify what is offered it as cognate

- A Clinical Section, which, at the Henri-Rousselle Hospital, is fulfilling its role of instructing young psychiatrists

A positive report. The experiment will therefore continue. At Vincennes, so long as it has the freedom to do so. If ever it gets restricted, then out of the university!

JACQUES LACAN
This 22-10-78

As a matter of fact, I hope Edgar Faure will do what it takes for Vincennes, that is, Paris VIII, his creation, to remain.
J.L. c/c

NOTE

This essay was originally published in *Ornicar?* 17/18 (1979): 278. It has been translated from the French by Adrian Price with Russell Grigg.

JACQUES LACAN

Yale University: Lecture on the Body

HYSTERICS PRODUCE KNOWLEDGE. An hysteric is an effect, just as any subject is. Hysterics force "signifying matter" to confess, by virtue of which they constitute a discourse.

Socrates is the one who started it. He wasn't a hysteric, but something much worse—a subtle master. That didn't stop him from having hysterical symptoms. He would sometimes remain standing on one leg, unable to move, there was no way of drawing him out of what we call "catatonia." And this didn't prevent him from having lots of effects. Just as an hysteric would, he would deliver anyone's knowledge—knowledge that, in short, he himself was unaware of.

That resembles what Freud, rather late in the piece, called the "unconscious." In his own way, Socrates wasn't such a bad analyst.

A slave is defined by the fact that someone has power over his or her body. Geometry is the same thing; it has a lot to do with bodies.

A body has the property of being able to be seen, poorly seen. People think of it as a bubble of air, a bag of skin. Here one is dealing with a support, a figure (of the imaginary, that is), with a material that I posit as real.

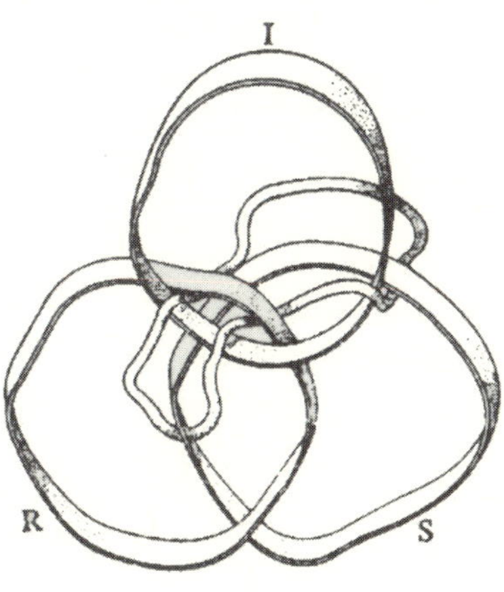

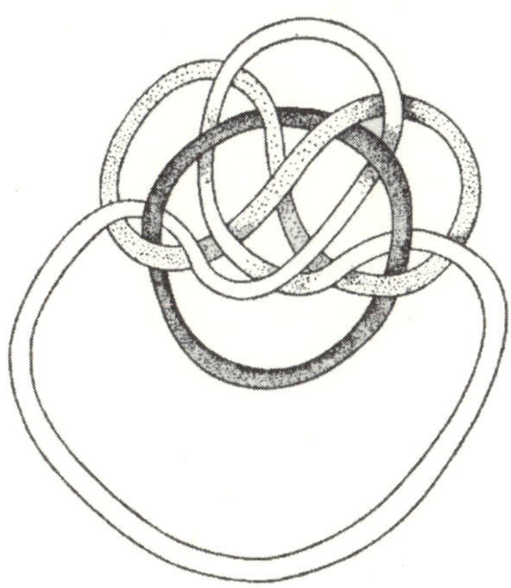

How would a slave have reacted?

Slaves knew that the master would set a price on their body; they were property, and in itself this protected them. A slave would know that the master wasn't about to carve up his body: small chance his body would end up fragmented. He thereby knew himself to be safe from a good many things.

R, S, and *I* are entirely independent of one another. If you draw *S* back, really far back, then the knot will end up pulling on *R* at four points—which no doubt could all draw closer together—though that requires that *I* is pulling on *S;* thus, you have the following:

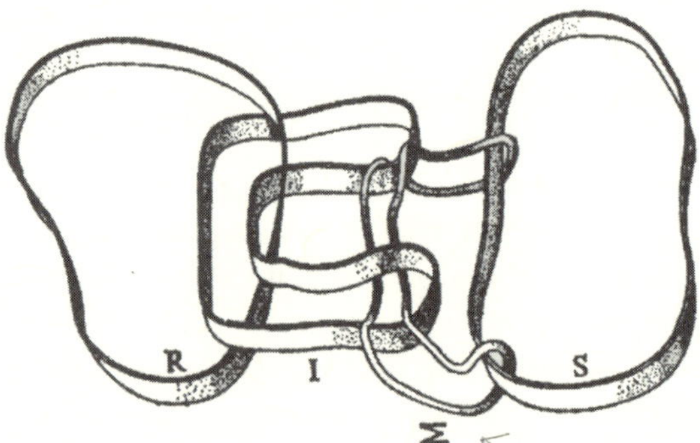

Ce qu'on dit ment. What one says lies—*condiment.* The fourth ring is the symptom.

Between the body insofar as it is imagined and what binds it (namely, the fact of speaking), man imagines himself as thinking. He thinks in so far as he speaks. Speaking has effects on his body. Owing to the fact that he speaks, he is almost as clever as an animal. An animal gets by very well without speaking.

The real—merely introducing the term makes one wonder what one is saying. The real is not the outside world; it is anatomy too, it involves the entire body.

The question is how all of that knots together.

The minimum requirement was that each of these three terms—imaginary, symbolic (that is, chit-chat), and real—should have been strictly equal to one another, tied in such a way that the parts are equal.

I have been striving to produce another geometry that comes to grips with what's going on in the chain. This has never, ever been done.

This geometry is not imaginary, unlike the geometry of triangles; it's a geometry of the real, of rings of string.

Suppose if you will that the body, chit-chat, and the real each go off on their own, wandering about. . . .

Freud's id is the real.

The symbolic, which the superego comes under, has to do with the hole.

If a fourth element is required, it is what the symbolic, in so far as it forms a circle with the unconscious, brings about.

If we want to put the real and the imaginary at each end, we get:

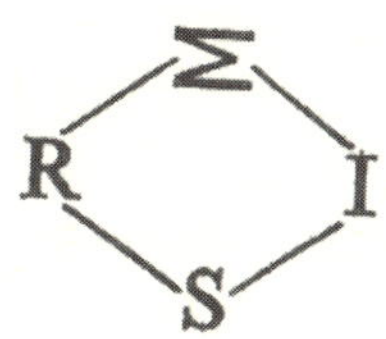

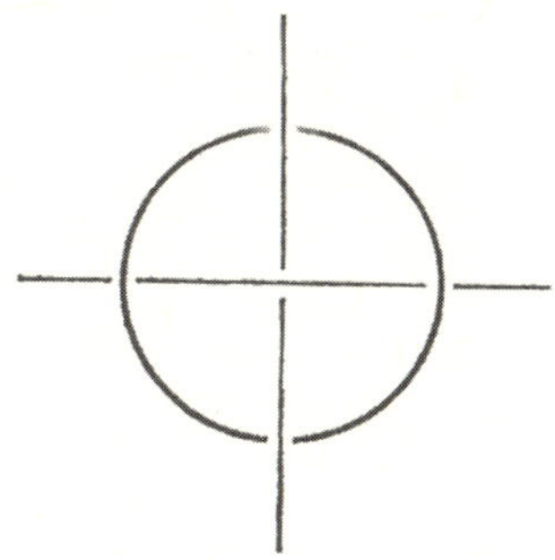

If you raise a horizontal bar or if you pull the vertical line to the right or to the left, you find yourself wedged in. This makes a knot.

The straight line is equivalent to a ring of string if one presupposes it has an infinite point.

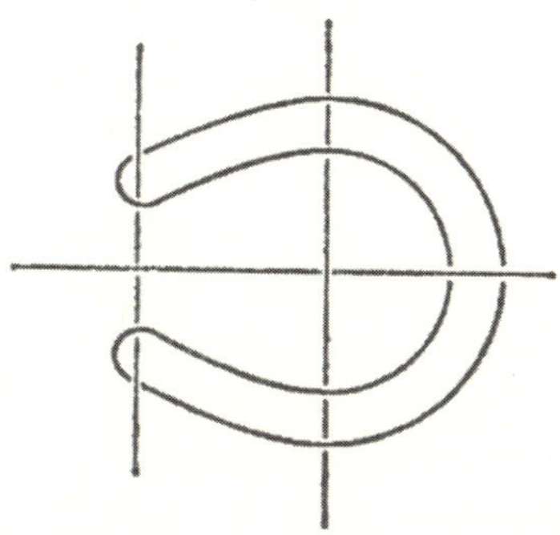

Their symptom is the most real thing that many people have. For some people, you could say: the symbolic, the imaginary, and the symptom.

Phallic jouissance lies at the joint between the symbolic and the real, outside the imaginary, outside the body, as a parasite on the sexual organs.

NOTE

This lecture was delivered on November 25, 1975, at the Law School Auditorium, Yale University. The text was originally published in French in *Scilicet* 6/7 (1976): 38–41. The translation is by Adrian Price with Russell Grigg.

JACQUES LACAN

Columbia University: Lecture on the Symptom

IN ANALYSIS, there are nonetheless, it must be said, certain results. They are not always what we expect; and this is because we are wrong to expect, which is the difficulty of being an analyst.

I tried to spell out something about analysts, which I called the "analytic discourse." The analytic discourse exists because it's the analysand who supports it . . . fortunately. His fortune—the fortune that is sometimes his good fortune, the good fortune of having met an analyst. This doesn't always happen. Analysts often believe that the philosopher's stone of his trade, as it were, consists in remaining silent. What I'm saying is well known. Even so, it's wrong, a deviation, that analysts should speak so little.

As it happens, I conduct what are known as "supervisions." I don't know why it came to be called supervision. It's a super-audition. I mean it's very surprising that on hearing what a practitioner has told you, through what he tells you, you can form a representation about the person in analysis, who is an analysand. It's a new dimension.

I'll speak shortly about this fact, the *dit*-mension that I don't spell exactly as it is usually spelled in French. The best thing would be for me to go to the effort of showing you how I spell it—dit-mension. That's how I spell it—dit-mension—*mention/mansion,* that is, in English, I mean—*mention,* the place where *un dit,* a saying, resides.

So, nevertheless, an analyst does have things to say. He has things to say to his analysand, to the one who, all the same, hasn't come along simply to be confronted by his analyst's silence. What the analyst has to say belongs to the order of truth. I don't know whether you get anything very tangible with truth. I mean—whether you have an idea of what truth is. Every discourse implies at least one place that is the place of truth. What

I call a discourse is in reference to a social bond. Analysis is of this order. With the qualification that, as it's quite new, because, after all, it doesn't go back all that far, it comprises a pact. An analysand knows that the analyst will expect him so many times a week and that, in principle, he is required to attend. Otherwise, the analyst—even if he doesn't come—will demand his fee. Naturally, this implies that the analyst has his duties, too. He has to be there.

When does truth begin? It begins when you start to use sentences. A sentence is an act of saying *[un dire]*. And this act of saying is one of *saying the truth*.

Somewhere I said—not just said, but wrote, There is a nuance. . . . There's more than a nuance; there's a mountain between saying and writing. The proof is that people consider themselves much more confident of a promise when it's in writing. As in a note that is an "IOU," for instance. This note lends support to the truth of the promise. It would be hard to imagine someone saying, "That note isn't mine." In any case, that's when the experts step in, namely the graphologists who say, "Yes, that's the same handwriting alright," which proves that writing also has something individual about it. But writing hasn't always existed. Beforehand, there was the oral tradition. This didn't prevent things from being transmitted from mouth to mouth. The origin of the principle of poetry lies there.

I've stated a number of points about what truth is. It's a defensible proposition to say that truth has the structure of fiction. This is what is normally called "myth"—many truths have a mythical existence—it is precisely for this reason that truth cannot be exhausted, that the whole truth cannot be said. This is what I stated in the following form—truth can only be half said. One speaks the truth as best one can, that is, in part. It is just that in the way it presents itself, it presents itself as a whole. And that's precisely where the difficulty lies—it's that you have to make the one who is in analysis sense that this truth is not whole, that it's not true for everyone, that it isn't—this is an old idea—that it isn't general, that it's not valid for everyone.

How is such a thing as that there are analysts possible? The thing is only possible due to the fact that the analysand is made aware—as it were—of a rule to be observed, to say only what he might have to say, only what is close to his heart, as we say. This echoes—but it's not because a thing is an echo that it is singled out—this echoes a very old idea of what the center of the being known as human used to be, the one they used to call *anthropos*. The center was the heart—*thumos*—at the very least that's how it used to be designated. What you had *on your chest*, in your heart, was *epithumia*. But it was a conception that gave man a privilege. There were two kinds of man. The one who was specified as being from a *polis* (π, ό, λ, ι, ς), as being a citizen—he alone was a human being who enjoyed full rights. Of course, all this has become blurred. It is still the case, however, that the relationship known as *political* goes on existing throughout the different structures. It exists more solidly than any other, nevertheless.

I've opened the way to something I've called "the saying of the truth." Before the candidate went into analysis, the analyst informed him that he would have to say everything. What does it mean to say everything? It doesn't make sense. It can only mean "Say any old thing whatever." In point of fact, that's what happens. It's how you enter into analysis. The strange thing is that something in the order of an inertia, a polarization, an orientation occurs. The analysand—if the analysis is functioning, if it's moving forward—comes to speak in an increasingly focused way, focused on something that has always stood in opposition to the *polis*—in the sense of the city—and that is, namely, one's own particular family. This inertia that means that a subject only ever speaks about mum or dad is nevertheless a strange business. It's strange that this tendency should ensue, that this should happen, that it should end up behaving like water, making a river, a river of return to that by which one clings to one's family, namely, childhood. It may be said that this explains the fact that an analyst only intervenes by way of a particular truth, because a child is not an abstract child. He has had a history, and a history that is specified by this particularity. It's not the same thing to have had your own mum and not your neighbor's mum. The same goes for your dad.

A dad is not at all what he's reckoned to be. He's really not necessarily the one who had this child with that woman. In many cases there's no guarantee whatsoever, given that, after all, a good many things can happen to a woman, especially if she gets around a bit. That's why Dad is really not necessarily the one who, as it were, is the father in the real sense, in the sense of animal life. The father is a function that refers to the real, and this is not necessarily the truth of the real. This doesn't prevent the real of the father being absolutely fundamental in analysis. The father's mode of existence stems from this real. It's the only case where the real is stronger than the true. Let's say that the real, too, can be mythical. This doesn't change the fact that, for the structure, it is just as important as any true statement *[dire]*. The real lies in this direction.

It's very worrying. It's very worrying that there is a real that is mythical, and it's very much for this reason that Freud clung so strongly to the father's function in his doctrine.

Well, so far I've been speaking slowly so that you might at least hear a few fundamental truths, but I have to tell you this: as I've been teaching for an excessively long time, I don't even remember anymore what I said the first time round, some twenty-two years ago, which you will find reproduced in *Seminar I*, and which has already been published as a reproduction of my seminar. I trust the stenographer, and also the person who was prepared to make sure that everything got put into his own French. He's very good, one of my immediate kin, and is quite prepared to undertake this task.

What I said at the outset concerning saying, the saying of truth, has been taught us by our practice. And I started, in what I was just stating, I started with this—an analysis is a part-said, with parts for someone who speaks, but who has been informed that his chatter is important[, and an analyst]. You know there are people one deals with in analysis with whom this is hard to obtain. There are those for whom saying a few words isn't so easy. It is what is known as autism. This is easily said. It's really not necessarily that at all. They are simply people for whom the weight of words is very serious and who are not easily disposed to feeling comfortable with these words.

I sometimes have to respond to cases like these in that famous supervision I mentioned earlier, which, more straightforwardly, we call *contrôle* in French—which doesn't mean of course that we think we are controlling anything. As far as I am concerned, often in my *contrôles*—at least at the beginning—I rather encourage analysts—or him or her who thinks he or she is one—I encourage them to follow their movement. I don't think it is for no reason—not that they should put themselves in this position, that's very little controlled—but I don't think it's for no reason that someone should come and tell someone something simply by virtue of the fact that he was told this person was an analyst. It's not for no reason, because he expects to get something from it.

And now, what we have to understand is how what I've just roughly sketched out is able to function in such a way that, nonetheless, the social bond constituted by analysis may progress and carry on. That's where I took a stand and I said—in something where, on the one hand, there's someone who's speaking without the slightest concern for self-contradiction, and then, on the other, someone who doesn't speak—because, most of the time, you have to let the person who is there for something speak—when he speaks, he's supposed to say the truth. But not any old truth; the truth that the analysand must hear. That the analysand must hear—whatever for? For what he expects, namely, to be free of his symptom.

What is implied by the fact that in speaking someone is freed of his symptom? It assumes that a symptom and this kind of intervention by the analyst—it seems to me that this is the minimum one can assert—are of the same order. Symptoms also say something. A symptom says something, and it is another form of truthful saying. All in all, what the analyst does is try to do a little more than skip over it. This is precisely why analysis, analytic theory, uses a term like *resistance*. Symptoms resist. This is not something that goes away by itself. But to present an analysis as being something like a duel would also be quite contrary to the truth. That's precisely why I've tried—over time, it didn't come along straight away—to construct something that accounts for what goes on in an analysis. I don't have the slightest "conception of the world," as they say. The world is that charming little shell in the center of which one places a precious stone, that unique thing that man is supposed to be. Man is supposed to have—given this scheme of things—these things that palpitate within him—an inner world. And then the world itself is said to be an outside world. I really don't believe that this is adequate. I really don't believe that there is an inner world that is the reflection of the outside world, nor the contrary either. I've tried to formulate something that incontestably presupposes a more complicated organization. If we say—we analysts—that there is an unconscious, this is based on experience.

The experience consists in the fact that from the origins there has been a relationship with *lalangue* that deserves to be called, rightly, the mother tongue, because it's from the mother that the child, as it were, receives it. He doesn't learn it. There's an inclination. It's surprising to see how early on it is that a child handles things as notably grammatical as the use of the words *maybe* or *not yet*. Of course, he's heard that, but that he should understand the meaning of it is something that deserves all our attention.

In language, there is something that is structured. Linguists confine themselves to this, making apparent the structure called "grammatical." And that the child should be so comfortable in it, that so early on he should familiarize himself with the use of a structure that—it's not for nothing that it was ascertained there, but in an elaborated fashion—is what are called "rhetorical figures," signals that grammar isn't taught to him. Grammar is developed on the basis of what is already operating as speech. This is not its most characteristic feature. If I've been saying, "The unconscious is structured like a language," it's because I want to maintain that *a* language is not language *per se*. There is something in language per se that is already too general, too logical.

It is the entire system, present as if it were innate, that the child plays in relation to one of his mother's departure with the statement that so struck Freud—from one of his grandchildren's utterances—*Fort-Da*. This is where it all gets inserted. This *Fort-Da* is already a rhetorical figure.

Someone by whom I was rather surprised to have been quoted, because I didn't even know he knew me—clearly he knows me through Paul de Man, who welcomed me at Yale, and who of course I can only be grateful to for all the care he has taken to open the way for me to travel to the Americas—but, all the same, I'm surprised that so many people should after all be saying certain things that really aren't that far from what I've been saying. It happens like that, in different places, a kind of whirlwind, a way of speaking that is what I personally call "style." I don't have a "conception of the world," but I have a style, one that, naturally, isn't altogether easy. But that's the whole problem. What is a style? What is a thing? What is the way in which a style is situated and characterized? For my part, at the time when I only used to speak with my colleagues, the most natural thing was to say, "It's not exactly that," and if what I wrote after saying it, elaborating on what I said, is at all distinctive, it's because it carries the mark of my attempt to grasp as tightly as possible what *that* is, *exactly*.

Of course, it's not easy; it's not easy to start off, as, for example, the structuralists do, with a division between nature and culture. Culture is what I have been trying to quarter into the form of four discourses, but of course it's not limited to these. Discourse is what floats, what skims across the surface of our own politics, I mean, our way of conceiving of a certain social bond. If the bond was a purely political one, we have added something else to it. We have added the discourse called the "university discourse," and the discourse called "scientific," which are not to be confused, contrary to what one might imagine. It is not for nothing that special faculties have been set aside in the academic field for the scientific discourse. It's kept at a distance, but not for nothing. Somewhere I have shown that there is a relationship, which is not insignificant, between scientific discourse and hysteric discourse. That might seem strange—except for a certain chain of certain functions that I've defined by employing a certain S_1 and a certain S_2, which don't have the same function, and also a certain S that I call the "subject" and a certain "object" *(a)*, except for a certain order of rotation of these four functions—scientific discourse is only distinct from hysteric discourse by the order in which all of that is distributed.

All of this has resulted in something that can be drawn using several different colors. I believed I could link the symbolic—that's this one here, the arbitrary one—the real and the imaginary.

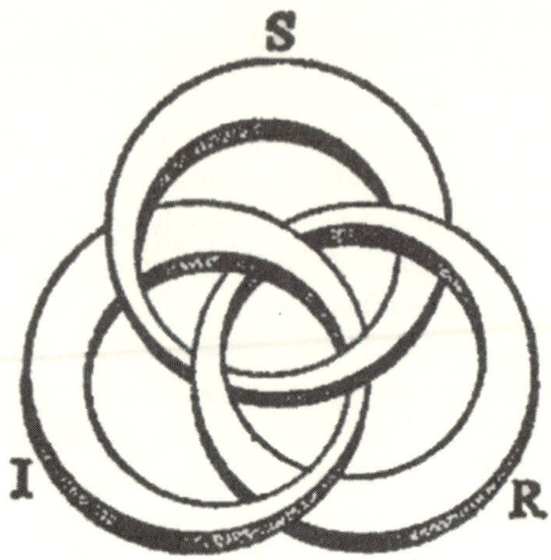

How is it that, having distinguished this symbolic, this imaginary, and this real from one another, and having specified them by the fact that the symbolic is our bond with language, based on this distinction, we are speaking *beings?* It's viciously circular to say that we are speaking beings, *êtres parlants*. We are *parlêtres*—a word it would be advantageous to substitute for the unconscious, equivocating, as it does, on *parleying*, on the one hand, and on the fact that *it's from language* that we get this crazy idea that there is being, on the other—for it is certain that we believe in it, we believe in it because of everything that appears to make for substance. But in what way is this being, apart from the fact that language uses the verb *to be?* It uses the verb *to be*, but only moderately. A man might say that he *is* a body, and this would make a lot of sense, for it's obvious that the fact he consists of a body is, for him, what is the most certain thing about him. A few doubts have been cast on the existence of an outside world in the name of the fact that, after all, we only ever have perceptions of it. But it is sufficient to get—as I did earlier—to get a bump on the head by running into something hard, for it to be quite obvious that there are things that resist, that there are things that don't move so easily. On the other hand, what man insists on is not that he is a body, but, as he expresses it—and this is something quite striking—*that he has one.*

In the name of what can he say that he has a body? In the name of the fact that he treats it any old how, he treats it like a piece of furniture. He puts it in a train carriage, for instance, and lets himself get carted around. That too was nevertheless true; it started when he began putting it in carts. So, I would like to say that this history of the *parlêtre* is encountered with this other apprehension of the body, and it's not self-evident. I mean that a body has another way of consisting than what I was just referring to as a spoken form, in the form of the unconscious, in so far as it is from speech, as such, that it emerges. These are marks whose trace we can see in the unconscious. These are marks that have been left by a certain way of relating to knowledge that constitutes the fundamental substance of the unconscious. We imagine that the unconscious is something like an instinct, but this isn't true. We utterly lack any instinct whatsoever, and the way we react isn't linked to an instinct but to certain knowledge conveyed not so much by words as by what I call "signifiers." Signifiers, they are what is said—there's a much more profound rhetoric of course—they are what lends itself to equivocation. Interpretation must always, on the analyst's side, take into account that, in what is said, there is the sonorous element. And this has to be consonant with the unconscious.

There's something important in this way of representing the bond—the bond among the symbolic, the imaginary, and the real—and here's what it is. It is that we are not necessarily to lie these three terms out flat. The body, of course, also has a shape, a shape we think of as spherical, but we must also know how to draw things differently.

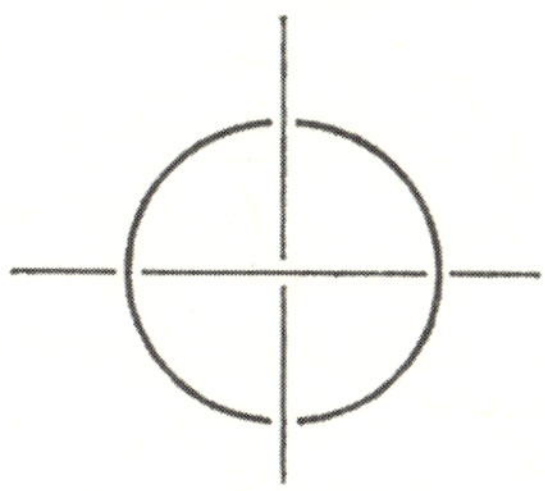

As you can see, it's remarkable that for an object as familiar to me as you can imagine this way of drawing the knot to be, I am obliged to use a piece of paper. That means that it's not so natural as all that to draw it like that. This, then, is a knot.

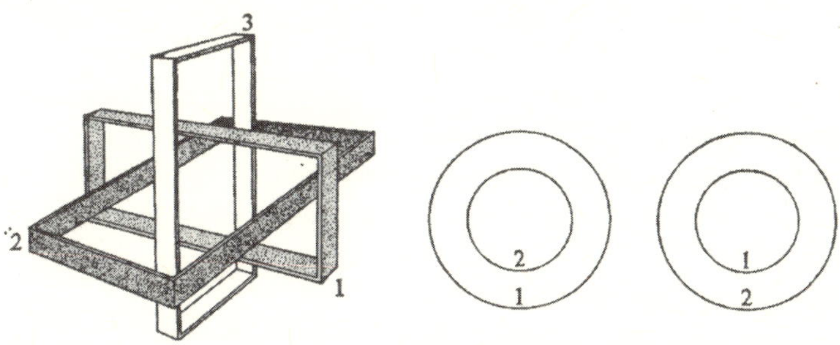

I hope you can all see that this is a knot. What does that mean? It means that, with respect to this reference to the sphere, 1 goes around 2. For 1 in relation to 2, you can get it to go around it exactly, just as you can, moreover, get 1 to go around 2 exactly. But what does it mean for 3 to be arranged like that? It's arranged in a way that is made tangible by this way of arranging things that on occasion we call "the sphere and the cross," except that here it's not a sphere, it's a ring. A ring isn't at all the same thing as a sphere. Suppose I make this narrower here in the middle, then we get this, which is a further form of what we can state as being a Borromean knot.

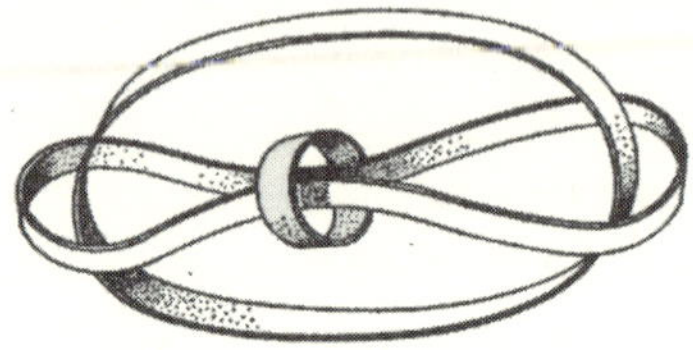

I mean that, whichever way number 3 here goes around 1, it still has the other one wrapped around it, but it has the other one wrapped around it in a third dimension. Contrary to what one imagines—those of us who are very ambitious and spend our time dreaming of a fourth one—we would be better off thinking about the weight that the third *dit*-mention has—the one I described earlier. We ought to marvel at the third before making another one. There's nothing easier than making another one. When they are all separate, that is, if we take three circles that can all drift off on their own, it's sufficient to make a fourth; it's sufficient to attach it with a circle in such a way that it makes a ring, for us to find ourselves back with what gives consistency to these circles.

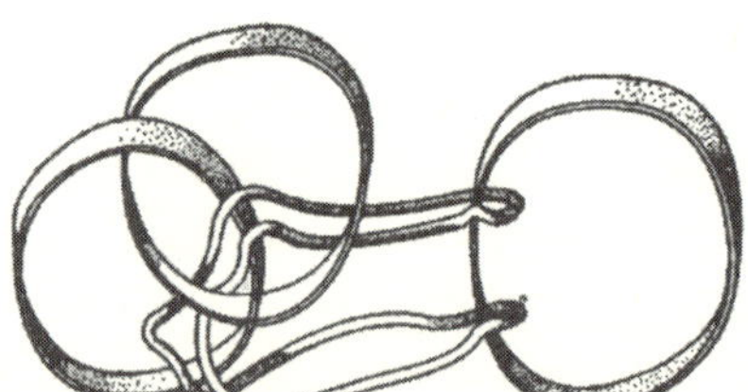

Having provided you with these facts about these knots, which lead to the notion that there is no such thing as space, that there are only knots—or, more accurately, that it's by means of knots that we think space—now, because I haven't finished too late, I'd be happy to take your questions. C/C

NOTE

This lecture was delivered on December 1, 1975, at the School of International Affairs Auditorium, Columbia University. It was published in the original French in *Scilicet* 6/7 (1976): 44–52. The translation is by Adrian Price with Russell Grigg.

JACQUES-ALAIN MILLER

Everyone Is Mad

■ A DISCOURSE THAT EXCLUDES DOMINATION

THEY'RE HANDING OUT, as I announced last time, the text in which the sentence "Everyone is mad, that is, delusional" [Lacan, in this issue] features. I'm not sure there will be enough copies for everybody, so please share with the person sitting next to you. It's a short text, and I will be reading it slowly, so don't be devastated if neither you nor the person next to you has got a copy. I've had copies made of a sheet that was obtained from the library of the École de la Cause freudienne by Madame Pascale Fari. The text is as it was published at the time in what presented itself as the bulletin of the Freudian field, *Ornicar?* Just look at the first six paragraphs, which are the only ones that interest us, the end of the text being a presentation of the moment for the department of psychoanalysis of the time.

So, "Everyone is mad, that is, delusional." I said last time I would be commenting on this sentence, which I've been using as a compass with which to steer through Lacan's very last teaching. And in so doing, to steer us also in our lattermost practice, since through an effect of retroaction, at least for those of us who are informed, we will no longer be able to elucidate Lacan's teaching without ordering it on the basis of his lattermost aim. And to the extent that this teaching goes on conditioning today's analytic practice, for those who are informed, well, this compass is set to have an impact there.

■ COMPASS AND ORIENTATION

The sentence I've read out is from Lacan, it is attested; it is written and published with its date: October 10, 1978. And this date is to be noted as it indicates that the drafting of this text dates from after the *Moment de conclure*, the twenty-fifth in the series of *The Seminars of Jacques Lacan*, which

I went through with you here quite recently. It is against the backdrop of this *Moment de conclure,* the last seminar, that this sentence ought to be read. So the sentence is from Lacan at a remarkable moment. That it should be a compass, that's my doing; it's a choice. And it's my responsibility, all the more so now that most of you have the context of this sentence in front of you, and in this context it is uttered in the place of Freud. It is uttered as a digest of Freud's teaching, or of what, in Freud's work, stood in for an impossible teaching. So this is a first reason why I must put it down to me to have constituted this sentence as a compass, as an ultimate Lacanian compass.

And Lacan, like everyone else, said a lot of things. In some respects he said everything and its opposite. That can be demonstrated. I've underlined it more than once. He said some essential things and some nonessential things. He tried some things out that he went back on; he contradicted himself from one week to the next. And so nothing of what he wrote or nothing of what is written of what he said can be read as a manual, if we understand that in a manual discourse unfolds in a homogenous way, and occasionally what is essential and what is nonessential is pointed out, but in any case, it doesn't contradict itself. What Lacan produced by way of books, including the books he got me to produce—and it's not over yet—none of these books can be read as if the statements were contemporary with each other, unlike the little work I designated as a manual. And therefore to punctuate these works, to discern within them the essential and the nonessential, is an act. It's a modest act, but in the end it's an act that conditions a good many things, the responsibility for which cannot be shirked, that is to say, the responsibility of answering for it.

So this is what I mean to do today. To put myself to the test of justifying my having made something of this sentence to the point that it has ended up as a slogan on the cover of a journal, in a slightly altered form. Did I weigh up all the ins and outs? I believe so. I believe so even though I taught myself something in forcing myself to come back to it today, publicly, in forcing myself to assess this choice once again. But I indicated last time that I'd been able, on occasion, to measure the errors that could ensue from punctuating Lacan's text askew, that could ensue from choosing as a compass such or such a sentence that is, on the contrary, if not to be ruled out, at the very least to be situated as parenthetical, as an attempt, the core of an attempt.

Here, it's not a core. On the contrary, if you like, it's more of a seed, or since I'm talking about a compass, it gives an orientation, the orientation of what Lacan was grappling with at the end. At the end, I mean, when he himself had tolled the bell, had tolled his own bell. It's part of what he put forward after the *Moment de conclure*. I don't mean to be gloomy, but it's part of the groans of his teaching. And yet we don't skip over this. It's clearly a fact of transference that we don't object to it, but on the contrary we see what is indicative of the thrust of his thinking in it. It indicates what attracts thought, what is always to be sought out behind the scaffolding and the rigging. What is, in fact, the point that attracts thought? Afterward, that gets set to music with whatever means one has. One writes a song, a light-hearted ditty or a grand symphony. But for anyone who gets involved in thinking, in communicating something of this thought, a chord is struck, the opening chord. And in this "Everyone is mad, that is, delusional," I hear the chord, the root chord.

So I was saying, to come back to it: *orientation*. I have already been led to distinguish several types of these orientations.

There is the orientation of the Roman road, the one Lacan himself brought us at the time of his third seminar. He was working on the paternal metaphor and what would become, a little later, the monument of his text on psychosis, the "Question Prior to Any Possible Treatment of Psychosis" [2006b]. This Roman road was evidently the Name-of-the-Father. And this is where, in this Name-of-the-Father, the root chord had to be found, which he made us hear on the mode of a *there is or there isn't* the Name-of-the-Father. To be or not to be. And it was with this chord that he caught hold of the question of psychosis, deploying a whole symbolic apparatus.

Here, the chord struck by this sentence ["Everyone is mad"] is utterly distinct. It's on the contrary an "Everyone"; it doesn't lead to sharing out, to segregation. So the Roman road clearly indicates a direction. When the Name-of-the-Father is there, the direction is univocal; it goes one way, and one way only. This can be indicated on a plane, on a surface. *This way*.

As you know, orientation becomes much more problematic on a Möbius strip, or on other such topological objects that may be described as unorientable, downside up, as it were.

WHENCE?

The sentence "Everyone is mad, that is, delusional" is unorientable. To say it like that signals precisely that it is not ordered by the Name-of-the-Father. Hence the question I was already bringing up last time: Whence is that said? Whence can such a sentence be said? Whence is it uttered? Whence is it posited? Whence, if I may, is it *thesised?* It seems to me that such a sentence is inseparable from this question, from this "Whence?"

If we hear it like that, with a "Whence?," it seems to me that we cannot fail to hear another "Whence?" that Lacan made ring out in his *Écrits* and that you will find on page 694 [of the 2006 edition], in response to a question he poses in the following terms: "What am *I*?" The *J* of *Je* is capitalized (in the French) to indicate that this *Je* refers to the subject, to the subject's Being. The response comes in the form of a quote—"*I* am in the place whence 'the universe is a flaw in the purity of Non-Being' is vociferated." It's a line of verse from Paul Valéry, from his "Sketch of a Serpent" [1986]. The next part of the text mentions the name that Lacan posts to this place, which I have just called the subject's Being, and this name is articulated as Jouissance—with a capital *J*—and it's no doubt the only occurrence in the *Écrits* of the word *jouissance* being written with a capital *J*. In what way is the locus called "jouissance," the place whence the voice must ring out? The enigmatic proposition that "the universe is a flaw in the purity of Non-Being" [2006, 694] is a sentence that can't be uttered without having to wonder "Whence?" "Whence can it be said?"

Is it uttered? Is it whispered? Saying that it vociferates implies that the voice has to pay its share, to pay its share to sustain it, in its paradox here too. So what can be known about the Non-Being and its purity when evidently one is bustling around in the universe? And how then is the universe to be measured against purity so as to be qualified as a "flaw"? Yes, I'm laying it on thick in order to make this passage resonate, this passage that I'm bringing in through the channel of this little "whence," but that is very much in question here.

Let me tell you that I've already commented on this passage on page 694 of the *Écrits* [2006c]. It's a digest of metapsychology. To see this, one only has to refer to a text that precedes "Subversion of the Subject and the Dialectic of Desire" [2006e] which this passage is from—a text entitled "Remarks . . . ," in particular to pages 558–59.

Provided that we are in tune with Lacan's music, we find ourselves drawn back to this text, because here Lacan mentions explicitly as metapsychology the place called *jouissance,* this time in the guise of "the place of *Plus-Personne,*" the place *of* No One Anymore. Following these references can help to clarify the details of the text you have in your hands. I'm getting to it. Following the footsteps of a colleague, commenting on his presentation, Lacan takes up the agencies of Freud's second topography, and, to do so, he goes through a very rapid but well-articulated critique of what he calls, roughly speaking, the classical theory of knowledge. Let's make the link with the text you have in your hands by noting that it's in starting off from a reflection on teaching, that is, what people believe can be communicated of knowledge, that Lacan comes to formulate "Everyone is mad."

In the text on page 558 that ends on page 559 [2006]—if I cut the text like that—Lacan starts off from knowledge and classical theory—he says "*a* theory"—I reckon we can say "classical theory" here by understanding that his "Remarks . . ." give us an insight into what is in Plato, in Plotinus, in Aristotle too, and, why not, in Descartes or in Kant. These "Remarks" shed a slanting light that aims at the root chord of the classical theory of knowledge, which doesn't deal with apparatuses. It designates the following point: in classical theory, knowledge of what we shall call the "object"—a term that is evidently not simple but that he uses at one point—implies that this object is united with the subject. Knowledge is a union; a union of which we shall say that it has an immediate form or mediate forms. An immediate form of the union constituted by knowledge is intuition. That's putting it rather quickly, but it will make us bring Plato and Bergson together. There are immediate forms that entail a process, and moreover, one can make intuition itself a method that, before giving us immediateness, does indeed go through mediations. But in every case, there is an accord between subject and object, and this accord has to do with their being of the same nature, their being homogenous.

If we gloss this, if we pathematize it, there has to be sympathy between them, in their nature, or, if we want to systematize it, they have to be simply in accord. Lacan speaks, in this respect, of "connaturality" in the same way that, following a *mot d'esprit* of Paul Claudel's, he highlighted the term *co-naissance,* being born together. There has to be a conjugation, a conjunction of senses and birth. Lacan says, *le connaissant . . . vient à co-naître au connu,* "the knower . . . comes to be born along with the known" [2006, 558]. Well, if Lacan makes this very quick remark that can lend itself to as many detailed rectifications as you like, but that nonetheless forms a root chord, if he takes this path, it's because he deems this theory of knowledge to be incompatible with psychoanalytic experience.

Let's say that, as in the text you're holding, he sets psychoanalysis apart. And to do so, he relies on two things, he presents two arguments. What goes against psychoanalysis is, first, "the fragmentation . . . from the outset in the combinatory of the unconscious"; second, "the breakdown of the drive into its component parts" [Lacan 2006, 558]. He doesn't really explain himself much further on this score. What we can say is that once more we find the two aspects that are always distinguished by Lacan in the *Écrits* in the guise of the unconscious and the drive. Later on it will be the subject and the object *a*. Here these two aspects are, in a way, assigned the same structure—"fragmentation" or "breakdown"—but they go against any accord.

This can be read in two different ways. First, neither the unconscious nor the drive is an object that a knowing subject can be united with, and thus it is rather on the mode of the stealing away of the want-of-Being that they inscribe themselves into wanting to be knowledge. The second way of reading this is that the unconscious does not stand with the drive in the relation of "knower born along with the known." In any case, we don't have unitary formations here. We don't have what Lacan [2006] calls elsewhere on page 558 "Whole-Ones . . . fixed in any range."

As much on the side of the unconscious as on the side of the drive, he says, we are dealing with elements of structure that, on the side of the unconscious enter a combinatory, and on the side of the drive enter what in his eleventh seminar he will call a "montage" [Lacan 1994, 169]. We are dealing with elements and systems. We are not dealing with natures. We are dealing with machines. And we have no relation of co-naturality whatsoever with these machines, which, for him, in the last analysis, are signifying machines.

THE CIRCLE CLEARED BY BURNING THE BRUSH OF JOUISSANCE

It is within the framework of this modified theory of knowledge that Lacan takes up, or rather refutes his colleague's proposition, that he quotes, namely that the organization of the id is best characterized by the "absence of a coherent subject." Lacan rectifies this proposition by underlining that, strictly speaking, the id is "unorganized." He only says this in a comment clause, in passing. Here he is implying the id precisely in its relation to jouissance and not to the signifier. To say that the id is "unorganized" is to say that not everything in the id is signifier. I think that here the term *organization* refers back to the term *signifier*.

So, first, the id is unorganized, and, second, "the absence of the subject . . . is produced somewhere [therein]" [Lacan 2006, 558]. This second phrase refers to what in the id is organized based on the absence of subject, since for the absence of the subject to be produced somewhere, there must already be a place to begin with. Therefore, Lacan is rectifying by specifying that the absence of the subject is not pure and simple; it's not the purity of Non-Being, or it's the purity of Non-Being in as much as it is localized in a place. So the subject is not there in the id; he's not there in person; and he can't make head or tail of it, but his absence makes for a place: "the place of No One Anymore." Lacan chooses metaphor to designate this place, to poeticize it as "the circle that is cleared by burning the brush of the drives" [558]. As a place, this is what he will encapsulate afterward with the line of verse from Valéry. It's the same place. It's the place at which the other agencies of Freud's topography can next be inscribed and erected: the ego and the superego. Freud always stressed that the ego belonged to the id. The superego, through its deepest phase, is far from belying this belonging; quite the contrary—this is what Lacan would go on to demonstrate in "Kant with Sade" [2006]—it stands in relation to the "brush of the drives."

So, what is he designating here? To de-poeticize this passage, I think I can use the capital *J* of the word *Jouissance* to inscribe it and bar it at this place designated as being equivalent to the place of the subject. I'm rounding up what I'm presenting here in the shape of this little matheme.

$$\not{J} \equiv \$$$

I'm saying that it's a metapsychology in reduced form because it's exactly here, at the place of the circle, at the place of No One Anymore, that Lacan inscribes defense. Primordial defense. Primordial defense—in relation to the defenses that are attached to the ego or the superego and that are called, for example, "repression"—primordial defense that consists essentially in not being there, while still having its place marked out as the place of an absence. This is the primordial form of defense faced with jouissance—to be there only in the form of an absence.

I've said "fundamental defense." The adjective is mine because Lacan says, "The defence that one might call 'natural'" [2006, 558]. He puts "natural" in inverted commas because the point is precisely to refute any naturality. One calls it natural in a certain improper use of the word, essentially so as to be able to say in a way that initially seems mysterious that the cleared circle within the brush of the drives is stamped with artifice. I believe that this "natural" here needs to be understood as a reference to a jouissance that stands prior to the signifier, while the circle, the place of No One Anymore, is relative to the artifice of the signifier. Lacan speaks of this place in terms that seem quite exalted. What one needs to bear in mind is that what he's designating above all else, based on this place, is the binarism of the signifier, namely, the binarism between the signifier and its absence. This is the elementary matrix of the signifier that, for him, determines this place, the place of the absence of the subject. This is how he puts it:

> This is the very place to which each and every thing is called to be washed of sin [*faute,* that is, "fault"], sin that this place makes possible since it is the place of an absence: for everything might not exist in the first place. . . . With this very simple matrix of the first contradiction—to be or not to be— . . . the judgement of existence founds reality. [558]

And he adds, "It is the structure of this place which demands that the nothing [*le rien*] be at the core of creation. . . ." (559). Here we already have an echo of the universe whose creation is a flaw in Non-Being. We have a projection of the binary matrix of the signifier at the level of creation, namely, that there might be something rather than nothing. As Leibniz's formula has it, "Why is there something instead of nothing?"

So, what can be got from this text is that at the place where a space is cleared within the brush of Jouissance, the subject of the signifier can be inscribed. This is the place at which one dreams of inscribing the creator, the creator giving rise ex nihilo (out of nothing) to something, and at the same time promising the disappearance of compromising elements, the attributes of fault and sin, in this place.

At this point, the "possible" that features in the sentence ought to be underlined, that is, what might exist or not exist. It's the echo that the adjective *possible* has in the title ". . . Possible Treatment of Psychosis" [2006b]. If Lacan said, "Possible Treatment," and not just "Treatment of Psychosis," it was precisely so as not to assign the universal to it, and, on the contrary, to assign it a *which might or might not exist*. Let's say that this place of No One Anymore holds up, or is designated in this way, to the extent that the Supreme Being, the creator, is not stuffed in there, but rather that this place is brought out in its absence, and on occasion we will put the subject-supposed-to-know there. Therefore, the No One Anymore comes in place of the Supreme Being, and, at the start, this place is the one that is due to an annulling practiced at the level at which there is jouissance, and the subject can then inscribe himself with his question "What am *I*?"

There you have it for what I'm suggesting you bear in mind, with all the difficulty it possesses, of course. Lacan writes it in the style of evocation. It's not written in a style of mathemes. It's written in a style of pathos, which at the end of the day I'm reducing to these elements. But there you have what I'm suggesting you bear in mind to read these six short paragraphs from the text you're holding.

TRUTH AND ITS SEMBLANCE

The text was written on the occasion of a difficulty in the Department of Psychoanalysis and the University of Vincennes at the time. It starts off from the idea of teaching. For Lacan it's an opportunity to come back to what, back in the day, he used to call the "matheme of psychoanalysis," what he happened to word in the terms—spoken I believe, and not during his seminar itself but during one of his papers, one of the congresses or conferences—"There is a possible matheme of psychoanalysis." A "possible" matheme. I remember this adjective well. There must be a recording somewhere. If I find it, I'll publish it in the series of Lacan's lectures. But I'm citing from memory. There was the formula—"a possible matheme of psychoanalysis"—with the same adjective, which says *maybe yes but maybe no*.

There's no title to this little text. The title you have on what you're holding was tacked on rather crudely by the editorial board of the time, which was myself. There was a blank space, and I'm ashamed of having used that typeface. It's hideous.

In this text, he is revisiting the matheme of psychoanalysis, the possible matheme of psychoanalysis, and therefore he takes as his point of departure the teaching of psychoanalysis. Well, he takes his own teaching as his point of departure, because the first sentence is "There are four discourses." Therefore, at the moment Lacan is wondering about the possible matheme of psychoanalysis, we already have this paradox that he's referring to himself, and assertively at that, with a "There are. . . ." He's referring to what he himself has taught, because that didn't exist at all before he taught it. This paradox is tangible in the very first sentence, once you've read the text.

"There are four discourses." I'll mention them for you, though you're familiar with them: the discourses of the master, the university, the hysteric, and the analyst. There is no reminder here. There is no reminder of the matheme he proposed for these discourses. Let's say he takes this fact as a point of departure, this fact that is a fact of speech, of what he said, that indicates what the coordinates of his present reflection are. That's the first sentence.

"Each one thinks it is the truth." This is an assertion to be considered, and that hints that each discourse is inhabited by pretensions to truth. The proper sense of "thinks it is" makes these pretensions lean toward imposture. It's all the more the emphasis of this sentence given that one says "*the* truth" and there are *four* of them, four discourses. And so in two sentences we have a little comedy sketch: four discourses, each one fancying itself as the truth. You can already see the battle, the quarrel, looming large. We cannot fail to recall either that the one who's writing this had uttered, had vociferated in his time: "I, truth, speak" [Lacan 2006X, 340]. And here there are four of them to say: "I, truth, speak." But when Lacan said, "I, truth, speak," what discourse was that in? It was supposed precisely to be situated in the psychoanalytic discourse. The truth that was speaking was the Freudian truth. I refer you to his text "The Freudian Thing" [2006a], in which you have the prosopopeia borrowed from Erasmus, the prosopopeia of truth. There it was the Freudian truth, the truth that speaks between the lines, the one that speaks in slips of the tongue, in bungled actions. That was the dwelling place where this truth was welcomed and treated in relation to the Freudian Thing, which is another name for the Jouissance with a capital *J* we have been speaking about.

Here, on the contrary, if we follow the third sentence, the imposture of truth is for the three others and not for the analytic discourse: "The only exception is the analytic discourse." This would be the only one not to fancy itself as the truth. Well, we still have to understand this, because in what Lacan calls "discourse," there are four places, always, and one of them is called "the place of truth."

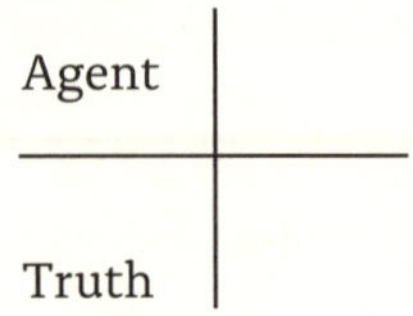

In each of the discourses, one term occupies the place of truth, which doesn't drive at the idea that each discourse thinks it is the truth because, on the contrary, each discourse has a place for truth. So, does the "thinks it is the truth" designate, in each discourse, in the three discourses, the element that is in this place? No, it doesn't. It designates, so it seems to me, the element at the place called "the place of the agent," by which each discourse is designated.

In the discourse of the master, the master-signifier is inscribed here, and we can argue that in the discourse of the master the master-signifier is proposed as truth, universal truth, truth destined to gather together, unite, and even exclude.

In each of the discourses, it is this term [of *agent*] that is explicitly assigned truth by the discourse. For the university discourse, S_2, knowledge, upholds this imposture.

In the discourse of the hysteric, it is the barred subject, the subject put in a bind by the bar, the subject slipping away. But it is the subject that glows as if it were the truth and that speaks the evangelical word, "I am the truth." Moreover, this is far from "I, truth, speak." The truth that speaks does not, indeed, say, "I am."

So, "the only exception is the analytic discourse." And in what way does it not have the same regime? The term it sets as agent is the *a*. This term has no pretensions to truth.

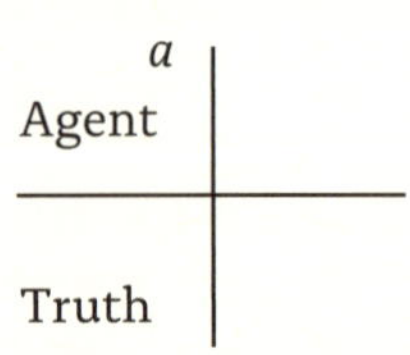

It has no pretensions to truth to the extent that it is only acknowledged in the analytic discourse as an element of semblance. Semblance isn't opposed to truth. On the contrary, when we designate the object *a* as a *semblant,* we include that truth is a *semblant*. The analytic discourse is cut out to show this because there one experiences a variable truth: each session has its truth, just as each lesson of Lacan's seminars has its truth. It's precisely here that one feels the variation in truth, which Lacan wrote *varité*. It's in his seminar, the one that precedes the *Moment de conclure*. That's where he brings out the *varité* [Lacan 1979, 13].

So, each one thinks it is the truth, only the analytic discourse knows it is *varité*, that is, it acknowledges truth as semblance. And in this respect it is an exception to the regime of the three others.

DOMINATION AND ITS EXCLUSION

The fourth sentence is "We would be better off if it did dominate, people will conclude, but in point of fact this discourse excludes domination." This sentence brings in something other than the theme of truth. It brings in the theme of power, of domination. Except that, as I've already remarked, when Lacan said "truth," he didn't mean the place under the bar on the left. He was designating the place of the "agent," which is the archetypal place at which power, domination, is inscribed. In the discourse of the master, it's the master-signifier. In the university discourse, it's knowledge. And therefore each of these discourses proposes a domination. In this respect there are four dominations, and the best one would be the domination of the truth that refutes itself, the domination of the truth that knows itself to be semblance.

This is what sometimes leads us to think, naïvely, that it would be preferable for politicians to be psychoanalyzed. It's the naïve idea of *the analytic discourse would be better off dominating*. That's never changed anything about anything. Lacan indicated that it could give rise to the worst. Having shaken Goebbels's hand at the 1936 Berlin Olympics, he thought it had left him with the feeling that Goebbels had been analyzed and that this was doubtless why he'd become the master and initiator of the most mendacious propaganda the world has ever known. [Goebbels] had fully grasped—let's make the link—truth's status of semblance. And it's very dangerous. It's very dangerous to teach that to people in power. Well, now they gravitate around them, the numerous spin doctors, as they're called, the numerous publicists and marketers who are there to train them in the truth's character of semblance. Therefore, the idea that *the analytic discourse would be better off dominating* in fact takes the form of the analytic discourse being put in the service of the master discourse; the master discourse including the capitalist discourse too, as we have seen in the sensational boost the inventor of modern marketing was given by reading Freud. I spoke about that back in the day.

Therefore, the practical form of domination by the analytic discourse is not so tempting. At the end of the day, the axiom that lies behind this is: a discourse dominates. A discourse is a form of domination insofar as it organizes. It organizes a world that includes the criterion of what truth is. And it is in this regard that the analytic discourse excludes domination, because it doesn't organize a world. It is more for undoing it. In any case, it isn't coordinated with a world to be known, if I refer to the critique of the theory of knowledge I mentioned. In other words, with the *a* as semblance, at the place from which the discourse dominates, this *a* cannot dominate, that is, it doesn't organize a world. Besides, of the three terms it's the only one that isn't a term of the symbolic. But it designates, to put it rapidly, what is excluded from the symbolic: S_1, S_2, and barred *S* are terms from the symbolic, and Lacan refers here to the object *a* insofar as it is not liable to represent symbolic domination.

It's striking here that Lacan should say, "This discourse excludes domination; in other words is teaches nothing." Just as in a while we get: "Everyone is mad, that is, delusional." We have here a surprising equivalence in which *to teach* is *to dominate*. It seems to me that here this equivalence refers essentially to the discourses, and so let's say to the university discourse. Well, it could be the discourse of the master as well. This equivalence refers to teaching as pedagogy. I have to be careful here, now that we've just been told about a projected abolition of pedagogy from the instruction of *maîtres*—the French word, and what a word, for teacher training students. I'll make it clear that I'm not taking sides, or at least, that's not my purpose here. Obviously, I can't find a good thing to say about pedagogy. It's along the same lines as what Lacan's saying here. The expression *formation des maîtres* is something to make a Lacanian keel over, but clearly it's not for all that something that should translate into taking a political position in the present matter. Well, that would require a good many more developments. Let's note the short circuit by which Lacan reduces teaching to pedagogy and thus to domination, and therefore excludes the analytic discourse from domination and from teaching as pedagogy.

THE UNIVERSAL AND ITS NEGATION

In the last sentence of the first paragraph there's a doubling of this opposition, of the incompatibility between teaching and psychoanalysis: "There is nothing universal about [the analytic discourse], which is precisely why it cannot be taught." This doubling up introduces a new term, that of the universal, a new criterion already foreshadowing the "Everyone . . ." of the formula I've highlighted and that distances the analytic discourse from the universal. Thus it seems to indicate that the three others are for everybody. The three others entail a "for all *x*," as we say on occasion: $\forall x$. The matheme, which can be taught, which can be "teaching matter," is attached to a "for all *x*." And indeed the criteria by which one can acknowledge mathematics as being teachable—the mathematics that speaks of two plus two equaling four—is supposedly that it is valid for everybody and for all time, universal and omnitemporal. Therefore we can admit that there is a co-belonging between the universal and the teachable; and that the analytic discourse is of the order of the *particular*, even of the *singular;* and that there is no science at this level, as Aristotle said. This Aristotelian reference is hidden between the lines of Lacan, and I was getting ready to bring it out by introducing an element that fits in perfectly with this one, though I might not have time to do it today.

In what way is the analytic discourse not coordinated with the universal? Why doesn't it have anything of the universal about it?

First of all, it's not sure that the analytic experience is for everybody, nor for all cultures, nor for all time. Nor for all, one by one. Therefore it is not intended to be taught in the same way as "two plus two is four"; it can't deliver propositions of this type.

Second, its essential reference is the *not-all,* and not the *all,* with the bar of obligation: $\overline{\forall x}$. Psychoanalysis takes mismatched subjects on a one-by-one basis, with the meaning that is valid for one not being valid for another, with reference to Freud advising us to take each case from scratch, not to assume that the value of a word for one subject is valid for another. That doesn't stop experience from accumulating. But there is no universal.

Third, this "nothing universal" can be justified by saying that everything is singular there, by formulating the universal proposition of the exclusivity of the singular. At the end of the first paragraph, Lacan underlines the incompatibility between psychoanalysis and teaching, but a teaching that is nonetheless of a pedagogical order, one that is open to becoming a pedagogy. As reference is made to the four discourses and to the university, to the place of psychoanalysis in the university (because that is the occasion of the text), we can say that he has accentuated, amplified the incompatibility between psychoanalysis and the university. In the end, when called upon to defend the place of the department of psychoanalysis in the university, his orientation, which this first paragraph attests to, is rather to bring out the incompatibility between psychoanalysis and the university.

It seems to me that this is the musical phrase that can be heard in the first paragraph. He has wrong-footed the request. He will indeed defend the department of psychoanalysis, but he begins at the opposite end, by underlining how the regime of the analytic discourse is fundamentally different from the regime of the university discourse and from all other discourses. This here is the last value of the universal that you can hear in the university, in what the university pretensions harbor by way of the universal.

■ PARADOX

This beginning is taken up, raised to the level of a paradox, with the first sentence of the second paragraph: "How does one go about teaching what cannot be taught?" Therefore, a resumption as a paradox, that is, the negative of the first paragraph does not prevent a forcing, that is, a posited thesis doesn't stop one from formulating a hypothesis beneath it, in the sense of the thesis-beneath, the thesis-beneath that contradicts it. Therefore, the first paragraph is there to say, Psychoanalysis cannot be taught, hence the question: "What are we going to do to teach it since it can't be taught?"

This movement is frequently met in Lacan, where the impossible doesn't cancel out the contingent, or doesn't cancel out the other modalities. It cancels out neither the contingent, nor the possible, nor the necessary. The impossible, the absolute of the impossible, does not kill off the relative. There is no sexual relation, and this is precisely why we wonder how to go about establishing the sexual relation that there is not.

Against the backdrop of this impossible, how does one go about obtaining something that can act as a stand-in, and that will allow one to get by? How does one get by with the impossible? Well, we'll be seeing that next week!

■ A VOCIFERATION FROM THE PLACE OF NO ONE ANYMORE

"Everyone is mad, that is, delusional." This is the sentence with which I shall be concluding the course this year. A year during which I've allowed myself to be carried along by what came to hand, which I gathered up. I thought that what would be less systematic would be more authentic. I feel I'm close, closer this year to what's been on my mind from one moment to the next. And concluding with this "Everyone is mad" provides me with the key, with the title for this year—and about time too!

This sentence is from Lacan. There's no doubt about that, but as I said last time, it's proffered from nowhere, from a *non-lieu*, from *nullibiety,* to put back on the map one of Lacan's neologisms, referring to a text by Jorge Luis Borges, that you will find in the *Écrits* [2006a, 16]. Last time I recognized this locus as being the place of No One Anymore. That too could have been the title for this year.

Because in a sense, I've been that: No One Anymore. I've allowed the occasion to pass through me, and I've made use of it. I've stayed loyal, without too many trappings, to what came to mind, as any analysand worthy of the name must, as any analysand who meets the definition and the status thereof must.

No One Anymore. Now that's a character! By the by, it's one of the names of the subject, the barred subject, but with a particular stress, the stress of his native relationship with jouissance. No One Anymore, now that's a character who hadn't been spotted in the Lacanian cast. And yet, I could say that No One Anymore is Lacan's spokesperson.

VOCIFERATION

His teaching, what he called his teaching and which I've taken up, to the point of effacing the names of the books, the works, the theories . . . well no, I said, "Lacan's teaching," after Lacan, but with insistence, with a univocal insistence, to designate that this work was *work in progress,* to use James Joyce's expression, whose conclusions, as strongly affirmed as they may be, are always transitory.

It was only for the facilities of university teaching that I promoted, that I spoke from this place in the department of psychoanalysis of Lacan's "theses," without ever *ne varietur*. I said, "teaching," and this is precisely what I'm revising today by commenting on the sentence, "Everybody is mad, that is, delusional," because it doesn't leave teaching intact, because it attacks the very possibility of a matheme of psychoanalysis. And it thereby makes for the pathos of what Lacan wended his way through. That said, I'm taking up the very expression that, in the text, is assigned by Lacan to Freud's name. Therefore this teaching—since from the start of this course that's what I've been calling it—is what is said, what is proffered, what is vociferated.

It takes a body to vociferate. You have to pay with your person, and not just with your subjectivity. This teaching is vociferated from the place of No One Anymore. Today I shall say that this is where Lacan set up camp. And what bursts through in this last text had in fact been present in waiting, waiting to unfold its consequences and its devastation, from the moment Lacan first spoke up.

In fact, "to speak up" dampens the splendor that is carried in vociferation. Vociferation adds value to "speaking up"; it adds dimension, the weight of the voice, that is, what comes along as an excess in what is called in the nicest possible way the relationship between analyst and analysand. The term *relationship* is just what it takes to conceal what's involved, and what this sentence is designed to restore for us. The place of No One Anymore is without doubt the place of the subject, but conceived of, named, as the circle cleared by burning the brush of jouissance. And to speak up, to simply speak up, is already to pass on, to roll on this part taken from the brush that is the object *a* as voice. Doubtless it should be added that the voice goes further than the object *a*, which can always be suspected of being mere semblance, a semblant of jouissance due to the apparatus of the signifier. The place of No One Anymore is without doubt the place of the subject, but designated beforehand, so to speak, before the signifier unrolls its fallacious scrolls that I'm giving you an example of by forcing the eloquence. Those fallacious scrolls that make you forget that right there where you're suffering, you're enjoying.

We say, "listen," and nowadays nothing's more common than that. We make it a policy, a means of mastery, and even "listen by interpreting," by interpreting that this means something else, that this means something more, that this means something that lies off to one side. Psychoanalysis is indeed sufficiently widespread for there to be clinicians who listen by interpreting. But what the sentence "Everyone is mad" directs us to is that, as an analyst, it's a matter of listening out, in what is uttered from the mouth of the patient, for what vociferates from the place of No One Anymore. There, vociferation is not a statement.

A statement is a proposition. A proposition is what can be true or false, or contradictory, or, if you want to widen this binarism, paradoxical. Fundamentally, a proposition is submitted to the matrix of the true and the false, while a statement isn't. It's a fact, it isn't a value. But a statement is submitted to the binary matrix of statement and enunciation. That makes two. I would say today that *vociferation*, which I'm making the third term after *statement* and *enunciation*, gets over the division between the statement and the enunciation, that it is both statement and enunciation as indivisible. Unlike the statement, vociferation does not suspend, does not hold itself at a distance from "who said it," and when there is no "who," then "whence it is said," that is, the vociferation includes its point of emission.

It is a reminder that Lacan always comes back to, that what gets taken for his statements, and gets hijacked—because it's often caught, for him, in his moans and protests of being plagiarized, of being robbed—what gets taken for his statements, and then trailed around, and taught in his name—which is now being done on a large scale—and I've got something to do with that—only has the right impact at the place where it was said. It goes beyond moaning and protesting. It amounts to asking for the status of vociferation to be granted to the teaching we received, his teaching. This is how we approach what I could call "how to listen to Lacan." There is a vociferation that has to be heard as being said from the place of No One Anymore, a vociferation that is apt—to use a term that I made the overall title for this course when I began it long ago and that I've kept over the ensuing years—to orient how one listens in psychoanalysis and that sets this practice apart, which makes for what I've occasionally called its "inhumanity." Indeed, it isn't humanist, even if it might be well known for being a parody of humanism. When I say, "inhumanity," that's a way of clothing the No One Anymore.

THE SUBJECT IS HAPPY

This vociferation, because I'm making this term a category, is as follows: The subject is happy. I heard Lacan say that, to me, with a smile; and to all of you, should you get to watch the film *Television*. In the written version, you'll find that on page 22 of the English translation of *Television* [Lacan 1990, 22]. "It is his very definition," Lacan added. It's the twist he gives to what Freud himself disguised, shut away; it has to be believed, if we go by how that's been understood, in the form of the pleasure principle. And there, we didn't hear, because we believed, and he did everything to make that happen, that it formed a couple, a contrasting couple with the reality principle. "The subject is happy" gives it back its cutting edge.

It would not be wrong to put this cutting edge down to Freud. In parentheses, one can always present that differently by saying that this is the cutting edge that Lacan adds. But this isn't the direction the text I've handed out to you orients us in. On the contrary, this text invites us to put it down to Freud.

The subject, the happy subject, Lacan specifies, "can owe nothing if not to hap [luck]." It's the "hap" that features in hap-piness. To hap, in other words to happenstance, to fortune. Fortune here is the Latin *fortuna* that Machiavelli made into a category of his politics, and that, if we want to furnish it with its logical equivalent, we would call "contingency," that which happens and which wasn't written. It wasn't written, it happens, and the subject seizes it in so far as—I quote—"Any luck [hap] is good as something to maintain him, insofar as it repeats itself" [1990, 22]. Repetition is of the order of what is written, of what doesn't stop being written. But the remarkable point is that what is not written, and which happens, serves the repetition. And that, that which isn't written and which happens, which cannot be deduced, which is called in the nicest possible way the "coordinates of the case," for example, when one is in the clinician's role, is of the order of contingency.

This makes for what we are trying to circumscribe as reality. This makes for reality in as much as contingency is inserted into the repetition of happiness. In other words, to keep something of the order of teaching nevertheless, you oughtn't to represent things like this: PP/RP—Pleasure Principle/Reality Principle, as Freud seems to direct us, leaving the pleasure principle to move into the new regime of the reality principle, and then finally giving up pleasure for the hard law of the world, bowing one's head to what is in place there. It's a lesson in renunciation. All the same, one cannot live only for pleasure! You have to make allowances, otherwise you're daft.

This reading wouldn't have been upheld if it didn't lend itself to capturing something of commonplace thinking, that is, the thinking of everybody, the stations of the cross that make up the existence of one and all. All right! But that's not how it should be written. It can be written like that, that says something, right enough. But what Freud says, as heard by Lacan, is that the reality principle is dominated by the pleasure principle, always.

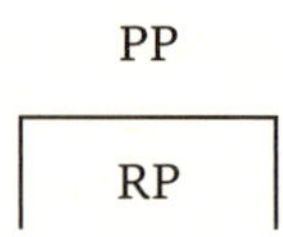

And this is vociferation: the subject is happy. And reality, that which arises for the subject—because it does arise, things arise, they arise before your birth and things come about as soon as the little fellow makes his appearance—but in each case, reality is put at the service of the happiness of repetition. The reality principle is the pursuit of the pleasure principle by other means—to parody Clausewitz. This is why the great difficulty in interpreting the Constitution of the United States of America is down to that one incredible clause inspired by the Enlightenment thinkers: that this great republic would be made to fulfill "the pursuit of happiness." Well, I'm not going to go into the various considerations and the sarcasm they might inspire. There you have it.

A vociferation—is it true? Is it false? It's not a proposition. It sums up and one could even say it inaugurates the position of the analyst, a position that does not just amount to scheming away in the signifier and interpreting, that amounts to aiming, from the outset, and verifying, that the subject is bound to jouissance, is inscribed in jouissance, lets go of jouissance, and that in the various maledictions that affect him, he forges the means to sustain this jouissance. This is also why good faith, help, the different patterns by which pity—to call it by its name—disguises itself nowadays do not conform to what this vociferation designates for us.

THE MOMENT OF *VARITÉ* WRESTLED FROM THE IMPOSSIBLE

I'm coming back to Lacan's text, which as I pointed out, he wrote at my request to ensure the protection of the department of psychoanalysis in the framework of the university. This is without doubt the situation he referred to in these four discourses, among which there is the university discourse. Hence his proposition: There are four discourses. But straight off the bat he gauges them up against a watchword, that of "truth," and we have to find out how to hear it. I hope to come to this at the end.

Each discourse reportedly thinks it is the truth. Each discourse softly hints, "I am the truth," with the exception of one of them, the analytic discourse, which can only formulate, as I said last time, "I am *varité*." And in this word, in this neologism, taken in the singular, clearly one is to hear *truths*. "I only give out truths," "I only allow the subject to reach a transitory and fleeting truth, which will be replaced by another one." Without doubt, this goes right up to the idea of the Pass, where there would be a marriage, wedlock; jouissance would wed truth. As you know, Lacan kept up this dream, precisely right up to his very last teaching when he came out of it. And that too is what this text says, when it says that the analytic discourse doesn't claim the truth, that it's an exception to taking oneself for the truth. What Lacan uttered regarding the Pass corresponds to a moment, a moment when the analytic discourse thought it was the truth. Here we're in the aftermath of this attempt. He doesn't do away with the Pass, he restores it. He restores it in *varité*. In analysis one goes from truths to other truths, and the truths become errors, the truths become deceptions, and the truths become mistakes. He doesn't go and set up a truth that one wouldn't fail to hold on to, which would be a hold as such. What Lacan called the object *a* is something that is spoken of as falling. The secret of its fall is that it would be the object of a holding, and a hold that could be let go of. So, it's along this path that the term "for all *x*"—$\forall x$—is invalidated in the analytic discourse. As I said, the notion of a truth that would be valid for all and for all times and for all situations [is invalidated]. Lacan says in this text that "there is nothing universal about analytic discourse." This "nothing universal" doesn't oblige us to efface the "for all *x*," but rather leads us to place, to indicate a bar of negation over it, to be read as "not-all," not universal: $\overline{\forall x}$. "Not universal," and in logical terms, we understand this as "the particular."

I'll come to this right away. This special quantifier, the "not-all," with its bar of negation, specifies an effect of "push-to-the-woman," says Lacan in *L'étourdit* [2001, 466]. And you know he constructed his formula for male sexuation on the "for all *x*" and that of feminine sexuality on the negated "for all *x*," on the "not-all." In this sense, saying "There is nothing universal" about the analytic discourse refers us back to the status he gives to women in sexual relation. In the end, he's targeting a dimension that hadn't found its theoretician, nor its *théoricienne,* whereas the other one, the "for all *x*," had no shortage of theoreticians. The first one to pay homage to, even if he didn't use the symbolic quantifier involved, is Aristotle. To say there is nothing universal about the analytic discourse is to say that it is non-Aristotelian, and to what extent, in not being Aristotelian, it is feminizing.

The first effect, a sardonic effect, here too, is to disconnect the analytic discourse from the matheme, if the matheme—and Lacan hadn't defined it otherwise—depends on, is under the sway of, the "for all *x*." In this respect, Aristotle was indeed the educator of logical thought, the archetypal mentor. Unjoining the analytic discourse and the matheme means that one cannot set up operators of the analytic discourse. What is said in and about psychoanalysis cannot be set up through teaching. It can only be set up through the experience. Here we have something that has been accepted, or admitted. Psychoanalysts are not trained by teaching; they are trained through the experience.

In view of which—this is a hypothesis—there has to be teaching too. But at the radical level, which is where I'm positioning myself, there's an opposition between teaching and experience.

To be able to teach, you need the matheme, an already present knowledge, a lay formula that corresponds to "for all *x*," whereas in the experience, knowledge is still to come and it is only ever valid for one *x*. I can even pass over to the singular. It will only be valid for one *x*. That's what the Pass is. It is to try, by some miracle, to transform the knowledge of one by itself—the knowledge of one by itself that comes from the experience, from its experience—into teaching matter for everyone. There's a gap between the "for all *x*" of the matheme and the "There exists one by itself" of the experience. I shall write this, logically, by adding an exclamation mark after the existential quantifier—that might make you snigger but it's a correct use: $\forall x/\exists !x$. It's not used very much, but in the furthest reaches of the logic of quantification you can find this quantifier. "There exists one, and one alone." It's not "at least one," it's "one by itself."

So, the second paragraph—because I'm still only here, and I wouldn't want to still be on this next year—encapsulates in a paradox what has been affirmed. What has been affirmed is an impossible. It is the thesis: The teaching of psychoanalysis doesn't stop not being written. What's involved is to bring about the occasion whereby it stops not being written. And this will only ever be of the order of contingency; it will be a fragile and revisable success. It will never be of the order of "the truths," and that's how Lacan treated all of his teaching—as a fabric of *varité*. It is in this regard that he says, "There are four discourses." It is with regard to what occurred to him at one point to try and counter the impossible, the impossible to teach. We start off from Jacob wrestling with the angel. Well, Jacques Lacan wrestles with the impossible, which makes for the pathos of his teaching, and which makes his successes, his transgressions, his forcing, his vociferations, a moment of *varité*. It takes all of our distress faced with what comes about, our distress faced with the analytic experience itself, to transform it into a thesis *ne varietur*, into "teaching matter," whereas it's to be seen as an episode, doubtless a heroic one, but one that is doomed to be short-lived, an episode of a wrestle with the impossible. This is how I hear "How does one go about teaching what cannot be taught?"

FREUD AND THE DREAM

You can see that the word *paradox* that I've hooked onto this sentence, and that I hooked onto the little collection of Lacan I created—*Paradoxes*—is a very gentle word to designate what's involved. In this text, at the same time as the wrestle with the impossible, we find the name of Freud, a singular return to Freud.

It isn't meant in the same way as Lacan said "return to Freud" in his article "The Freudian Thing," whose subtitle is "A Return to Freud" [2006a]. It's not the same meaning. Here he's bringing out a meaning that lies beyond this first one, which was what? It was the evidence that Freud taught, that he didn't simply invent psychoanalysis but he gave it a theoretical consistence that he retranscribed while burying his experience in mathemes that made for "teaching matter." It is in the name of what in Freud constituted mathemes that Lacan, to begin with, vociferated his return to Freud, to make Freud's teaching resonate, to lend it the ear it called for in the guise of what Freud really said. That then was the first meaning of a return to Freud.

The return to Freud indicated in this text has a different value. Let's say it precisely: "How does one go about teaching what cannot be taught? That is something Freud ventured into." This word, *il a cheminé*, he "ventured into" or "he wended his way," is enough to burst apart the teaching matter, the Freudian manual, the Freudian matheme. What Lacan affirms with this *il a cheminé* is the kinship between Freud's path and his own. Saying that he ventured into it means that he didn't resolve the paradox of the teaching of psychoanalysis, that he didn't overcome it, that he stayed in the paradox. He ventured into it and he remained, like Lacan, at the mercy of the impossible, in his effort to treat the impossible by way of the contingent, as it were.

When I said that this year I have agreed to give up on the systematic so as to gather up what's come along, what's fallen into my lap, I meant that I was resigned, in my own way, to wending my way, that is, each time trying to foil the impossible to say, the impossible to teach, that which I have experience of from day to day based on analysands' experience; to foil the impossibility of teaching this, by each time seeking to reset the stakes through a fresh twist and one that at any rate surprises me at least a little myself.

One wends one's way precisely when one hasn't found it. "Wending one's way" means that one is reduced to getting by, one is reduced to compromise, one is reduced to scouring, to being evasive, to finding a way 'round, to gaining ground, to crossing a moat with the means to hand, to the point of giving an idea of what it might be to teach what cannot be taught. After all, this can also be valid as a preparation of the operators for the experience, as I was saying earlier.

The thesis, in quotation marks, "Everyone is mad, that is, delusional" is introduced by "he thought," referring to Freud. This means that Lacan, in this text, doesn't assume responsibility for this in the first person. He doesn't say "Everyone is mad" in the same way he says that "there are four discourses." He takes his distance from this thesis. He says that it's someone else's. Precisely because it's extreme and because it constitutes a reading of Freud that he can see has been his from the start.

This thesis is twofold, it splits into two. First of all, it is that "all is but a dream," and second, "everyone is mad, that is, delusional," all of which does not presuppose a suspension of the universal: "everyone (if one can say such a thing)." Here, the universal, the "for all *x*" of this formula, which clearly contradicts what's in the opening paragraph—there's "nothing universal" about the analytic discourse—designates this gap and this interplay between the impossible and the contingent. The "for all *x*" of "Everyone is mad" is written in inverted commas. It's a "so to speak" that is here in brackets. And this can only be resolved by targeting, by thinking from the place of No One Anymore where "Everyone is mad" means the same thing as "The subject is happy."

Did Freud say that "all is but a dream"? Certainly he entered psychoanalysis via the dream, the royal road of the dream, but apparently by saying: sometimes you dream, and sometimes you don't. What Lacan deciphered was: it's the generalization of the dream, that is, one is always dreaming. This means that the pleasure principle doesn't stand in opposition to the reality principle. The pleasure principle is not mere dreaming with the reality principle as the wake-up. It's that the dream is there night and day. There is no binarism of dream and not-dream. If we are in teaching, from time to time, we know that Lacan did indeed formulate that in his last teaching: one only wakes up so as to go on dreaming.

It's rather in the dream that one stands a chance of encountering the real. We call that a nightmare, and precisely the nightmare casts you into reality so that you might forget the real encountered in the dream and go on dreaming with your eyes wide open. The waking state is merely the pursuit of the dream by other means. So this dream isn't merely the dream of everyone; it's the dream of all time. It's "The subject dreams" just as "The subject is happy." And all that may be said of analysis is that there is a subject, as Lacan said, who dreams a little less, and that also means that he doesn't take up every contingency in the regime of repetition.

DREAMING THE ARTICULATION BETWEEN THE UNIVERSAL AND THE PARTICULAR

The generic madness in question here is general, or rather, universal. It's not psychosis. Psychosis is a category of the clinic with which one tries to capture something that is at any rate inscribed into the universal. It's a madness that is delusion, and in the end the delusion begins with knowledge. Delusion begins when to one signifier all by itself you add the articulation to a second one, whereby the "all by itself" becomes "one."

$$\frac{S_1 \longrightarrow S_2}{s \equiv d^1}$$

And at that moment, the effect of signification that is produced—which I'm writing with a lower case *s*—is equivalent to d^1, is equivalent to delusion, and this is how it's understood in the text. It's in the sense that Lacan could say of the Aimée case, the first case that he wrote a book on—moreover he didn't write books on any other cases, he wrote articles—that it showed how a delusion, what one calls a delusion, is a folding screen. It can be blown over, it can fall down, if one touches on the real in the right way, or even the wrong way, since Aimée touched on the real by attacking an image, supported by a character who was a star of the stage.

I said the word earlier, I spoke earlier of Aristotle. Lacan spoke about Aristotle a few months before this text, before an eminently academic audience, an international audience, at UNESCO, on June 1, 1978. It was a short talk he gave, which I didn't put in the *Autres écrits* because there was no written version—I was the one to write it up, so it will be for the little collection. Lacan said, to the astonishment of the audience, who were quite sure not that everyone was mad but that Lacan was—I went with him and I felt the wing of incomprehension that passed over that august assembly: "Aristotle was dreaming, like everyone does" [1978, 23]. This was to say that what needed to be heard was that the very syllogism of Aristotle results from the dream, results from the dream of "for all *x*." The example that Lacan dragged up in front of that audience—it goes way back in his teaching—is the august syllogism "All men are mortal; Socrates is a man; therefore Socrates is mortal." This is, *in nucleo,* the dream of a coincidence, a perfect articulation, an eminent juncture between the general and the particular. We go from the general, "All men are mortal" to the particular, "Socrates is mortal." Here therefore, as if by miracle, the union of the general and the particular is brought about.

Only, this introduces, says Lacan, a snag. In the end, that's what Lacan spends his time doing, introducing and showing snags where people see harmonies. Like Oedipus's [lame foot]. Lacan introduces a snag. The snag here, with which he manages to disarticulate the syllogism is the snag that Freud introduced saying, according to Lacan, that man desires death, that he doesn't die because of a syllogism, that all men are mortal but a man desires death and, it has to be said, Socrates did everything for that. He didn't die in the name of being mortal; he died in the name of having been a clumsy idiot in front of the judges, such a clumsy idiot that one can only be led to think he was happy in all that, that is, that he wanted that, that to satisfy his repetition, he needed death. So this "to desire death" is what was universalized in the guise of the death drive. But it only happens on a one-by-one basis.

I don't have time to look at this text any closer, as I'd intended, but the same path wending from the impossible to the contingent is to be found there because, on one hand, how does one escape Aristotle? How does one escape the "for all *x*"? And at the same time it is not appropriate but Lacan came to say, "In every psychoanalyst, there is a student of Aristotle." Simply saying, "in every psychoanalyst" already makes the "for all *x*" function, and saying "is a student of Aristotle, of the archetypal master" means that one doesn't break off from the aspiration toward the "for all *x*," and that clearly this status of "student of Aristotle" has to be fought against by trying to be a student of Freud as read by Lacan. Anyway, in every psychoanalysand there is a student of Aristotle too because he accepts the rule, he keeps coming back, and therefore he thereby "believes in the universal."

I would underline the definition, which one can take as such, that Lacan gives here of what he calls the dream. He says precisely, "The psychoanalysand . . . dreams, that is. . . ." so once again this closing clause, this formula, as in the ["Everyone is mad"] text, ". . . he dreams, that is, he clasps onto the particularity of his symptom." Indeed, the terms *analytic discourse, dream, delusion, madness, symptom* all collapse to produce this shutting away of each subject in his own world, and therefore the impossibility of any common world. In view of which, one makes do. Everyone is in his own world, that is, in the world that his symptom instigates, in view of which, one makes do as best one can to understand each other and try to forge a path together.

I, TRUTH, AT THE PLACE OF NO ONE ANYMORE

So, "Everyone is mad"—I'll end on this, I shall nevertheless manage to end here—someone did say that. Someone said that before Lacan, and he was that singular character called Erasmus, who wrote a book that has endured over time. The others too, though they are not much read, but this one has echoed down the centuries: his *In Praise of Folly* [1509]. It is madness itself that sings its own praises. Madness is put on stage to sing its own praises: everyone is mad.

If I'd had time, I'd have shown what this praise owes to the classical tradition of praising tiny things. It's an erudite distraction, praise for dirtiness, for tiny repugnant things, praise for sloth, praise for ignorance. It's part and parcel of this tradition, and it provides the figure that has turned out to be the most lasting, and as the very embodiment of humanist wisdom, and of the eye it invites us to cast upon the world, namely, everyone is mad; with all the values that can be given to this madness, from the one that gets rejected right up to the one that gets celebrated: the folly of Christ; which invites us to look at our labors and our honors as pitiful clowning around.

Well, it's no accident that it is here, in this discourse that begins with the statement "Folly speaks," that Lacan went and found the inspiration for his prosopopeia of the truth, "I, truth, speak," a formula he had a particular dilection for and that he gladly repeated over the course of his Seminar, and whose different facets he brought out. His "I, truth, speak" is an Erasmian shoot, and it is this truth that Lacan places in Freud's mouth. The "I, truth, speak" passed through Freud's mouth.

This truth, this truth that is the analytic mode of truth, the truth that is in speech, the truth that speaks in speech—to use Lacan's terms at the time—this truth is clearly akin to jouissance. Read it again—I don't have time to do it with you—starting at page 340 of Lacan, *Écrits* [2006]. This truth is clearly the circle cleared by burning the brush of jouissance, because the word Lacan ends this discourse on is "I belie myself, I defy you, I slip away: you say that I am being defensive" [342]. And this word *defense,* in its verb form, is there to tell us that the truth is the same thing as the Freudian Thing, that truth is a transformation of jouissance, and that jouissance, truth, and madness are a ternary of nouns to be placed right there where the No One Anymore came to be.

There you have it. I've got myself to this place of the No One Anymore. Nonetheless I'll still have to stand in for No One again next year to make my voice sound out. I haven't altogether resigned myself to it, but you shall see what comes of it in September.

Good-bye. C/C

BIOGRAPHY

Jacques-Alain Miller is the editor of Jacques Lacan's seminars and the founder of the World Association of Psychoanalysis. He is the director of the Department of Psychoanalysis, Paris VIII University.

NOTE

This is the text of the last two sessions (June 4 and 11, 2008) of Jacques-Alain Miller's 2007–8 course, *L'orientation lacanienne*, III, 10: "Tout le monde est fou." Translated by Adrian Price from the unedited French transcription.

BIBLIOGRAPHY

Erasmus, Desiderius. 1509. *Morias Enkomion.*

———. 1509 [1970]. *The Praise of Folly,* trans. Hoyt Hopewell Hudson. Princeton, N.J.: Princeton University Press.

Lacan, Jacques. 1963–64 [1994]. *The Seminar Book XI: The Four Fundamental Concepts of Psychoanalysis.* London: Penguin.

———. 1978. "Le rêve d'Aristote." *Colloque pour le 23ᵉ centenaire d'Aristote*, 23–24. Sycomore: UNESCO.

———. 1979. "There Are Four Discourses." In this issue of *Culture/Clinic.*

———. 1979. "Vers un signifiant nouveau." *Ornicar?* 17–18.

———. 1990. *Television.* New York: Norton.

———. 2006a. "The Freudian Thing." In *Écrits: The First Complete English Edition.* New York: Norton.

———. 2006b. "On a Question Prior to Any Possible Treatment of Psychosis." In *Écrits: The First Complete English Edition.* New York: Norton.

———. 2006c. "Remarks on Daniel Lagache's Presentation." In *Écrits: The First Complete English Edition.* New York: Norton.

———. 2006d. "Seminar on *The Purloined Letter.*" In *Écrits: The First Complete English Edition.* New York: Norton.

———. 2006e. "The Subversion of the Subject and the Dialectic of Desire." In *Écrits: The First Complete English Edition.* New York: Norton.

Valéry, Paul. 1986. *Sketch of a Serpent and Other Poems,* trans. Jan Schreber. Florence, Ky.: R. L. Barth.

MAIRE JAANUS

Happiness and Madness

C/C ■ **THE SMILEY ICON**

IN AMERICA EVERYONE KNOWS THE SMILEY FACE. It is a childish image, disarming in its simplicity of design. Seen often at the end of e-mails, it serves as if as a reminder of the pact we have all made with the pursuit of happiness. ☺ Keep smiling. Cheer up. (The original smiley face was designed by Harvey R. Ball for the State Mutual Life Assurance Company to cheer up workers afraid of being laid off during a merger.) The smiley face is a mask, although much less expressive than were the tragic and comic masks of the Greek theater. There's no trace of pain in it or of pleasure great enough to really make one laugh. This icon is not about the maximization of pleasure—the greatest good for the greatest number—that inspired the utilitarians, nor about ardent desire. Desire would be too disturbing. Do not allow yourself to be disturbed, the image seems to say, implying a kind of *ataraxia* (from the Greek *a* "not" and *tarassein*—"disturb"), a state in this instance not of a serene calmness but of a deliberately maintained, steadfast cheerfulness. I'm okay. We're all okay as long as we keep smiling and are nice. The verbal equivalent of the image is the mantra, "Have a nice day." Smiley promotes a kind of mildly delusional sense of collective okayness, cheerfulness, and good will toward everyone that we ourselves can produce with our smiles.

But what lies behind this smiling icon? What's in the empty mustard pot or in the Heideggerian vase, as Lacan liked to ask (1992, 127)? Desire, he answered initially: "The flowers of desire are contained in this vase. . . . The form of the human body is the cloak of all possible fantasms of human desire" (298). However, jouissance is "desire's formidable center" (246). And jouissance, he added later, is what "really fucks us up" (Lacan 1973–74).

■ THE ENJOYING SUBSTANCE (LA SUBSTANCE JOUISSANTE) AND FAITH

"The meaning of the feelings of pleasure and unpleasure which act so imperatively upon us," said Freud, "is the most obscure and inaccessible region of the mind" (SE, 18:7). Lacan understood that these feelings are manifestations of the enjoying substance *(la substance jouissante)* that we at core are (Lacan 1998, 24). He compared them to the unreadable traces or "textual work" that the web emerging from a spider's belly is and that testifies to an existence that remains unknown and illegible. In "the trace of these writings taking form," says Lacan, "one can grasp the limits, impasses, and the dead ends that show up the real acceding to the symbolic" (1998, 93). In literary works in which the structure of desire exposes desire as unrealizable or overwhelming or exposes realized desire as insufficient, we momentarily see "these limits, impasses, and dead ends" and also something of the ferocity of jouissance that drives desire. Such writings are symbolic webs that have caught and encrypted deeply lived experiences of happiness and unhappiness. For Lacan the investigation of such a symbolic web can produce as if a momentary revelation of what he calls the "law of a particular subject," or his *Atè*—his delusion, blindness, "misfortune," and potential ruin—that has brought him with his suffering and demands into analysis (Lacan 1992, 300).

The analysand comes to analysis with a demand for happiness, says Lacan. The demand is all the more urgent since the Enlightenment, when happiness became a political matter, the right of everyone to happiness or at least to its pursuit (Lacan 1992, 292). Who received the demand for happiness before? It is inconceivable that St. Augustine could ever have wanted an analyst in place of the God he believed in, who was "the life of lives. You live, O Life of my soul, because you are life itself, immutable" (Augustine 1962, 61–62). Augustine attributes his very life or *substance jouissante* to God. His faith is the certitude that the moment of death will be a transference to an eternal and more perfect enjoyment and a more perfect knowledge of himself and of God than is now his. "What I do not know about myself I shall continue not to know until I see you face to face" (211). Augustine wanted knowledge of himself *(de anima)* and of God *(de deo)*. "God and the soul. Nothing more?" he asked himself, and answered, "Nothing!" (Marrou 1962, 72). "You, my Father, are eternal," whereas my soul is "torn this way and that in the havoc of change. And so it will be until I am purified and melted into the fire of your love and fused into one with you" (Augustine 1962, 279). Thus Augustine's "line of desire" ends as if in a "false" death—a death that is a fusion with a more complete form of Life—a death denied by love of a God who, Augustine is certain, exists.

This love restructures and transfigures his conception of desire: "But what do I love when I love my God?" Augustine asked:

> Not material beauty or beauty of a temporal order; not the brilliance of earthly light, so welcome to our eyes; not the sweet melody of harmony and song; not the fragrance of flowers, perfumes, and spices; not manna or honey; not limbs such as the body delights to embrace. It is not these that I love when I love my God. And yet, when I love him, it is true that I love a light of a certain kind, a voice, a perfume, a food, an embrace; but they are of the kind that I love in my inner self, when my soul is bathed in light that is not bound by space; when it listens to sound that never dies away; when it breathes fragrance, that is not borne away on the wind; when it tastes food that is never consumed by eating; when it clings to an embrace from which it is not severed by fulfillment of desire. This is what I love when I love my God. (Augustine 1962, 211–12)

In the love of God, all the soul's desires are satisfied and transfigured into an immortal desiring. Existence is purified of any loss, diminution, or ending. Nothing ends, nothing dies, nothing is borne away, nothing is ever consumed, from no embrace is one ever severed by fulfillment. The negativity of desire vanishes. Every mortal satisfaction is immortalized, extended into the infinite, remaining forever desirable despite the complete jouissance already attained. "O Love, ever burning, never quenched! O Charity, my God, set me on fire with your love!" (Augustine 1962, 233).

Augustine believed that one must understand in order to believe: *intellige ut credas*. He desired ardently to know, but his deepest joy came from his faith. For him, there was the knowledge given by faith and the knowledge given by reason (Marrou 1962, 71). What the knowledge by faith gives, beyond a new ideal of desire, is certitude and trust: "My hope lies in the *knowledge* that you do not play us false" (Augustine 1962, 211). Faith abolishes distrust, the fear of deception, and incertitude. Augustine's feeling for God is "not some vague feeling, it is positive and certain" (211).

As his faith in the existence of God becomes ever more certain, his conviction that he must devote himself exclusively to God grows. The idea of falling away from devotion to God, of resting even momentarily in other pleasures, seems more and more sinful. Thus, he grows wary of all his other human desires. He blames himself for enjoying eating, drinking, smelling, listening, even to religious music, and seeing and taking pleasure in the beauty of the world with his eyes (Augustine 1962, 234–52). All that he enjoys becomes a perpetual temptation that distracts him from being mindful of God, who alone is worthy of being the supreme object of his love.

Augustine's ethics become an ever more focused and narrow *eudae-*

monism compared to which Aristotle's ethical teaching seems positively liberal. Ethical for Augustine is to enjoy *(frui)* God, all the rest is a means to be used *(uti)* for that end alone. "In God alone is it lawful to rest and to have joy" (Marrou 1962, 79). This love demands the sacrifice of nearly all his other human desires. He speaks of his struggles to be free of his delight in "this earthly light" so as to see "the true Light." He sees his failure to deaden himself to the world as an illness: "Have pity on me and heal me, for you see that I have become a problem to myself, and this is the ailment from which I suffer" (Augustine 1962, 239–41). Here we see enacted the "amputation, sacrifices, indeed a kind of Puritanism in the relationship to desire that has occurred historically," that Lacan sees greatly aggravated in his own time (1960) by the reduction of desire to the level of a want for material goods under the pressure of a consumption-driven capitalism (Lacan 1992, 303).

For Augustine, the impossible jouissance is something that he *can* have. For him *das Ding* that would fill the void of existence *exists*. "Religion in all its forms consists of avoiding the emptiness" within us, said Lacan (1992, 130), but after his conversion, Augustine did not for a minute believe in his emptiness. Augustine's God is knowledge and jouissance without any limits. Augustine had Christian certitude that the *summum bonum*, the Supreme Good that the classical philosophers had so ardently searched for by reason alone, was his by the knowledge given by faith.

Lacan said, "We imagine that we think; we imagine that we believe what we say." But he asked, "How can we tell the difference between knowledge and belief?" Isn't it evident "that three quarters of so-called knowledge is nothing but belief?" (Lacan 1975, 12). Knowledge has to do with believing, not with being as the ancients thought. Lacan's effort was to make this cut between knowledge, dependent on the semblance of language, and being more evident. As he said, "The discordance between knowledge and being is my subject" (1998, 120). Both faith and belief obscure this discordance though to different degrees. Belief *(croyance)* does not have the same force as faith *(foi)*. Faith wants absolute certitude. It aligns itself with law, truth, and knowledge. Belief is more relaxed and loose; it is not about law, but about hope and possibility. Jouissance is most satisfied by faith, desire by belief and possibility. Because the real can never be filled with knowledge, we fill it with beliefs or a faith.

For Freud, the religions of mankind were mass delusions. They were "remouldings of reality" in order to obtain a wish or to eliminate some unbearable feature of reality. "Whoever sets out upon this path to happiness will as a rule attain nothing," said Freud. "Reality is too strong for him. He becomes a madman, who for the most part finds no one to help him in carrying through his delusion" (SE, 21:81). What Freud downplays, what did not suit his temper as a rationalist, realist, and ardent believer in Darwin, is how happy a "delusion" such as Augustine's made him feel. For reasons that we will never know, Augustine's happiness was the absolute faith his desire searched for and finally found, despite the fact that it demanded so many sacrifices, for example, of his beloved mistress and of so many of the other passions of this most passionate of men, who even comes to ask whether it was a sin that he finally wept for his mother, having forbidden himself to do so at her funeral (Augustine 1962, 203). God was Augustine's inner law, his *Atè:* his ruin as a man and his success as a saint. If St. Augustine is for Catholicism the venerated Father of faith and for Freud one of the leaders of a mass delusion, what becomes evident in either case is that jouissance exists and that its demand for something absolute is fierce. For the late Lacan, such a *unio passionalis* with God as Augustine's is a metaphor of a sexual rapport that doesn't exist and that exposes the "mental debility of systems of thought that suppose it does" (1974–75a).

Such delusional beliefs seem now to have shifted for a large part of the world to science and capitalism. Nonetheless, 82 percent of Americans say they believe in the afterlife, 95 percent believe in God, and "substantially more people believe in angels than believe in evolution" (Obama 2008, 235). That a large percentage of America may, therefore, also not feel in need of psychoanalysis might follow from such statistics. However, regardless of such surveys, religion is no longer the political or legal institution that governs America or that it obeys, and religious discourse is no longer its master discourse. The part of the world that was once Augustine's has chosen history over eternity.

"A delusion," Miller reminds us, "is symbolic. A delusion is a symbolic tale. And a delusion is able to order a world" (2009, 152). It exists in many other fields besides religion, perhaps in all. Delusions are what jouissance and desire together with the semblance that is language readily construct, perhaps even daily, to fill in large and small deficiencies in quotidian experience. Because it is symbolic, a delusion can be communicated and adopted by others or a group. Then its power obviously grows, though that is no guarantee of its beneficence. Symbolic delusions or entire delusional metaphysical systems organize "fragmented and panic-stricken drives" (Lacan 1992, 302), localize jouissance, and design paths of desire. A delusion is not a psychosis. Psychosis is the implosion of a subject that disables its participation in reality.

■ THE DELUSIONAL ANIMAL

Animals cannot be happy, so Aristotle reasoned, "because they have no way of participating in contemplation" (1962, 333). Thus, happiness, the *summum bonum,* is reserved only for us. Today, we believe that animals feel many of the emotions that we do. We also know that animals dream (Wilson 2010). It is also argued that animals in a radically deprived environment, such as a zoo, may develop zoochosis (zoo + psychosis), but given that the "language" (ours or their own) that programs animals limits them to a referential relationship to objects in their environment, they cannot construct delusions. Delusions are, therefore, reserved exclusively for us. We are the delusional animal. And it is our pursuit of happiness and equally of unhappiness that seems to show up our delusional power more clearly than anything else about us. Delusions may be our *summum bonum,* the main and distinctive form of a human adaptation to survival.

When we have happiness, Diotima tells Socrates, we possess the good things we desire, and, therefore "there's no need to ask further, 'What's the point of wanting happiness'" (Plato 1989, 50). In the *Euthydemus,* however, Socrates says, if happiness is desired by all, "how can we be happy, is the next question?" (Plato, 380 b.c.e. [1994]). For Lacan, this was the beginning of a new scientific way of thinking that Aristotle continued by writing the first differential "science of happiness" (Lacan 1992, 258). According to Aristotle, the good is attained through rational discipline, the practice of logical thinking and moderation. Aristotle posited the ideal of a god of pure thinking, his Unmoved Mover, but he did not really think a creature compounded of reason and unreason was capable of pure thought, and thus he, wisely, relegated the activity of pure thinking to the gods and chose the secondary happiness of an active life of teaching and politics for himself. For Aristotle, reason was about logicality, and unreason was a failure to use logic correctly. Aristotle's field of ethical examination excluded the real of sex, unconscious desire, and fantasy. This left a great deal for Lacan to deal with in his own ethics seminar.

Freud did not think that the aim of life was the good or that it had any purpose (*SE,* 21:75–76). Freud said, "*The aim of all life is death.*" It seemed to him "a truth beyond exception . . . that everything living becomes inorganic once again" and returns to the inanimate (*SE,* 18:38–39). Freud did also not believe that contemplation was man's *summum bonum* because it is obviously not the strongest or the most intense experience of pleasure for the majority of human beings. For Freud, "sexual love" is "the prototype of all happiness" and gives human beings their strongest experiences of satisfaction (*SE,* 2:101). Other satisfactions may "seem 'finer and higher,' but their intensity is mild compared with that derived from the sating of crude and primary drives; they do not convulse our corporality *(sie erschüttern nicht unsere Leiblichkeit)*. . . . The feeling of happiness *(Glücksgefühl)* derived from the satisfaction of a wild drive *(Triebregung)* untamed by the ego is incomparably more intense than that derived from sating a tamed drive *(Trieb)*" (*SE*, 21:79–80).

For Freud, sex is the root *(radix)* of all other forms of love. All the others paths of love are attenuated forms of sex. They are aim inhibited, sublimated, and displaced forms of sex. St. Francis of Assisi, says Freud, went perhaps as far as anyone can go in "exploiting love for the benefit of an inner feeling of happiness." But what such rare individuals in fact "bring about in themselves in this way is a state of evenly suspended, steadfast affectionate feeling, which has little external resemblance any more to the stormy agitations of genital love, from which it is nevertheless derived" (*SE*, 21:102).

The body is polymorphously perverse, and many forms of jouissance arise from it. Lacan singles out four basic fields of jouissance: phallic *jouissance* [J (ɸ)], feminine *jouissance* [S (Ø)], *Jouis-sens*, and the *en plus* given by the *objet a*. Each is capable of utterly convulsing our being. The symbolic jouissance that creative scientists or artists have at breakthrough moments measures as high as the strongest drug hit. The mystic's feminine jouissance is not attenuated. Freud did not make as many critical cuts, nor did he examine as intently as did Lacan the divide between sex and love. He stood away from erotic feelings that were beyond sex—such as Romain Rolland's "oceanic sensation of eternity," love, or the feeling for the beautiful or the sublime—almost as if they were suspect in some way of a neurotic condition. He disclaimed having such feelings himself (*SE*, 21:65).

Freud was certain that the feeling for beauty was derived from the field of sexual feeling as well, and "a perfect example of an impulse inhibited in its aim." That explained, for him, why the enjoyment of beauty had only "a peculiar, mildly intoxicating quality of feeling" (*SE*, 21:82–83). Not even the sober-minded Kant, who understood that the feeling of the beautiful had to do with the subject's "feeling of life," would have agreed (Kant 1986, 161). And Stendhal, who fainted when he saw the beauties of Florence on his first arrival there, would not have understood Freud at all. What is termed the "Stendhal syndrome"—the dizziness, fainting, confusion, increased heartbeat due to an encounter with art—commemorates this psychic event. The variety of the plays of pain and pleasure in a polymorphously perverse body, so Lacan understood, is immense, the occurrence of these plays is unpredictable, and their exact description ever eludes us.

■ POETIC FAITH

Don Quixote bears witness at the beginning of modernity to the great shift of language itself from heaven to earth. He reads and believes. Seduced and invaded down to his very bones and muscles by words that are only profane, he is moved to enact them as if they were sacred commands. In his world of exalted knighthood, he is the main agent and actor. His megalomania gives him the position of a master. There is no question that he is delusional: an inn is not a castle, and his poor old body is not that of a knight. But not long after, why do so many others follow him? Who then is mad?

Sancho Panza has a sense of reality given to him by his body, which Don Quixote has lost. To preserve himself from the beatings that his master's delusions subject him to, he learns to make crazy compromises with Don Quixote's ideas. For example, there is the object that is a barber's basin for Sancho that a barber happens to be carrying on his head, but that the Don perceives as Malbrino's golden helmet:

> "By God, it's a good basin, and worth a *real* if it's worth a farthing."
>
> He then gave it to his master, who placed it on his head turning it round and round to find the vizor. But unable to discover it, he remarked: "Certainly the pagan to whose measure this famous headpiece was first shaped must have had an enormous head; and the worst of it is that one half is missing."
>
> When Sancho heard the basin called a head-piece he could not restrain his laughter; but suddenly he remembered his master's anger, and he stopped short.
>
> "What are you laughing at?" asked Don Quixote.
>
> "It makes me laugh," he replied, "to think what a big head that pagan must have had, who owned the headpiece. It's like nothing so much as a barber's basin. Just *like* it, it is."
>
> "Do you know what I think, Sancho? This famous piece, this enchanted helmet, must have fallen by some strange accident into the hands of someone who did not esteem it at its true value. So, not knowing what he was doing, and seeing it was pure gold, he must have melted down the other half for the sake of the metal, and made from this half what looks *like* a barber's basin, *as you say*. But, however that may be, its metamorphosis is of no consequence to me, who know *what it really is*. For I *will have it set right* in the first village where there is a smith, and so well that it will not be surpassed or even equalled by the helmet which the god of smithies forged and made for the god of battles. In the meantime, however, I will wear it as best as I can, for something is better than nothing; and, besides, it will do very well to defend me from a stoning." (my italics, Cervantes 1967, 162–63)

Don Quixote and Sancho need to solve the problem of the object and its name: Is it Sancho's object of material value and pleasure, worth at least a *real*, or the object of the Don's desire and delusion? Sancho's naming the basin disturbs the Don's desire, as does the size of the object itself, because it does not fit his head and half of it is missing. But the Don's first reaction that the "helmet" is partial and too big is already a considerable concession to the failure of the object as it were or to the existence of a gap between the true helmet that would be a whole helmet, with a visor, versus what is only half a helmet. The incorrect size and the shape of the object have to be accounted for. A considerable remolding of reality is necessary on the Don's part to accomplish this and to assure that the basin continue to be a helmet. There has to have been a giant with a large head and some event or accident that caused the loss of the visor.

This wacko explanation strikes Sancho as hilarious, but to avoid another beating, he decides to accept his master's version of the basin by way of the simplest of metaphors, the simile "like." "Just like it, it is." *Like* is not *is*. It is a similitude that isn't the same. It merely *seems* to be. It is a semblance. With this simile Sancho can continue to assert his own version of the facts, the truth of *his* basin, the barber's basin. But Sancho's insertion of this simple, ambiguous "like" creates considerable difficulties for the Don, operating somewhat like an apt analytic intervention. It demands a new effort of thought, ingenuity, and verbal inventiveness on his part to make it harmonize with his own delusional narrative. That simile, pointing to an unwelcome discrepancy, requires the production of a far more elaborate and extensive narration (there was someone who valued it only for its gold, who melted half of it down, and so on). Finally, he is able to bring himself to a compromise with what Sancho "says" by way of Sancho's own ruse: "What looks like a barber's basin, as you say." It is only in the symbolic field of metaphor that their irreconcilable difference can momentarily be bridged. It is by means of the semblance that they can find a common ground and maintain a peaceful human bond. Although theirs is not an analytic transference, their recurrent need to resolve such differences builds a human transference that ends in love.

The Don's concession to semblance seems to be as far as he can, at this point, go, before having to reassert the absolute certitude of his sublime and noble delusion once again: *his* golden helmet: *his* jouissance. He can accept what Sancho "says" because beyond that "he *knows* what it really is," and he will "have it set right," and it will be more beautiful than ever before. He exerts himself to the utmost to find words to reestablish the absolute existence of a helmet that will be beyond the excellence of any ever made, even beyond the one that "the god of smithies forged and made for the god of battles." Then, exhausted, he falls down as if to another rhetorical level, to the colloquial tone and diction of Sancho, to received proverbs, to the acceptance of the more practical and expedient, and his need for self-protection in case of a stoning. He has enough energy to weave this poetic web of words once again over the miserable existence of this unacceptable barber's basin that shouldn't exist, but he does not have enough energy to transform all that needs transforming in the world.

In this incredible dialogue, the master and servant attain together, but only for a moment, what Coleridge called "poetic faith." He defined it as "the willing suspension of disbelief." He came up with this felicitous phrase to justify the reintroduction of the supernatural, which the Enlightenment had banned from its poetry. Poetic faith was Coleridge's way of realigning poetic language once again with a pleasure that was being denied. It is a "belief" given to words because they have the power to release pleasure, but on condition that we obey the requirement of "the willing suspension of disbelief for the moment." Poetic faith is not a truth relationship or a knowledge relationship to the word. It establishes no laws, though it is not lawless. It advocates no specific knowledge, though it is not without knowing. It doesn't say, "It is"; it says, "It seems." It has only what Kant called "exemplary necessity" (Kant 1986, 194–200).

The law commands, "Thou shalt not lie," lending powerful support and authority to language as a place of truth, but what kind of truth can this commandment produce? Only as much truth as is under the command of language. Jouissance is outside of language, as Lacan wrote with the matheme S (Ø). It is part of the real or "what is strictly unthinkable" (Lacan 1974–75b). Language "lies" by omission because it cannot directly tell nor does it even know the whole truth about that which is beyond it. Our whole world is built upon a knowing that does in fact not know the most basic things that we would like to know, for example, how long we will live or what we should do to be happy. The commandment to tell "the whole truth and nothing but the truth" cannot be obeyed because it is based on a false assumption about language and its limits. The law commands us to do something with language that it is impossible to do. Only poetic or fictional writing is inherently liberated from this commandment because it has never claimed to be the truth. It doesn't ask to be believed. It only asks us not to disbelieve, and only "for the moment." This is part of the secret of its lightness and pleasure. It is a free domain.

THE MAD BODY

The Letter of Lord Chandos, dated 1603 and addressed to his friend, Francis Bacon, is a fictional letter, written by Hofmannsthal in 1902. Originally published simply as *A Letter (Ein Brief),* it describes the writing crisis of a successfully published and acclaimed young artist that ends in a complete collapse of his ability to use, comprehend, or enjoy language: "I have lost completely the ability to think or to speak of anything coherently" (Hofmannsthal 1902). He cannot understand what is said. He cannot speak. Words are meaningless. He cannot even make ordinary conversation. The impairment and the communication failure are extreme.

Most striking is the loss of his ability to enjoy language. First comes distaste for abstract words like *soul*. This distaste grows into a violent physical aversion. Words fall apart in his mouth "like rotten mushrooms." One senses that he will have to "vomit" them out. He compares this evacuation of jouissance from the field of language to seeing nothing but holes and hallows where there had one been a solid texture and meaning, a seamless and continuous reality, upheld and elaborated by the symbolic: "As once through a magnifying glass, I had seen a piece of skin on my little finger look like a field full of holes and furrows, so I now perceived human beings and their actions" (Hofmannsthal 1902).

As he loses his hold on the signified and signifying control over signifiers, his ability to conceptualize collapses: "For me everything disintegrated into parts, those parts again into parts; no longer would anything let itself be encompassed by one idea." The signifier and signified split in a way that is irreparable. He can no longer think coherently. He becomes acutely aware of the spaces between words: "Single words floated around me; they congealed into eyes which stared at me and into which I was forced to stare back—whirlpools which gave me vertigo and reeling incessantly, led into the void." He loses the signifier as such. He is no longer in the symbolic. Words are no longer words. They become eyes. What was sound becomes a look. Words are now enigmatic, speechless eyes, leading him to the void, the real of the symbolic. This is the moment of the implosion of his symbolic world.

The collapse of the symbolic into the erogenous zone of the eyes is followed by a tremendous uprising and accretion of jouissance in the imaginary. Now ordinary objects, even the ones present only in his imagination, can give rise to "a flood of divine sensation." A rat or stone can become "exalted and moving," "the vessel of my revelation." In his moments of ecstasy, nothing is void of life or love though which object will produce this sense of dazzling intimacy with itself is uncertain and contingent. His eyes are always scanning his surroundings with hunger and longing for that one object "whose insignificant form, whose unnoticed being, whose mute existence, can become the source of that mysterious, wordless, and boundless ecstasy." He has lost the symbolic world that orders, but he now has a passional world of exalted sensations and intimate erotic relations with objects that fill up the void of his existence with "unnamable" and "unnamed blissful feelings."

These epiphanic moments of idenficatory unity with different objects are his one form of solace in a life of "vacuity," "stagnation," and "indifference" to all his human relationships and affairs, which he is able to continue thanks only to the "good and strict education that I owe to my late father and the early habit of leaving no hour of the day unused." What is left of the Name-of-the-Father, namely habit or routine movements stored in long-term memory, are sufficient at least at this time to help him "maintain towards the outer world the stability and the dignified appearance appropriate to my class and my person."

Chandos's delusional imaginary world is reminiscent of what Baudrillard called "the world of metamorphosis," where there is a free interplay, shifting, and exchange of all forms and a direct slippage from one's own bodily form into another. Baudrillard speaks of it as a constant betrayal of one's own form and an exposure to the giddiness of a sumptuous theater of multiple forms. "The body of the fable," says Baudrillard, is part of a "phantasmagoria of species," where the yielding of one's own form leads to self-perpetuation and immortality. "The body of the fable" disappears only to reappear. In the network of forms that is metamorphosis, one is always somewhere, dispersed, but never dead. By comparison, sexuation signifies a fall from this richer imaginary of the subject, and a reduction to one form, that of the sexed human body with its mortality (Baudrillard 1988, 45–48).

Chandos's breakdown and subsequent delusion were preceded, as he tells us, by "a state of continuous intoxication" and an immense desire to write and to find a new form of writing. This new form would lead to its own dissolution in that it would no longer have anything to do with organizing its subject matter, but with penetrating and dissolving it, "creating at once both dream and reality, an interplay of eternal forces, something as marvelous as music or algebra." The subject matter that had obsessed Chandos was the disordered world of the fable, with its metamorphoses. He wanted to talk from within the bodies in the fables, and to talk, as they did, no longer humanly. He wanted to "enter these naked, glistening bodies, these sirens and dryads, this Narcissus and Proteus. . . . I longed to disappear in them and talk out of them with tongues" (Hofmannsthal 1902).

Lord Chandos's "encyclopedic book" or collection, entitled *Apophthegmata* (from the Greek *apo,* "from" and *phtheggomai,* "to cry out") that would have expressed his "felt sense of the whole of existence as one great unit," fails to be written because he cannot find the words for that "one great unit" or the liquid form of writing that would dissolve everything into this great one Name-of-the-Father—Pan or God—that no longer exists. No Name-of-the-Father is able to condense and contain so much jouissance. The world of jouissance has no names. This failure to be able to symbolize as if jouissance itself seems to be what triggered his break.

The implosion of his bodily ego that centers the imaginary order and that Chandos now experiences is signaled by his one final identification with a human figure, namely that of Crassus, the Roman senator, mocked for mourning the death of his tame lamprey– a dumb, apathetic, red-eyed fish—of which he had become enamored. The weeping Crassus with his fish is the "mirrored image of my Self," says Chandos. This image, which sits in his brain "like a splinter," provokes a "feverish thinking" that is "more immediate, more liquid, more glowing than words. It too forms whirlpools, but of a sort that does not seem to lead as do the whirlpools of language, into the abyss, but into myself and into the deepest womb of peace" (Hofmannsthal 1902). Thus this liquid thinking leads not as before to the real of the symbolic with its void, but into the real of his organism, which, in the form of a holding womb or a tomb, can contain all that he is and give him peace. It seems to lead him into what Miller calls "the place of No One Anymore," into his own possible nonexistence, which is, for Miller, the primordial defense (see this issue, 23). Lord Chandos is mourning the potential loss of his own being together with the singular objects (such as Crassus's fish) that gave him happiness and bound him to the world.

He says that he will never ever write again as long as he lives "because the language in which I might be able not only to write but to think is neither Latin nor English, neither Italian not Spanish, but a language none of whose words is known to me, a language in which inanimate things speak to me and wherein I may one day have to justify myself before an unknown judge." He has no being anymore besides that dream of his fusionary oneness with inanimate things. In that fantasy, his body is "nought but ciphers which give me the key to everything; or as if we could enter into a new and hopeful relationship with the whole of existence if only we begin to think with the heart" (Hofmannsthal 1902). It would seem that his ancient wish to write lies behind this delusional transformation of his imaginary body form into a new body of ciphers. A body of ciphers is no longer alive. His desire to write "with tongues" out of things failed, but by a fantastical remolding of his body into inanimate ciphers he attains what was his original dream of a union, albeit now of lifeless things with dead letters. His cipher body is writing and seeking the jouissance that writing once gave him and that his jouissance still inexorably demands. It is an erotomaniac body, a polymorphously perverse body gone mad. The push to writing continues in delusional form, but one suspects that without that he would not want to live at all.

Lord Chandos's letter is addressed to Francis Bacon, with great respect and in grateful friendship, but it is Bacon who destroyed what Lacan calls the "sacred world" of Pan as surely as Machiavelli destroyed the sacred world of symbolic vows and promises. Chandos's letter may be an ironic or an accusatory answer to Bacon's call for a return "to things themselves" and the restoration of the "commerce between the mind of man and the nature of things . . . to its perfect and original condition," for it is Bacon, who wanted scientific thinking to begin with particular things and to proceed inductively. Bacon's goal was "a total reconstruction of sciences, arts, and all human knowledge, raised upon proper foundations" (Bacon 1960, 3–4). He wanted progress and works that would be of use to human life (24). He proposed making instrumental and practical use of nature to enhance our material life and our power over nature (29). His ideas and desires were the deathblow to a world of rituals and libations where wine was poured to the gods of the earth before a field was plowed or a mine was opened.

Bacon's thinking was oriented to material happiness. His jouissance was science and the scientific revolution. He had little interest in the obscure field of desires and jouissances in which human beings struggle for psychic survival and happiness. He was indifferent to the already known and to the classical humanist concerns with past authors and their thoughts. He wanted nothing to do with Aristotelian metaphysics or mere contemplative activity. He wanted to separate our minds from nature as much as possible because he saw that the deficiencies and limitations of our symbolic system and our imagination distort nature. He wanted laboratories, instruments, machinery, experiments, observation, and proofs as "helps and guards" against the feeble human intellect with its delusions (Bacon 1960, 27).

Bacon is the most modern of the late Renaissance thinkers and the father of the scientific revolution that, starting from the seventeenth century, pushed us ultimately into the Industrial Revolution and contemporary global capitalism. That revolution, as now becomes more and more evident, was a break with humanism and the humanistic disciplines. Descartes tells us that "as soon as age permitted me to escape the tutelage of my teachers, I left the study of letters completely." He saw that in the world of humanistic letters "there is nothing about which there is not some dispute—and thus nothing that is not doubtful," and what Descartes above all craved was something doubt free and certain, which he felt the sciences and his method alone gave him (Descartes 1980, 5). He writes that from his method he derived "such intense satisfaction . . . that I did not believe one could receive sweeter or more innocent satisfaction in this life. . . . I had a satisfaction that so filled my mind that nothing else was of any consequence to me" (15). It is this jouissance in scientific methods, so different from Augustine's or Aristotle's or Hofmannsthal's Lord Chandos, that set his own, and in many ways, our destiny.

STUPIDITY AND PLATO'S *SCHWÄRMEREI*

In analysis, Lacan tells us, the key is to get the patient "to utter stupidities." "It is with those stupidities that we do analysis and that we enter into the new subject—of the unconscious" (Lacan 1998, 22). In other discourses, as he says, "Stupidity is what one flees," one aims at the least stupidity, but analytic discourses bases itself on the dimension of stupidity (13). Why? Because the analytic discourse is "situated at the level of enjoying substance" (24). In it, the object *a* is given agency, and object *a* does not speak. The dimension of stupidity begins where language ends, where nothing is any longer certain, understood, or coherent, where there is bewilderment, where one may feel overwhelmed by affects, or be raving, delusional, or make false moves or slips, or lose the ability to speak altogether as does Hofmannsthal's Lord Chandos.

In the seminar on transference, Lacan points out that everyone at the banquet of Agathon utters stupidities about love except for Alcibiades, Socrates, and Aristophanes, who gets an extreme case of hiccups trying to cover up his laughter over the ridiculous things being said. Lacan is at great pains to point out that Plato distances Socrates from the speech of his teacher Diotima, because this revered speech on love is, in fact, "a speculative stupidity." For Lacan, it is an example of Plato's high, ironic, and extremely subtle derision and play. It testifies to Plato's infernal humor and his "metaphysical dandyism" (Lacan 1991, 105).

According to Lacan, Christian desire mandated a misreading of Plato's meaning and a distortion of the *Symposium*. The Christian Neoplatonists seized on the ladder of love as a way of ascent to the divine. They intoxicated themselves with this thinking that dispossesses itself of everything mortal because it fitted in with their desire for the resurrection of the body, even if only a disembodied, purely spiritual one. As Diotima says, the reward of purifying one's thinking is a vision of "the Beautiful itself, absolute, pure, unmixed, not polluted by human flesh or colors or any other *great nonsense of mortality*" (Plato 1989, 59). One can recall here Castiglione's Bembo so transported out of himself after the vehemence of his speech on love, which replicates Diotima's, that Signora Emilia feels compelled—seeing him so dazed, silent, and still, gazing upward toward heaven—to pluck the hem of his robe and say, "Take care, Pietro, that with these thoughts of yours you too do not cause your soul to leave your body" (Castiglione 1967, 343). Love is two, as Aristophanes's myth and Alcibiades's rage demonstrate, not the self-adoration and oneness in which Diotima's speech ends and on which I have commented elsewhere. As Lacan says later, "When one gives rise to two there is never a return. *Aufhebung* is one of philosophy's pretty little dreams" (Lacan 1998, 86).

For Lacan, Diotima's speech is simply Plato's *Schwärmerei,* his giving way to a delirious raving of his own to demonstrate that he can give a speech superior to that of anyone at the banquet and in the same hyperbolic style. But this "oceanic development" of fullness and completeness cannot be identified with Socrates, says Lacan (1991, 159). Socrates introduces emptiness, the void of the signifier, into Greek reality. Emptiness is constitutive of his position, says Lacan (185–86).

STULTITIA *AND* INSANIA

Stultitia defends what is. Stupidity is. She exists. Her name is Stultitia and her epithet is "most foolish" (Erasmus 1970, 11). To be stupid is to be ignorant and happy. Sophocles understood that when he gave her a nice tribute and said, "To know nothing affords the happiest life" (Erasmus 1970, 16). Therefore, Stultitia knows that wherever and whenever she is excluded, there is no happiness. She knows why the world is not a happy place: she is foreclosed; wisdom rules instead. And wisdom is what ruins the world. Momus, the critic, god of blame and censure, was cast down to earth because the gods wanted to be rid of the presence of a censor and have more careless felicity (21–22). So does everyone. Stultitia bestows it (65). She has nothing to do with laws that restrict or prohibit. Her project is to make evident instead the law of foolishness as a "law without limits" (Lacan 1992, 259). She proposes a serious investigation of nonknowing. She is the first to promote what Lacan termed "the essential articulation of non-knowledge as a dynamic value" (295). For Freud this was one of his early paths into the unconscious, and for Lacan it was the beginning of his way into the real.

What else exists? Life. She is the "alpha of all gods," because she bestows life. Life as such is owed to her. "The wise man must send for me, I repeat, if ever he wishes to become a father." Speaking more frankly, she asks, whether it is the head or other such body part that "generates gods and men"? "Nay," she says, "rather that foolish, even silly, part which cannot be named without laughter is the propagator of the human race." Along with life she rightly, therefore, claims to be and have the phallus, the dumb organ of pleasure, necessary for making life. Let us not forget, she says, that we owe our existence to the marriage bed, and marriage itself to Anoia (*a*, "without" + *nous* "mind"), to mindlessness or to madness (Erasmus 1970, 14–15). But, evidently we did forget, because Freud's account of human sexuality was such a shock and so offensive to his era. More recently, Lacan had again to remind everyone that the "law does not ignore the bed" (1998, 2).

Bestowing life is, however, the least of her powers, because "Can life be called life at all if you take away pleasure?" (Erasmus 1970, 15). She is the way to pleasure as pleasure is her own very beginning. She came into the world laughing, not weeping; her father is the god of riches and her mother the goddess of youth. Her two nurses were drunkenness and ignorance. Her other attendants are self-love (Philautia), flattery (Kolkia), oblivion (Lethe), laziness (Misoponia), pleasure (Hedone), madness (Anoia), wantonness (Tryphe), intemperance (Comus), and sound sleep (Negretos Hypnos). She has nine attendants rather than the traditional, so-called seven deadly sins: greed, sloth, pride, lust, envy, wrath, and gluttony. Anoia, "the lady with the uncertain eyes rolling here and there," is a new and interesting addition (Erasmus 1970, 12–13). The nature and function of these attendants or so-called sins has been completely misunderstood, as she will clarify.

Stultitia claims folly, illusion, madness, and finally also insanity *(insania)* as part of her domain. Her pleasure principle extends, as does Freud's, beyond the pleasure principle. It is liberal, nonjudgmental, impartial, and democratically all-inclusive. "It is only I, Folly, who embrace all men without distinction in my provident goodness" (Erasmus 1970, 65). Isn't it evident, she asks, that a considerable "variety of madness is much more widespread than people generally realize" and indeed "so widespread that I do not know whether out of the whole world of mortals it is possible to find one who is wise at all times of day, and who is not subject to some extravagance"? (53). Only those ever-ingrate wise men try to deny the fact that "the universal is my temple" (66), but their great error in doing so proves them "foolosophers" (10).

She never stops speaking of the infinite value of what she offers. She offers self-love, for one, and exemplifies it. She praises herself. If others think that is foolish, she can let that pass, but she would like her audience at least to agree that it is proper for her to do so: "Who, indeed, could portray me better than I can myself? Unless it could so happen that I am better known to some else than I am to myself?" (Erasmus 1970, 8). Unlike Augustine, she does not believe that another knows her better than she knows herself. And this is true in the analytic encounter as well: the analyst does not know the analysand. Since the analysand, however, does not know himself either, together they are reduced to producing interpretations, "not meant to be understood," equivocations, and "waves" (Lacan 1975, 35). For Stultitia, this kind of foolishness is exactly *the* essential thing to understand.

Wanting to be wise is not wanting to be who you are, but other than you are. But she is stupid and accepts what she is. In general, it is wiser to accept what is and what one is than not to do so. After all, didn't Aristotle teach that we must accept, develop, and fulfill our nature in order to be happy? Unfortunately, though not surprisingly, he was completely mistaken regarding what human nature is. For Stultitia, the entire project of philosophy, both Greek and Roman, is mistaken. The fundamental notion of the wise man is an extremely foolish and, above all, an unnatural concept.

What then is our nature? Mainly passion rather than government by reason because Jupiter did not want our life to be too harsh or sad, and therefore he put in:

> How much more of the passions than of reason? Well the portions run about one pound to half an ounce. Besides, he imprisoned reason in a cramped corner of the head, and turned over all the rest of the body to the emotions. After that he instated two most violent tyrants, as it were, in opposition to reason: anger, which holds the citadel of the breast and consequently the very spring of life, the heart; and lust, which rules a broad empire lower down, even to the privy parts. How much reason is good for, against these twin forces, the ordinary life of men sufficiently reveals when reason—and it is all she can do—shouts out her prohibitions until she is hoarse and dictates formulas of virtue. But the passions simply bid their so-called king go hang himself and more brazenly roar down the opposition, until the man . . . knuckles under. (Erasmus 1970, 23)

This radical ratio of one part reason to thirty-two parts of passion is what is required, first of all, to have a human being. Subtract passion, and what you have is just a "marble simulacrum of a man, a senseless block, completely alien to every human feeling" (Erasmus 1970, 89). Passion is our nature and our *telos*. "Nothing can be called unhappy if it fulfils its own nature. . . . Hence just as a horse ignorant of grammar is not miserable, a man who is a fool is not unhappy; the reason being that in each case the attribute is consistent with the nature" (43). To go against nature makes for an unhappy world and civilization. Later Rousseau tried similarly to tell his supposedly civilized era that their unhappiness was grounded in their defiance of what he believed to be their original savage and gentle nature, but without much success.

Man's center is in passion. Ignorance is one of the three great passions, as Lacan taught. In ignorance the basic stance is "I don't want to know anything about it" (Lacan 1998, 1). Stultitia is in complete agreement that this is eminently so. Didn't God charge mankind "upon the pain of death" that they should not eat of the tree of knowledge, "exactly as if knowledge is the bane of happiness?" (Erasmus 1970, 117). Total ignorance is requisite in order for human beings to be in undisturbed and pure possession of their enjoyment. Knowledge causes nothing but strife and dissension, as Erasmus personally knew all too well. (The central section of *The Moriae* is a kind of comic Inferno for the scholastics and monastics of his time.) Thus, Stultitia has no regrets or complaints about the limits of knowledge or reason that has troubled so many foolosophers. Ignorance is unlimited and infinite. Its power extends to death against the fear of which it protects men. Stultitia cannot and does not share Plato and Aristotle's deep belief in reason and knowledge as our *summum bonum* or as our way to happiness or pleasure. And for salvation, as she shows us at the end, one needs not only folly or ignorance, but insanity *(insania)*. Knowledge is insufficient and limited. Ignorance, by contrast is unlimited and alone capable of reaching the infinite.

She knows, as does the analyst, according to Lacan, that "the question of the Sovereign Good is closed." Not only does the analyst not "have that Sovereign God that is asked of him, but he also knows there isn't any" (Lacan 1992, 300). The good can only emerge from those goods that men already have, as Stultitia is trying to demonstrate. Speaking extemporaneously is one such good. She says, "Whatever pops into my head" (Erasmus 1970, 9), because that is more satisfactory, more pleasurable, and truer. She is too foolishly pleasure seeking to bother about thinking, which involves order and discipline. She obeys the psychoanalytic rule naturally.

Stultitia rejects Aristotle's philosophic man, the subject-supposed-to-know, and imaginary wisdom. The wise fool replaces the wise man. It is a formidable act of liberation in an age of humanism that insisted, as in Pico's *Oration on the Dignity of Man*, that reason brings man close to the angels. What Stultitia has against wisdom is that it does not address life nor does it seem to have much know-how about living. The late Lacan was also not interested in wisdom. He rejects philosophy because it "puts at its center the idea that man is made for wisdom. I have, conforming to Freud's thought, no friendship with wisdom. I do not do philosophy because it is very far from this someone [the analysand] who addresses us, to answer him with wisdom" (Lacan 1975, 53). How could wisdom be useful in analysis when the analysand who comes demands happiness?

Nothing proves better that we have little in common with wisdom than the Christian religion, which, as Stultitia says, "has no alliance whatever with wisdom" (Erasmus 1970, 118). Christian zeal and piety is testimony to this:

> For they pour out their wealth, they overlook wrongs, allow themselves to be cheated, make no distinction between friends and enemies, shun pleasure, glut themselves with hunger, wakefulness, tears, toils, and reproaches; they distain life and dearly prefer death; in short, they seem to have grown utterly numb to ordinary sensations, quite as if their souls lived elsewhere and not in their bodies. "What is this forsooth, but to be mad?" (*Quod quidem quid aliud est, quam insanire?*). (118)

Stultitia goes on: "Paul in the eyes of his judge, Festus, looked as if he had gone mad *(insanire)*. . . . The happiness of Christians . . . is nothing else but a kind of madness *(insania)* and folly *(stultitia)*" (119). Stultitia's shift to the use of the stronger verb *insanire* ("to be insane") and the word *insania* ("insanity") from the words she used earlier like *foolish* (*fatuus*), *stultitia* (from *stultus*, "stupid, foolish"), or *moriae* ("idiocy," "imbecility, " "fatuity," "foolishness") does not show up in the English translation I am using. Also, when Stultitia speaks of the pious, it is as a distant "they" compared to the close vulgar, whose stance is more comprehensible. Stultitia compares the pious to mad *(insaniam)* lovers who "are truly outside themselves *(vere toti extra se sunt)*" and who when they return want "nothing but to be mad *(insanire)* always with this madness *(insania)*" (124).

In her argument for Christian madness, Stultitia makes a point of backing up every reference by a citation from the Bible. This leads not only to a demonstration that the Bible encourages us to be insane, but to the implication that this entire text is itself insane. Stultitia, then, works herself up into a sweat to inspire us to really feel as vertiginous and insane as we need to be to identify with the pious and to deliver ourselves over to their madness. To get us to take the final step on this self-destructive *Via Dolorosa* to the divine, she needs frenzy. Folly is an unusual humanist, beyond her time, because nothing human is alien to her, not even the alienated, those insane enough to follow the martyrs. In this, she anticipates Shakespeare, born twenty-eight years later.

In what way is this ecstatic climax Erasmus's *Schwärmerei?* Is it a hilariously funny and ironic version of Christian ecstasy, as most commentators and readers have assumed, or is this more subversive, more like a commentary both on Diotima's adherents and those of Christian Platonism as delusional, perhaps even psychotic (the word didn't come into use until 1845). Was Huizinga totally wrong when he said, "This is bolder and more chilling than Machiavelli, more insightful than Montaigne?" (Huizinga 1957, 71). Can one at the least assume the same kind of irony and distance between Stultitia and the pious that Lacan felt there was between Diotima and Socrates, as well as Diotima and Plato? At the end, Erasmus certainly distances his Stultitia from any such *Schwärmerei*. She goes off to have a drink. Her final farewell words are about life. She tells us to forget everything that she has said and to live *(vivite)* and to drink *(bibite)*.

We know that Erasmus did not claim or search for religious ecstasy (Bainton 1969, 60). He abhorred the various forms of fanaticism of his time and war in particular (124). He wrote the stunning *Complaint of Peace*, refuting Augustine's arguments for the theory of just war that had held sway for over a thousand years (195). Erasmus was often denounced as a Lutheran (161), and some held that if he had not been a pacifist, his, in certain respects, more radical views could have stirred up a greater revolution than did Luther (165), though in the opinion of others ultimately to a more rational and peaceful one. Like Luther and More, he was deeply invested in reform. Luther wrote to him accusingly: "You with your peace-loving theology don't care about truth." "But," responded Erasmus, "what happens to truth when men are embroiled in a war of religion?" (Bainton 1969, 192). Luther had absolute faith that the "freedom of the Christian" resided in a sinlessness given "by faith alone." It is a somewhat delusional ideal of an impossible self-purity (a sinlessness best reserved perhaps for the gods) that served, however, to relieve Luther of his own abysmal suffering from a sense of being literally nothing but a piece of waste. However, this was the idea and promise that inflamed Europeans who were ready to be free of sin and many other oppressive things, such as indulgences, too many sacraments (Luther abolished several), Papal supremacy, and perhaps above all of having to believe without ever having heard or read the words of the Bible in their own language. It stirred up the continent to violence and a calamitous series of wars that lasted for more than a hundred years. But Folly, with her unhesitating acknowledgement of her stupidity, ignorance, and humility, feels utterly sinless as she is, and it is by means of the cathartic laughter that she induces in us that we feel utterly sinless as well, at least for the moment.

Both tragedy and comedy concern the relationship between action and desire, but in the space of comedy, said Lacan, there is no triumph such as in tragedy. Death is because the action of desire can never catch up with the phallus which is life and jouissance as such. The phallus, not death, is at the center of comedy, and life slips away. Life is what triumphs, whatever happens (Lacan 1992, 313–14). Erasmus kept to belief in life and pleasure, Luther to his faith alone. Where are we now? What will triumph?

If there are no wise men and if there is no wisdom, then only the *sub-*

stance jouissante in its stupidity, and the imaginary, and a symbolic that enables us to build semblances or fictions are left. Literary semblances seem to have opened themselves to madness before philosophy did. One of the great texts to have done so is Erasmus's. That it is a powerfully ironic argument, bearing comic truth, and going against a venerable tradition of rational semblance, the many attempts to repress it prove. Rather than being able to claim his work as his own, as Cervantes does at the end of *Don Quixote,* Erasmus had to deny and play down the value of his own greatest and most brilliant achievement (Huizinga 1957, 77). It was attacked numerous times as heretical and he had purposely to diminish its significance (Bainton 1969, 201). During the Inquisition, after his death in 1559, everything he had ever written, including *The Moriae* (277–78) was placed on the Index of Forbidden Books. Does that once again indicate that we may not all be insane, but we are very likely all mad, as Erasmus said? C/C

BIOGRAPHY

Maire Jaanus is professor of English and comparative literature at Barnard College and the Columbia School of Graduate Studies. She is the author of *Kirg ja Kirjandus: Esseid Eesti ja Euroopa Kirjandusest ja Psühhoannalüüsist* (2011) [*Literature and Passion: Essays in Estonian and European Literature and Psychoanalysis*], *Literature and Negation* (1979), *Georg Trakl* (1974), and a novel, *She* (1984). She coedited *Lacan in the German-Speaking World* (2004), *Reading Seminars I and II: Lacan's Return to Freud* (1996), and *Reading Seminar XI: Lacan's Four Fundamental Concepts* (1995).

BIBLIOGRAPHY

Aristotle. 1976. *The Nicomachean Ethics,* trans. J. A. K. Thomson. London: Penguin.

Augustine. 1962. *Confessions,* trans. R. S. Pine-Coffin. Baltimore: Penguin.

Bacon, Francis. 1960. *The New Organon and Related Writings.* New York: Bobbs-Merrill.

Bainton, Roland H. 1969. *Erasmus of Christendom.* New York: Charles Scribner's Sons.

Baudrillard, Jean. 1988. *The Ecstasy of Communication,* trans. Bernard and Caroline Schutze. Brooklyn: Autonomedia.

Castiglione. 1967. *The Book of the Courtier,* trans. George Bull. Baltimore: Penguin.

Cervantes. 1967. *The Adventures of Don Quixote,* trans. J. M. Cohen. Baltimore: Penguin.

Descartes, René. 1980. *Discourse on the Method for Rightly Conducting One's*

Reason and for Seeking Truth in the Sciences, trans. Donald A Cress. Indianapolis: Hackett.
Erasmus, Desiderius. 1970. *The Praise of Folly,* trans. Hoyt Hopewell Hudson. Princeton: Princeton University Press.
Freud, Sigmund. 1953–74. *The Standard Edition of the Complete Psychological Works of Sigmund Freud [SE]. 24 vols.* London: Hogarth Press.
Hofmannsthal, Hugo von. 1902. *The Letter of Lord Chandos.* http://depts.washington.edu/vienna/documents/Hofmannsthal/Hofmannsthal_Chandos.htm.
Huizinga, Johan. 1957. *Erasmus and the Age of Reformation.* New York: Harper Torchbooks.
Kant, Immanuel. 1986. *Critique of Judgement.* In *Philosophical Writings,* Vol. 13, 160–223. New York: Continuum.
Lacan, Jacques. 1973–74. *Le séminaire de Jacques Lacan livre XXI: Les non-dupes errant.* Lesson of November 20, 1973 (unpublished).
———. 1974–75. *Le séminaire de Jacques Lacan livre XXII: R.S.I.* a. Lesson of December 17, 1974 and b. Lesson of December 10, 1974 (unpublished).
———. 1975. *Conferences and Conversations at North American Universities. Scilicet* (6/7): 7–63.
———. 1991. *Le séminaire. Livre VIII. Le transfert (1960–1).* Paris: Seuil.
———. 1992. *The Seminar of Jacques Lacan, Book VII. The Ethics of Psychoanalysis,* trans. Dennis Porter. New York: Norton.
———. 1998. *The Seminar of Jacques Lacan, Book XX. Encore. On Feminine Sexuality: The Limits of Love and Knowledge,* trans. Bruce Fink. New York: Norton.
Marrou, Henri. 1962. *Saint Augustine and His Influence through the Ages,* trans. Patrick Hepburne-Scott. New York: Harper Brothers.
Miller, Jacques-Alain. 2008. "*Tout le monde est fou.* Dix-septième séance du cours, 4 juin 2008. " Published in this issue as "Everyone Is Mad."
———. 2009. "Ordinary Psychosis Revisited." *Psychoanalytic Notebooks* 19: 139–67.
Obama, Barack. 2008. *The Audacity of Hope. Thoughts on Reclaiming the American Dream.* New York: Vintage Books.
Plato. 1989. *Symposium,* trans. Alexander Nehamas and Paul Woodruff. Indianapolis: Hackett.
Plato. 1994. *Euthydemus.* http://classics.mit.edu/Plato/euthydemus.html.
Wilson, Matthew. 2010. "Animals Have Complex Dreams." *Neuron* (January 25). http://www.anapsid.org/ethology3.html.

PIERRE-GILLES GUÉGUEN

Who Is Mad and Who Is Not? On Differential Diagnosis in Psychoanalysis

THE EXPRESSION "differential diagnosis in psychoanalysis" may seem contradictory, or could at least be considered an oxymoron, and yet there cannot be a sound practice of psychoanalysis without a thorough diagnosis. It is true that differential diagnoses primarily refer back to psychiatry and thus to a practice originating in medicine. It is also true that psychoanalysis is not primarily oriented by therapeutic goals, and thus it differs from psychiatry.

But in its origins, the psychiatric discipline, from which psychoanalysis detached itself thanks to Freud's invention, attracted those (even when they were laymen like Ernst Kris, the famous art critic, for example) who shared with Freud the belief in the scientific, experimental, rational model of medicine. Today some ill-informed commentators may look down on this, and scorn Freud's blind scientism, thereby refusing to acknowledge that his insistence on rationality preserved psychoanalysis from hermeneutics (as was proven with the Jungian deviation, which ended as a collaboration with the ideals of Nazism) and from religion and its moralistic stands. Freud had to fight—sometimes very hard and painfully—to keep that orientation.

THE COMMON ROOTS

During the late nineteenth century and the beginning of the twentieth century, "madness"—as many historians and philosophers have shown—progressively tended to be considered as an illness and a matter for health care. This gave rise to the creation of several typologies based on the careful and systematic observation of patients, both over short periods of time and on a longitudinal historical basis. Essentially it was a time when there was very little medication that would change, improve, or alter the patient's state; recovery was mainly reported to be a natural effect of the evolution of the disease.

This was the state of affairs when Freud started his private practice, until he discovered that talking, under some precise circumstances, engendered therapeutic effects per se, and from there on invented the psychoanalytic method.

In addition, psychiatrists also treated people who did not seek their help because they considered their misery to be due to an external cause: an evil Other. These patients were brought to them against their will by family members or the police.

Psychiatrists would then be faced with the decision of treating the person medically for the sake of society in order to protect those around the patient or the patient himself from his own destructive tendencies. Nowadays psychiatry still has to make decisions of this kind to protect the public and the patient. It is part of the psychiatric duty, which has its own value and deserves respect.

We must keep in mind that the walls of the psychiatric hospital, so harshly criticized during the last quarter of the twentieth century, can also offer shelter, in accordance with the etymology of the word *asylum,* which may sound outdated today but was once synonymous with "refuge," "harbor."

The classifications developed before the invention of neuroleptic medication offer a framework for major distinctions among mental disorders, mainly based on observation (Foucault called it the "clinic of the visible"), because they usually offer very little insight concerning the etiology and the causes of such ailments and even fewer clues concerning their relation to biology, although some psychiatrists like Henri Ey, for example,[1] tried to build a bridge between neurology and psychiatry. Today's blind belief in the paradigms of the neurosciences tends to forge the illusion that the gap has been filled. Furthermore, one branch of psychoanalysis (represented by the International Psychoanalytic Association [IPA]) has officially adopted this delusion, whose only possible outcome is to ruin the very nature of psychoanalysis (see Laurent 2008).

In spite of their shortcomings, the classical topologies relied faithfully on the phenomena appearing in situ and over time, and transcribed them minutely. Several of these classifications, thanks to some outstandingly erudite professors of psychiatry, allowed for the elaboration of a broad yet subtle general overview of mental illnesses.

They depended greatly on the subjectivity of their inventors and also were sometimes related to a national body of knowledge concerning specific items. Now and then another voice would rise up against an existing typology and impose a new item, or a new classification, or branch, through discussion. This was the case for Clérambault, whom Lacan considered to be his "only master in psychiatry" (Lacan 2006, 51) and who invented the concept of mental automatism.

Another example is that of the German psychiatrist Ernst Kretschmer (1918), who, in specifying some of the traits gathered by Emil Kraepelin around paranoia, created his own syndrome, which he called "sensitive paranoia." In his work, dating back to 1918 and based on an extensively documented compilation of case stories, he described a mild form of paranoia where the "evil Other" is not as strongly defined as in the Kraepelinian paranoid delusion of persecution but is rather insidious, and corresponds mainly to a sensation of being continually observed. In so doing he opposed Kraepelin and joined in with a number of other psychiatrists of his time who had been observing forms of what they called "abortive paranoia," while the great Kraepelin first believed that paranoia would in all cases sooner or later develop into a fully fledged persecutory delusional state.

For a long time psychiatry evolved through this kind of discussion between eminent and respected figures of authority, who were building up their own classifications and had to demonstrate to other clinicians that their assertions, and also their premises, were well founded and could be used to distinguish "normal" behavior from unhealthy or pathological behavior. It also required steady presence and lengthy interviews with the patients. The lines were not easy to draw, and specialists were fighting among themselves. Freud played his part in the evolution of psychiatry, partaking in the great conversation that allowed for much slack and personal interpretation, while pushing his psychoanalytical theory forward. Among others he was well versed in Kraepelin's work (as a matter of fact the Wolf Man had met with the master before he came to see Freud).[2] Freud's discussions with Jung on schizophrenia and paranoia, published in his *Correspondence* (Freud 1977, see letters 22F and 23F), are still of utmost interest for today's clinicians. We can also mention his invention of the category of obsessive neurosis, unheard of until then. He himself evolved in his usage of psychiatric classifications: while at first he did not make a clear-cut distinction between neurosis and psychosis (he spoke of the neuropsychoses of defense), he soon enough distinguished between psychosis and neurosis and expressed caution concerning the treatment of psychosis with the psychoanalytic method. From its inception psychoanalysis is thus deeply rooted in, and intertwined with, psychiatry. And as mentioned earlier, Freud himself believed in the scientific ideals of the psychiatry of his time inasmuch as he was a rationalist opposed to magical, religious, or moralistic treatment of psychic suffering. He nonetheless took a very strong and lasting stand against making psychoanalysis a part of the medical body of knowledge (see also Sokolowsky, this issue). He fought against the will of many of his colleagues (especially the American ones) to restrict the right to practice analysis to medically trained physicians.

What holds true for Freud also stands for Lacan, who was attracted to psychoanalysis, and away from psychiatry, through the special interest he had developed for Aimée, the patient he wrote his dissertation about (Lacan 1932), and more broadly for women's desire.[3]

Of course many psychiatric categories were, and still are, used to protect the individual, his or her family and friends, and society as a whole from the violent manifestations of some clinically recognized "illnesses." This noble—and useful—purpose certainly carried its load of errors and injustices due to segregating prejudices toward madness, especially in times when psychotropic drugs were nonexistent (notwithstanding the fact that moralistic and patrimonial issues could also play a non-innocent part in decisions of psychiatric confinement).

During the second half of the twentieth century, the anti-psychiatry movement was in full swing and was allied with libertarian ideals that, in a largely utopian and unconsciously dangerous form, ended up ruining the psychiatric health care system in some countries like Italy. Meanwhile Michel Foucault, on a more grounded basis, echoed these protests by demonstrating the links between power in general and the creation and application of norms. His seminar *The Abnormal* (2004) illustrates rather convincingly the relation between the state of a given society and what is considered to be within or beyond the limits of what can be socially tolerated. These norms fluctuate and are part of an ongoing movement across all societies and countries (for example, gay rights and "liberal social issues" nowadays on the American continent and in Europe). But psychoanalysis is on board the train of what Lacan called the "master's discourse." Its task is to subvert it, not to denounce it. It should therefore steer clear of both the anti-psychiatry utopia and reactionary backlashes.

THE "BOOK OF DISORDERS"

Then came the *Diagnostic and Statistical Manual of Mental Disorders* (DSM). The classification that has invaded and taken over psychiatry was based, to put it bluntly, on an attempt to erase subjectivity in diagnosis in order to reduce discrepancies across various practitioners. As a result, numbers outdid personal judgment; medication-based categories such as depression or hyperactivity were created to suppress the influence of both the judgment of the psychiatrist and the subjectivity of the patient. Everyone knows the appalling inadequacy of the scales and questionnaires that have, over time, replaced lengthy observation and frequent talks between the doctors and their patients. Éric Laurent, in an unpublished paper delivered at a "forum" in Paris in 2009, depicted the effects of the generalized spreading of evaluation, of which *DSM* classifications and similar "diagnostic" tools are part and parcel: "It leads to a vanishing of the real of the illness" (it signals, and also means the death of language, as an ongoing process of conversation between the patient and the therapist because it is replaced by a multiple choice questionnaire).

Once the death of language has been obtained, it then becomes impossible to say anything about the phenomenon besides what is included in the scales.

Ultimately it paves the way for the destruction of the social bond and the mutual agreement and support it entails. Thus the subject is led to what Éric Laurent most appositely names a "default position." The patient is no longer someone who suffers and addresses a demand to a specialist; instead he or she becomes a mishap in the order of the universe, and thus a potential misfit to be reeducated (see Watters 2010).

LACAN AND THE QUESTION OF DIAGNOSIS IN PSYCHOANALYSIS

There is a cross-fertilizing movement at play between two streams of thought throughout Lacan's work. On one hand, in the name of psychoanalysis, he discards any kind of segregation of our fellow humans (for example, when he defines madness as the essence of human liberty in his first *Écrits* [Lacan 2006, 121] or when he proclaims in 1978 that "everyone is mad" [1979b, 278, also this issue]); this is the Lacan who is in favor of a continuum.[4] On the other hand he tries to build very precise definitions of what the phenomena to be addressed through psychoanalysis might be: their logics, their minute descriptions, their clear-cut differences. And this is the Lacan who advocates a discrete model of the psychical apparatus. For him phenomena are always events of language: the signifying chain is made out of discrete elements that he calls "signifiers" after Saussure. These elements are linked together through metaphor and metonymy in order to produce the flow of meaning and signification that, by its own nature, cannot be thought of as discrete. Again, within the field of speech and language, continuity and discontinuity are interwoven, and the Lacanian aphorism "The unconscious is structured like a language" has become famous, meaning that the concept itself entails the discrete as well as the continuous.

The "Question Prior to Any Possible Treatment of Psychosis" (Lacan 2006, 445) thoroughly illustrates Lacan's approach to structural diagnosis. In this fundamental text on psychosis he deciphers, with more precision than any other psychiatrist of his time—more than Freud himself—the massive amount of psychotic phenomena brought out by Schreber in his autobiography. We should keep in mind the logic of Lacan's contribution: psychoses, and especially Schreberian psychoses, are to be approached through language impairments and communicational disorders. In psychosis the relation to the Other is broken down and thus the fundamental phenomena are to be read within the disorganized symbolic order with—as a result—a cascade of repercussions being produced upon the imaginary: the foreclosed real returns within the symbolic with devastating effects.

According to the matrix of Lacan's classical conception of psychosis, diagnosis is primarily (if not exclusively) to be constructed starting from the language disorders that result from "the gulf formed by the simple effect in the imaginary of the futile appeal made in the symbolic to the paternal metaphor" (2006, 456). He immediately adds on this page that the phallic signification is then foreclosed for the subject owing to an "elision of the phallus, which the subject would like to reduce, in order to resolve it to the lethal gap of the mirror stage" (456). Ultimately Lacan trusts that the subject will invent a useful—if fragile—"delusional metaphor" that will stabilize his or her relationship to a modified Other.

On this side of his thinking Lacan can be called a mechanicist. As a consequence of his interpretation of the Freudian body of work through the prism of the "Function and Field of Speech and Language" (2006) (a text that is both a breakthrough and a landmark of his stormy arrival on the scene of traditional psychoanalysis), he was considered a structuralist, although he rejected this label. The structuralist, and thus mechanicist, part of his work is only one part of his clinical approach, although it is a long-standing one (Miller 2000).

Jacques-Alain Miller spent much time exploring this aspect of Lacan's teaching under its different facets, until he switched to the late Lacan, beginning in 2005 and culminating in 2007–8 with his lecture series at Paris VIII University, to which he gave the generic title: *Tout le monde est fou*—or "Everyone Is Mad" (see Miller, this issue). The reference is not only to idiosyncrasies or eccentric behavior but to the very core of clinical delusional madness as underlined by Lacan in a short text written in 1978 to support the then-experimental Department of Psychoanalysis at the University of Paris VIII (1979b, also this issue).

A large part of an unpublished lecture—that of March 26, 2008—by

Miller is devoted to the importance of the mechanicism of Lacan's early and most publicized theory:

> You must understand that, for Lacan, the subject is drawn into these mechanisms; he is sucked in by them. The introduction of the Lacanian subject, the first Lacanian subject, into these mechanisms [namely metaphor and metonymy as developed by Roman Jakobson] is completely unlike the use most frequently made today of the category of the subject, *i.e.* in order to signal a degree of liberty, some unreachable part, something that cannot be tamed and especially tamed by quantification. If Lacan introduces the subject he is dealing with in the analytic experience as something that comes into motion by virtue of these mechanisms, it is because he considers this subject to be entirely calculable. (Miller 2011b, 29)

However, starting from the last lessons of seminar 20 (Lacan 1998)—though to be more precise, we could date it back to seminars 18 and 19—Lacan's clinical approach no longer advocates the preeminence of the symbolic. He shifts to a clinic of semblants (which means that human beings can never totally separate the imaginary and symbolic registers, the object itself being a semblant, *that is,* an imaginary part of the body, symbolically elevated in the fantasy to an equivalent of the real).

This leads him to an elusive clinic, a clinic of the continuous, of the transformational, that culminates with the knots along with the idea, repeatedly expressed, of a strict equivalence between the three registers. The Name-of-the-Father, both a signifier and a concept because no particular signifier can be pinned down to incarnate it (and even less the presence or the absence of the father in reality), was the keystone of the discrete architecture of psychosis in the early Lacan, which allowed for a distinction between the neurotic structure that vouched for the presence of the Name-of-the-Father and the psychotic state that originated in its absence, its foreclosure. Clinical approaches using the knots, on the contrary, suppose that the Name-of-the-Father works as a *function* (in the mathematical sense)[5] and not as signifier of a totality. It can thus be upheld through many devices, many values ascribed to the variable: it becomes one among many other ways of ensuring a strong hold on what we call reality and that in effect is more something of a shared social bond among human beings through their common dependence on language than a fact of language. It corresponds to what the philosophy of logical empiricism calls the "Charity principle" (Davidson 1984 [1974]).[6]

As a consequence, in the late Lacan, the normative aspect of psychoanalysis and its segregating potentialities (them, the mad ones, versus us, the normal ones) is erased.

Of course this "new" set of concepts has bearings on the theory of the end of analysis. It is also congruent with the status of psychoanalysis in our world, where the norm of the patriarchal family ruled by the law of the father has declined, if not totally crumbled.

In his late teaching, Lacan assumes that analysts do not put their trust in the conservative and traditional form of society supported by religions, nor do they have faith in the salvation of humankind through progress. A fragment of J.-A. Miller's address to the École de la Cause Freudienne in October 2007 can be quoted in support of this assertion:

> The great majority of psychoanalysts in the world . . . are traditionalists: they take up humanist and clerical positions quite naturally, in the hope of prolonging the world they have known, in the hope of reining in, even halting the current movement of science.

He considers that this was encouraged by Freud and by the early Lacan, who in spite of their subversive stands still believed that psychoanalysis was working in favor of the life drive against the death drive. While the late Lacan teaches us something else: namely that there is no such thing as an internal opposition in the drive, as Miller (2001) argued vigorously during his 1998–99 lectures, the drive in itself, inasmuch as jouissance is allowed, is both construction and destruction and thus:

> Psychoanalysts do not have to join in the choir of mourners who yearn for times past. They can be humanists if they want, Christians, why not, but as analysts they cannot be traditionalists because this reactive, reactionary, conservative position goes against the grain of their act. This does not mean however that analysts should share the enthusiasm of the managers of scientific progress, who are lining the pockets of their institutes with revenue from the licensing contracts they will be signing to grant use of their patented chromosomes. (Miller 2007)

And Miller calls for an "ironic clinic." It corresponds to a clinic of our times and its changes in the modes of jouissance, a clinic that takes into account the movement of society that is both constructive and destructive, for example, in family matters. It is only possible if the analytic aims and finalities go beyond the father as the only possible anchor for normativization. It refers to a clinical approach resting metaphorically on the schizophrenic's fundamental disbelief in the consistency of the Other. Such a clinical approach takes the Lacanian invention of the sinthome, and of the subject's final identification with his sinthome, seriously. The Lacanian concept of sinthome refers to a mixture of imaginary and symbolic that is the closest a subject can get to the "pieces of real" to which he or she is attached.

To be more concrete: the version of the end of analysis first favored by Lacan in his "Proposition of 9 October 1967" (2001b) on the pass conveyed that analysis was totally reduced to an experience of knowledge and truth and, in a way, equivalent to the revelation of the "subject supposed to know." It was also implicitly suggesting that the end was a quilting point, a full stop that sublimated the object through an acquired knowledge of the truth about oneself.

The end of an analysis, if we follow Lacan in his considerations on Joyce-the-Sinthome, can no longer correspond to a normativization of the subject under the ruling of the Name-of-the-Father, which secured a widely shared solution, valid for a majority and leaving on the side a number of dropouts of the Name-of-the-Father: the madmen. The end through identification with the sinthome means two things:

1. There is no standard possibility to end the treatment: the identification with the sinthome is a matter of one by one. It relates to how each subject plays his part in a social bond with a nonstandard solution that allows for a form of jouissance and links it to a sense of responsibility, duty, and solidarity in the world.
2. It also means that there is some madness in the original solution he or she has elicited because it never is a standard one. In this sense it is ironic because it does not relate to a ready-made instance or a consistent register. In all cases it denounces the failure of the paternal metaphor to accomplish what it was ideally supposed to effectuate as an anchor for the subject and as an access to a fully assumed identification with the ideals of his or her sex.

The identification with the sinthome means that "we are all mad" in the sense of we are all different, all unnatural and still related through our common dependence on language, which informs our relation to the imaginary and the symbolic, never totally separated from others through the mediation of language, but also never accomplishing the dream of achieved heterosexual, harmonious sexuality, and even less, the dream of a loving union.

This version of the end and aims of psychoanalysis also means that the unconscious stays open, even after the end of analysis. In the last part of his teaching Lacan implicitly sets aside his previous idea that a matheme could articulate the end of an analysis or—to put it slightly differently—that there could be a matheme of psychoanalysis. He was then led to question the relation between the end of psychoanalysis and a final revelation of truth.

In Aristotelian logic, there is no such thing as a partial truth: a truth is or is not and thus there is solidarity between truth and universality.

In the conclusion to his 2008 lectures (in this issue), Miller notes that conversely, in his last teaching, Lacan formalizes the end of psychoanalysis along the lines of the logic presiding over feminine sexuality: the not-all (*le pas-tout*), grounded on a torsion of classic Aristotelian logic. This very torsion is an invention by Lacan. It paves the way for an end that does not resolve itself fully through knowledge. One of the consequences is that psychoanalysis cannot be taught: thus the training of an analyst, as Miller reminds us, is first of all due to his or her experience of his or her own analysis, pushed as far as possible and ideally to the point where there is no subject supposed to know left.

The unconscious can never be wholly sutured. Miller has frequently stated it, and particularly so in a note on the Freudian concept of *Urverdrängung* a propos of seminar 23 in its appendixes (Miller 2005, 239).

Of course, a thorough education in the discipline of psychoanalysis is also mandatory in the training of an analyst—extensive knowledge, even—but it is secondary to the experience in itself.

When Lacan says "Everyone is mad, that is, delusional," we could take it to be strictly equivalent to "We are all psychotics." If it were so, this would wholeheartedly favor the late Lacan and erase the first part of his teaching. It is of the utmost importance to stress the very subtle way in which J.-A. Miller comments on this sentence. His indications in this matter are fundamental because they have bearings on the very practice of psychoanalysis.

In his last lecture of 2008 (in this issue) Miller adopts a very clear standpoint: "The generic madness in question here is general, or rather, universal. It is not psychosis. Psychosis is a category of the clinic with which one tries to capture something that is at any rate inscribed into the universal." And in a course at the university of Paris VIII (unpublished) Miller indicates that the signifier "delusional" in this particular sentence of Lacan's ("Everyone is mad") is to be understood as "taken within the network of meaning" (which cannot be avoided because human beings are captured within the network of language). He also mentions that Lacan had made an allusion to a similar issue in the first part of his teaching when he mentioned, for example, that awakening is just another way of keeping on dreaming. Finally, we can add the passage in seminar 11 that relates the anecdote of the Chuang Zu butterfly (Lacan 1977, 76).

CLINICAL ENTANGLEMENTS

Miller's systematic lecturing on Lacan's teaching post–seminar 20 began in 2005 with the lectures he called *Pieces détachées* (in English "spare parts" but also "fallen parts"). In the first lecture he announced that he was going to study the sinthome as a concept invented by Lacan in the last part of his work and also as the title of a seminar: *Joyce le Sinthome*. Many among those who have studied this seminar or who attended it have noticed that Lacan never declares explicitly whether he thinks Joyce was psychotic or not. Since he never explained why—at least to my knowledge—it stays open to many an interpretation, interpretations that are not mutually exclusive.

One, and not the least of them, is that the respect for an artist of this importance demands not diminishing his aura by labeling him with a psychiatric nametag (although a few years earlier Lacan had not shied away from speaking of Wittgenstein's psychotic ferocity; Lacan 2007, 63). Another interpretation also holds true: Lacan knew that he was addressing an audience extending far beyond the confines of the medical world and did not want to stigmatize psychosis in general, being aware of the possible segregating effect of the signifier *psychotic*. Yet another would be that in light of the late teaching and the clinic of the knots, the clinical category of psychosis had become irrelevant.

Within the Freudian field the debate on nontriggered psychosis turned out to be a widely shared concern in the years leading to 1998, when the category of ordinary psychosis was created by Jacques-Alain Miller during a research program of the Clinical Sections of the Freudian Field.

The concept of ordinary psychosis was at first applied restrictively, but it soon became popular. In the beginning it was presumed to concern only some rare cases in which the foreclosure of the Name-of-the-Father could not be established. A consensus soon developed (Brousse 2009, 7) that it was not rare to have to deal with an indetermination in the diagnosis of a case even after lengthy preliminary interviews. As a matter of fact there were already hints of it in Lacan's first teachings when he mentioned nontriggered psychosis. And sometimes, even though psychosis has set in, it takes very discreet forms (an isolated elementary phenomenon, for example).

However, in some schools of the World Association of Psychoanalysis from 2004 to 2008, the enthusiasm for the category of ordinary psychosis—and it is a fact that there are more and more cases correlated with the ongoing decline of the Name-of-the-Father in our civilization—and the emphasis put on rapid therapeutic effects in psychoanalytic treatment as developed in the free psychoanalytical clinics created by the École de la Cause Freudienne in France produced an inflationist bubble of indecisive diagnoses and perhaps some disarray for many clinicians who did not see the point of using clinical categories that were obsolete in modern psychiatry when the "new clinical trend" was the clinic of the knots.

Because of these and many other flaws discovered and analyzed by Jacques-Alain Miller in a long series of interviews called *Entretiens d'actualité* and published electronically during the autumn of 2008, some precision and reflection about the overextension of ordinary psychosis was necessary. Miller presented these details in a lecture he gave in English under the title "Ordinary Psychosis Revisited." This text of reorientation is to be read as a landmark and a turning point in our clinical work (Miller 2009b, 139).

1. In this essential article he strongly emphasizes that the category we call ordinary psychosis is situated within the field of psychosis.
2. It is a form of psychosis propped up or stabilized by a sinthome (an "invention") in spite of an existing foreclosure of the Name-of-the-Father. Although it has not developed and perhaps never will, some indicative elements can be found and have to be looked for during the first interviews with the patient (sometimes it might require a long time because the phenomena are often subdued and lack precision). Miller advises to look into what he calls the "three externalities."
3. In the social, there should be some kind of "disconnection" *(débranchement)*. The link to the Other is loose, woolly, drifting.
4. In the body the subject can often be suffering from obscure pains (to be distinguished from hysterical conversion symptoms), or from difficulties in focusing (to be distinguished from obsessive ruminations or compulsive verifications). Often, as Miller puts it, "The subject is led to invent some artificial bond to re-appropriate his body, to tie his body to itself" (2009b, 156). Tattoos or piercings, fashionable today, can sometimes play this role.
5. In subjectivity itself, there is usually a "fixity of the identification" (2009b, 157); it refers back to a special form of relating to object *a* (either because there is a strong identification with waste or, at the opposite end, an extreme form of mannerism with which the subject defends itself against this identification). At both ends of the scale it is a relation to object *a* that cannot be dialecticized, that is not marked by the dimension of semblant.

In the same text Miller also indicates that in the differential diagnosis of ordinary psychosis the clinician has to adopt a negative differential approach: if it is not neurosis then it is psychosis, although it is not triggered. He mentions that the most solid reference to distinguish ordinary psychosis from neurosis is hysteria, for which there is a very sturdy structural apparatus in the Freudian and Lacanian corpuses.

GENERALIZED FORECLOSURE

The proposition "We are all mad but we are not all psychotics" should also be examined in light of the theory of generalized foreclosure formulated by J.-A. Miller in 1986 during his research seminar because at first sight they seem contradictory (2009a).

This concept can be related to the last part of "Subversion of the Subject and the Dialectic of Desire" when Lacan declares, "The neurotic underwent imaginary castration at the outset, it sustains the strong ego that is his, so strong, one might say, that his proper name bothers him, so strong that deep down, the neurotic is Nameless" (2006, 700). This passage reminds us of the issue of the absence or presence of the Name-of-the-Father, and it also suggests that for neurotics and psychotics both, the Name-of-the-Father is, to say the least, in question.

Starting from this part of "Subversion" and from the pluralization of the Names-of-the-Father effectuated by Lacan himself in his sole lesson from 1963, christened "The Inexistent Seminar," Miller (2006) emphasized more than once the questionable status of the logical function of the Name-of-the-Father and stressed the existence of the hole in the Other for both neurotics and psychotics.

In a commentary on Freud's Wolf Man case in Milan in 1994, Miller provides an interesting rationale for this theory: first he explains that from a certain perspective, reconstruction and remembering can be opposed, and yet they are made of the same material: signifiers.

> This is how Freud came to formulate that what is repressed is historical truth . . . ultimately what is repressed is truth, *Warheit*. The equivalence between the memory and the construction with regard to truth is decisive for opening up the path to Lacan. . . . From there, Freud suggests we consider that both hallucination and delusion correspond to the same mechanisms. He extends to psychosis a mechanism he had been restricting to neurosis. . . . . [If] hallucination and delusion correspond to the same structure as the neurotic mechanisms[:] it means that at the [core] of the hallucination and the delusion there is a repressed truth. This is the crux of his clinical demonstration. (2011, 73–74)

And indeed the clue, or to be more precise the Archimedean point in the question of differential diagnosis, revolves around the status of truth in psychoanalysis and can only be understood with the concept of "stratification of the Other" (introduced by Éric Laurent and Jacques-Alain Miller in their joint lecture series in 1996–97). The stratification of the Other allows for an explanation of what is common and what is different in neuroses and psychoses.

Lacan continuously asserted that truth is not One. In his late teaching he even speaks of the "varity" (*varité:* 1979a, 13) of truth, a pun conveying that truth always has several aspects. What has sometimes been called a debasement or dismissal of truth is clearly due to the rise of the category of the real in Lacan's thought. Truth relates to knowledge and signification, while the real rests on a hole: the same hole that lies in the "umbilicus of dreams" and that Freud recognized as the *Urverdrängt*. The sinthome as a remainder of the analytic operation leads us to take the Lacanian definition of the symptom as "what one has that is closest to the real" to the letter. And in some instances (as discussed by Miller in November 2007) Lacan will go as far as declaring that the sinthome is real because it is as close as one can get to the real with a semblant that knots together body, language, and image.

In this respect psychosis and neurosis are equivalent. And indeed in some cases, a psychotic sinthome can hold as strongly, or even more strongly, than a neurotic one. That seems to be the gist of Lacan's demonstration on Joyce.

At the beginning of his teaching Lacan thought that psychosis could be stabilized with the help of a delusional metaphor. This situates the process solely on the symbolic plane. In his late teaching, with the concept of the sinthome, the stabilization ties together the three "externalities" that Miller isolated in "Ordinary Psychosis Revisited" (2009b). But this is only valid for some cases where possible structural flaws cannot be found. Nonetheless, for many cases of psychosis and even ordinary psychosis, as Miller points out, there are usually inconspicuous hints of difficulties in the social, in the body, or in subjectivity, the three externalities. The sinthome can be approached from two sides. The first one is the side of the remainder of the treatment. This is obtained through the extraction of jouissance in the analytic treatment, and then the sinthome appears as the name of what is incurable. On the other side, the sinthome constitutes the ultimate defense against the real or the best that can be invented to prevent the catastrophe of the onset and its consequences. It is an original invention of the subject, one that is more or less solidly put together. Some of these inventions can be highly valued by society (works of art, for example); some will be less tolerated (a strong trait of perversion). They stand for absent phallic signification and in many cases they go unnoticed; they are not socially considered as signs of pathology; and still they belong to the realm of ordinary psychosis. A sinthome can also be constructed, usually at the cost of many efforts, when psychosis has already been triggered. In any case, a diagnosis has to be made and pushed as far as possible by the analyst for practical aims related to the direction of the treatment: it is a prerequisite to the act of the analyst.

Among the many side effects of the overexpansion of the category of ordinary psychosis brought to light recently by various psychoanalysts is a tendency for the analyst to refrain from taking his or her part in the treatment and to listen passively to the patient (Laurent, 2010b, 110). This tendency has been counterbalanced by the new surge driven by Miller during the Thirty-Eighth Study Days of the École de la Cause Freudienne in 2009. These study days were widely considered to have produced a "de-massification" of enunciations, while the preceding period tended to underestimate, if not totally erase, the inclusion of the analyst in the treatment (at least in research papers delivered at scientific meetings).

THE INCLUSION OF THE ANALYST IN THE TREATMENT

In an important article, Éric Laurent examined what he was already calling "the crisis of the case-study" in psychoanalysis (Laurent 2011). He shows how Lacan's conception of the case study evolved through time, with successive points of emphasis that are not mutually exclusive. He also stresses how Lacan started from a phenomenological conception of the case study inspired by Jaspers (the narrative focusing on a succession of phenomena) and then moved to a more logicized conception as he was eliciting an ever more logicized idea of the unconscious. In the classical moment of his teaching, the case study represents a paradigm for him, in which the particularity of the "formal envelope" of the symptom includes it within a classification (and here we are confronted again with the issue of differential diagnosis): "The symptom's character of logical coherence affirms that classes of symptoms exist and at the same time it deconstructs them" (Laurent 2011, 85).

This moment of Lacan's thinking about the case would belong entirely to the mechanicism of Lacanian theory if Lacan had not also been preoccupied with making place for the Freudian drive and the dimension of jouissance in psychoanalysis (which is not discrete). Laurent sums it up by stating that "the fundamental indication that Lacan gave on this point is that demonstration in psychoanalysis is homogeneous to the form of the witticism" (2011, 86). And he reminds us that in the Freudian *Witz* we have a "stratification of the Other," so to speak: at one level there is a mechanics, a logic of the pun, made essentially of an encounter between two registers usually kept apart. It produces an effect of rupture, of nonsense, of surprise. And at another level there is a surplus of libido that provokes laughter (Lacan indicated that in the comical effect of the pun the phallus was always at stake). If a case study is to "prove" something in analysis, as Laurent mentions, it is more thanks to the libidinal surplus obtained than owing to the rightness of the propositions. Both are necessary, but the proof, the partaking of the logic of the assertion, is only accepted if a libidinal satisfaction accompanies it. This type of *Aufhebung* that links together "mind" and "body," signifying chain and drive, is absolutely specific to the psychoanalytic discourse. Thus the enunciation cannot be separated from the enunciated. This is one of the meanings of the first sentence of Lacan's *L'Étourdit:* "That one says remains forgotten behind what is said in what is heard" (2001a, 449).

Laurent asserts that for a case study to have evidential value, there must be a shared practice and even a shared lifestyle in the analytic community (2011, 86).[7] One should never forget that psychoanalysis primarily aims at changes in the libidinal economy of the patient. It is far from being a pure matter of narratives.

Two consequences ensue:

1. The case study will never tell the whole truth about an analytic problem. It belongs to the "not-all" logic; no case will ever say the last word about the real.
2. In the place of truth comes a satisfaction that serves as proof for the listener. This satisfaction demands the implication of the analyst in his or her enunciation and also that the analyst does not identify with the knowledge produced by the exposition of his or her clinical cases to the analytic community. As Laurent points out, psychoanalysis never has, and never will, respond to the epistemology of the model (2011, 87).

PITFALLS IN INTERPRETATION

> Assuredly a psychoanalyst directs the treatment . . . in the capital outlay involved in the common enterprise, the patient is not alone in finding it difficult to pay his share. The analyst too must pay:
>
> Pay with words no doubt, if the transmutation they undergo due to the analytic operation raises them to the level of their effect as interpretation;
>
> But also pay with his person in that, whether he likes it or not, he lends it as a prop for the singular phenomena analysis discovered in transference;
>
> Can anyone forget that he must pay for becoming unmeshed in an ac-

tion that goes right to the core of being *(Kern unseres Wesens),* as Freud put it, with what is essential in his most intimate judgment: could he alone remain on the sidelines? (Lacan 2006, 587)

This is a famous passage from Lacan's "Direction of the Treatment." These considerations apply whether the patient belongs to the clinical category of psychosis or neurosis: an analysis requires the implication of both analyst and analysand. Nevertheless, the situation is not symmetrical: the analyst directs the treatment; the analysand is the one who demands.

As Éric Laurent states in his article "Ordinary Interpretation" (2009, 277), although the analyst is free in his or her interpretation, there are also rules of interpretation, or to be more exact, principles of interpretation. First and foremost there is no metalanguage, no Other of the Other. Thus interpretation is always taken from what the analysand says and returned to him so that he can read what he had said without noticing it. In this sense the analyst's task resides in inserting a signifier within a preexisting signifying chain that is developed by the patient. Miller added, formalizing Lacan's practice, that instead of another signifier, it could be a punctuation or a cut of the session that produces the effect of reading the unconscious.

In his classical period, Lacan stresses that interpretation is not open to all meanings and that it should aim at the cause of desire. It is consistent with the idea that interpretation should not reinforce the interpretative tendency of the unconscious along the lines of always building up more meaning. But in the case of neurosis, interpretation will use phallic signification *per via de levare* in order to uncover object *a* and the part it plays in the fantasy. It is possible inasmuch as, in spite of its flaws, the paternal metaphor is operating and fixes a limit to the possible invasion of the real that happens with the onset of psychosis. However, this type of interpretation, which opens up the subjective division and produces a fall of identifications, is risky in psychosis, especially when it is triggered, since it can unleash the delusional production of signifiers (the unconscious out in the open) without limit and in particular put the analyst in the place of the persecutor. This is the reason why some caution is necessary when treating psychotic subjects.

It does not mean, however, that the analyst should stay put and not interpret. In "Ordinary Interpretation," Laurent specifies it in a very clear manner:

> On the one hand we accompany the taking charge of jouissance by language. . . . We install the locus of the Other, we authorize the place that can enable translation. . . . The work of translation continues but, at the same

> time, we must know that what we are seeking to obtain is a stabilization, a homeostasis, a punctuation. (2009, 288)

This in itself advocates for the necessity of differential diagnosis.

The second period of Lacan's clinical approach, based on the symptom and the beyond of the Oedipus, does not cancel out the first. It puts it in a different perspective. First, if we follow Miller in his "Ordinary Psychosis Revisited" (2009b), he is still making a claim for the necessity of establishing a sound diagnosis. And in the case of ordinary psychosis, it is more a diagnosis by elimination: if it is not a neurosis and if there are no signs of a structural diagnosis of psychosis, then we are in the field of psychosis but an ordinary one. And again, the kind of interpretation that is possible rests on the capacity of language to take charge of the excessive jouissance. We will then preferentially, as Laurent states, "target the symptom": which means target in this case what in one or several of the "externalities" described by Miller seems to indicate a weakness of the knot between the imaginary, the symbolic, and the real. In this indication I understand the "targeting" as inviting the subject to expand, with signifying elements, what has not been deployed so far through signifiers in one or the other externalities. It is a way of naming the fragile part of the symptom. In the case of ordinary psychosis it is equivalent to analyzing the part of what is acted by the patient (as a disconnection expressed, for example, as a difficulty in focusing) of a jouissance that has not been taken up by the signifying chain. The goal of this operation, again as in classical psychosis, is to obtain a stabilization, to obtain that the subject finds himself or herself at peace.

It is also what is expected with neurotics: what can be called the satisfaction of the end of an analysis when the subject can finally accept the impossible and be at peace with a final "This is what I am!" When this is obtained, the sinthome, or the "symptomatic remainder" as Freud called it, will be the name of the part of jouissance that the Name-of-the-Father had not been able to appease. C/C

BIOGRAPHY

Pierre-Gilles Guéguen is a practicing psychoanalyst in Paris, member of the École de la Cause Freudienne and the World Association of Psychoanalysis, and former president of the New Lacanian School. He teaches at the Department of Psychoanalysis at Paris VIII University.

NOTES

1. Henri Ey was a French psychiatrist close to Jacques Lacan, who was, however, opposed to Ey's organo-dynamist theory.

2. Freud was well versed in the French school after studying with Charcot in Paris, but his main reference was the German school of psychiatry.

3. As Lacan mentions in his "Preface to the English-Language Edition of *Seminar XI*" (1977, 571) (where *Aimée* is translated as "Beloved"), and as developed by Éric Laurent (2010a).

4. Namely, that there is no rift between psychosis and neurosis: they are in continuity one with another.

5. If not an additional device in itself that has the value of an effect of creation (the fourth knot).

6. This is to be distinguished from social constructivism theories.

7. Éric Laurent is quoting Jacques-Alain Miller in a lecture delivered in Ghent in 1997.

BIBLIOGRAPHY

Brousse, Marie-Hélène. 2009. "Ordinary Psychosis in the Light of Lacan's Theory of Discourse." *Psychoanalytical Notebooks* 19: 7–19.

Davidson, Donald. 1984 [1974]. "On the Very Idea of a Conceptual Scheme." In *Inquiries into Truth and Interpretation*. Oxford, U.K.: Clarendon Press.

Foucault, Michel. 2004. *Abnormal: Lectures at the College de France 1974–1975*. New York: Picador USA.

Freud, Sigmund. 1977. *The Freud–Jung Letters: The Correspondence between Sigmund Freud and CG Jung*. New York: Taylor & Francis.

Kretschmer, Ernst. 1918. *Der sensitive Beziehungswahn*. Berlin: Springer.

Lacan, Jacques. 1932. *De la psychose paranoïaque dans ses rapports avec la personnalité*. Paris: Librairie le François.

———. 1977. *The Seminar Book XI: The Four Fundamental Concepts of Psychoanalysis*. trans. Alan Sheridan. New York: Norton.

———. 1979a. "L'insu que sait de l'une-bévue s'aile à mourre." *Ornicar?* 17/18: 15.

———. 1979b. "There Are Four Discourses" *Ornicar?* 17/18; this issue.

———. 1998. *The Seminar Book XX: Encore,* trans. by Bruce Fink. New York: Norton.

———. 2001a. "L'étourdit." In *Autres écrits,* 449–95. Paris: Seuil.

———. 2001b. "Proposition." In *Autres ecrits*. Paris: Seuil.

———. 2006. *Écrits: The First Complete Edition in English,* trans. Bruce Fink. New York: Norton.

———. 2007. *The Seminar of Jacques Lacan. Book XVII: The Other Side of Psychoanalysis,* trans. Russell Grigg. New York: Norton.

Laurent, Éric. 2008. *Lost in Cognition,* ed. Cecile Defaut. Nantes: Editions Cécile Defaut.

———. 2009. "Ordinary Interpretation." *Psychoanalytical Notebooks* 19: 277–93.

———. 2010a. "Lacan, Analysand." *Hurly-Burly* 3: 143–47.

———. 2010b. "Quelques réflexions sur les rapports des derniers cartels de la Passe." *La Cause Freudienne* 75: 110–13.

———. 2011. "The Case: From Unease to the Lie." *Psychoanalytical Notebooks* 22: 81–93.

Laurent, Éric, and Jacques-Alain Miller. 1996–97. *L'Autre qui n'existe pas et ses comités d'éthique* (unpublished).

Miller, Jacques-Alain. 1998. "Le symptôme: savoir, sens et réel." In *Le symptôme charlatan*, 53–60. Paris: Seuil.

———. 2000. "Paradigms of Jouissance. *Lacanian Ink* 17.

———. 2001. "Lacanian Biology." *Lacanian Ink* 18.

———. 2005. "Notice de fil en aiguille §17." *Le séminaire, livre XXIII, Le sinthome*. Paris: Seuil.

———. 2006. "The Inexistent Seminar." *Psychoanalytical Notebooks* 15: 9–40.

———. 2007. "The Future of Myscellania Laboratorium." (forthcoming: *Culture/Clinic* 2).

———. 2008. *Entretiens d'actualité*. http//www.wapol.org.

———. 2009a. "L'Homme aux loups (2e partie)." *La Cause Freudienne* 73: 64–117.

———. 2009b. "Ordinary Psychosis Revisited." *Psychoanalytical Notebooks* 19, 139–67.

———. 2011a. "Marginalia to 'Constructions in Analysis.'" *Psychoanalytical Notebooks* 22, 47–74.

———. 2011b. *Sutilezas anlaliticas*. Buenos Aires: Paidos.

Spiegel, A. 2005. "The Dictionary of Disorder." *Annals of Medicine* (January 3).

Watters, Ethan. 2010. *Crazy Like Us: The Globalization of the American Psyche*. New York: Free Press.

RUSSELL GRIGG

Treating the Wolf Man as a Case of Ordinary Psychosis

THE WOLF MAN was not in good shape in October 1926 when Freud referred him to Ruth Mack Brunswick. Pankejeff's analysis with Freud, long for its day at four years, on which Freud based his "From the History of an Infantile Neurosis," had been completed in July 1914, which was the date Freud had set at the start of that year for the termination of the analysis. When the analysis ended and Pankejeff departed, Freud must have assumed it would be for the last time, satisfied as he was at the time, as he later wrote, with the thought that his patient's cure was "radical and permanent" (Freud *SE,* 23:217). In the event, it was not to be the last time Freud was to receive Pankejeff for analysis; he came to see Freud for four months on his return from Russia in 1919. Moreover, Pankejeff was to undertake two more courses of analysis, both of them with the American analyst resident in Vienna, Ruth Mack Brunswick, who, when she received Pankejeff for the first time, was also Freud's analysand.

I discuss several aspects of Pankejeff's analysis with Mack Brunswick in the light of the hypothesis that Pankejeff was psychotic, a case of what we would call "ordinary psychosis."[1] My thesis is that Pankejeff's psychosis had been triggered in a mild form at some moment, probably in 1926, between his analysis with Freud and his first period of analysis with Mack Brunswick. I explore the thesis that, unwittingly, Mack Brunswick all but provokes a major psychotic episode by the manner in which she intervenes in the treatment.

The Pankejeff who consulted Mack Brunswick in October 1926 was a very different man from the patient Freud had received between 1910 and 1914. It was not just that his condition had deteriorated, but that his symptoms had taken a new turn. What he had initially presented to Freud with, namely, diverse obsessional symptoms, had subsequently developed into a series of somatic and significantly paranoid complaints related to his teeth and nose, the origins of which he at times attributed to the malevolent actions of the dentists and physicians from whom he had been seeking treatment. Thus, when he arrived at Mack Brunswick's consulting rooms, he appeared highly anxious above all about a scar and a hole or groove in the scar tissue on his nose that had been caused by the medical electrolysis he had undergone as treatment for a sebaceous cyst. Not only was there no sign of any disfigurement, Mack Brunswick reports, but also he would obsessively inspect his nose at every opportunity, using a small lady's pocket mirror he carried with him for this purpose. The feminization of this activity (should we see here a crypto *pousse-à-la-femme?*) is not lost on Mack Brunswick, who describes "a profound character change" in the Wolf Man, due, she reasons, to the more prominent role his unconscious passivity is permitted to play in his life and to a turn to dissimulation and unscrupulousness by this formerly conscientious, honest, and diligent man.

Despite Mack Brunswick's observation that her analysis of Pankejeff "corroborates in every detail the first" analysis with Freud, she provides details in recounting the case that tell a rather different story and that even lead her to wonder, in apparent contradiction with herself, whether Pankejeff "was perhaps always latently paranoid" (Mack Brunswick 1928, 474). The hypochondriacal tendencies, the feelings of persecutions, the ideas of reference, Pankejeff's obsession with his appearance, and the delusion of grandeur—all of this combines to suggest the view that Pankejeff is not the person he was when he consulted Freud. As one reads her discussion of Pankejeff's treatment, one cannot but be struck by the extent to which a picture emerges of a dramatically different analysand with a radically different presentation. Consider Mack Brunswick's own summary of her diagnosis (470), which includes the following features:

1. A hypochondriacal delusion
2. A delusion of persecution
3. Regression to narcissism (as shown in the delusion of grandeur)
4. The absence of hallucinations
5. Mild ideas of reference

If we accept Mack Brunswick's analysis, it is very difficult to avoid the conclusion, despite her own declarations to the contrary, that somewhere along the line the Wolf Man has become psychotic. And yet opinion in the literature has always been divided. Muriel Gardiner consistently maintains that Pankejeff was obsessional, as Freud had concluded, and dismisses, on the grounds of the success of the treatment and the rapid disappearance of his symptoms, the crisis that occurred during the Wolf Man's treatment with Mack Brunswick as not significant for the diagnosis of psychosis. She refers to the views of three analysts who had carried out assessments formally and informally—Pankejeff seems to have successfully managed to put the psychoanalytic community to work around his person—all of whom concur with Freud's original assessment of obsessional neurosis. As further evidence, she adduces Pankejeff's *awareness* that his attitude toward the injury to his nose was abnormal (Gardiner 1973, 389). She also maintains, and with some justification, that his "feeling of being favoured" by Freud was "logical enough," and that there were therefore no grounds for Mack Brunswick to consider his belief that Freud took a special interest in him to be "delusional or a complete 'regression to narcissism'" (389). Indeed, she claims, "Freud himself would have been the last person to deny his interest in his patient's welfare" (389). And, of course, Freud's own analysis of the case leaves little room for Pankejeff to be diagnosed as psychotic. The indications that have sometimes been appealed to, such as the hallucination of having severed his finger and the sense of reality of the wolf dream (see Blum 1974), are not probative. Jacques-Alain Miller, in his extensive discussion of Freud's case study, conducted within the limits of a reading of Freud's case on the question of foreclosure and the paternal function, emphasizes Lacan's position apropos of Pankejeff, namely that the presence of a psychotic phenomenon, especially in childhood, is not sufficient evidence of the presence of psychosis (Miller 2010, 69).

However, everything points to the conclusion that at around the time Pankejeff consults Mack Brunswick he has triggered a psychosis, as discreet as it may have been, and that when he enters analysis with her he is in the preliminary stages of a psychosis the final outcome of which at that point is uncertain—after all, at thirty-nine years of age he is younger than Schreber was when he became psychotic and is easily young enough to develop a paranoid psychosis. As it turned out, this never eventuated, but rather than regard this as evidence for Freud's diagnosis, as Gardiner does, it seems more reasonable to view the differences between the presentation of the case in Freud's case history and in Mack Brunswick's supplement as differences between an untriggered psychosis and a discreet case of ordinary psychosis (see Lysy-Stevens 2002).

The term "ordinary psychosis" was introduced by J.-A. Miller in 1997 (Miller 1999). It refers to a form of psychosis in which the subject does not manifest any of the classical psychotic symptoms, such as delusions, hallucinations, and bodily phenomena of various kinds, but manifests itself rather in a mild form in which the symptoms are often quite discreet. There is evidence to suggest that ordinary psychosis is quite widespread and possibly even on the increase—it certainly seems true that there has been an increase in the frequency of cases of ordinary psychosis encountered in clinical settings, and one can speculate on the reasons for this (see Grigg 2002). The reasons why the concept of borderline, which apparently covers precisely those cases that seem not to fit into the neurosis–psychosis divide, is unsatisfactory have been well argued (Brousse 2009; Maleval 2000).

There are several advantages to the concept of ordinary psychosis. For instance, it draws a clear distinction between untriggered and triggered psychosis, which, owing to the discreet nature of symptoms in ordinary psychosis, can be otherwise easily confused. And yet, in the clinical setting, it is crucial to know whether the subject one is treating is someone with a psychotic structure that has not yet been and indeed may never be triggered or someone whose psychosis has at some moment been triggered, but in a subtle way that may therefore have occurred undetected and undiagnosed. Furthermore, and most important, in speaking of ordinary psychosis, we intend it to be understood that making a diagnosis of psychosis does not require the presence of florid psychotic symptoms. The category covers those cases where it is very difficult to detect any neurotic symptoms or, a fortiori, any definite neurotic structure in the patient. This reasoning that leads from the uncertainty over seeing a patient as neurotic to a diagnosis of ordinary psychosis would make the concept merely an "epistemic category," as Miller (2009, 151) calls it, and an expression of uncertainty, were it not for the fact that use of the term implies the further inquiry into the particular features of the case that both reveal its kinship with classical categories (paranoia, schizophrenia) and explain how it has come about that the psychotic phenomena manage to adopt a mild form. Enquiries into this second aspect of ordinary psychosis have led to the discovery of a range of strategies that act for the subject as a prop or crutch—or, to use Lacan's term, a "suppletion" *[suppléance]*—to maintain a stability in their being in the world absent from florid cases (for more detail, consult the issue of *Psychoanalytic Notebooks* referred to in note 1).

The view that Pankejeff is a case of ordinary psychosis and, therefore, had become psychotic by the time he was received by Mack Brunswick has some admittedly indirect support in the International Psychoanalytical Association literature (see Blum 1974), which is most likely drawing on some remarks made in the late 1960s by Max Schur (Mack 1969, 219). This is the crux of the matter, and the period of analysis with Mack Brunswick is crucial to the discussion of the question of ordinary psychosis. As J.-A. Miller has said more recently, "You can doubt the psychosis when you read the Freudian case, but when you get the follow up with Ruth Mack Brunswick, it's difficult to question it," adding that "because he had a lot of neurotic traits," we must conclude that we are dealing with a case of ordinary psychosis (Miller 2009, 165).

To reiterate, then, the most likely scenario is that Pankejeff is a case of untriggered psychosis at the time of his analysis with Freud, that something triggers a discreet form of psychosis, probably in 1926, and therefore that when he consults Mack Brunswick in October of that year, he presents as a case of ordinary psychosis, which is not to be confused with untriggered psychosis. Max Schur (Mack 1969, 219) also speculates that Pankejeff's paranoia may have been triggered by Freud's illness—he had just had his first cancer operation—and possibly the illness and infertility of Pankejeff's wife. While this explanation has the odor of apriorism and one can wonder what real empirical support it has, we also know that it would not be the first case when the illness of an essential loved one who fulfils the role of suppletion provokes the onset of a psychosis.

Indeed, it seems strange that subsequent to Mack Brunswick's account, opinion in the psychoanalytic literature has been divided over Pankejeff's diagnosis, because, at least from the perspective of recent work in the Lacanian orientation, but also with the popularity of the category of borderline personality disorder, it is reasonable to think that we would consider Pankejeff a discreet case of psychosis. As for Mack Brunswick's own opinion, she considered that the absence of signs of delusion and loss of reality count against a diagnosis of psychosis, but ultimately she defers to Freud, as when she states that "the chief evidence against this theory is his conduct during his analysis with Freud," in which there was no evidence of a transference of a paranoid nature nor "the slightest manifestation of any paranoid mechanisms" (Mack Brunswick 1928, 475). I think we can conclude that Mack Brunswick puts the onus back on Freud's analysis too quickly, for it is at least possible and I think quite likely that there were no signs of paranoia in the treatment with Freud for the good reason that Pankejeff's psychosis did not appear until *after* his analysis with Freud, possibly during, but more likely before, his treatment with Mack Brunswick. In my opinion, then, Mack Brunswick does not countenance the most likely scenario of all, which is that, somewhere in the period between July 1914, when his treatment with Freud ceased, and October 1926, when Pankejeff consulted Mack Brunswick, there had been a triggering of psychosis.

This would explain the clear discrepancy between Freud's opinion, supported by Gardiner, and Mack Brunswick's observations as reported in her subsequent publication. It is unlikely that Freud would have missed clear signs of a psychotic disorder in his patient, who was in analysis with him for more than four years. The summer of 1926 therefore seems crucial. Pankejeff himself reports that, having written to Freud on June 6, 1926, by the end of that month he was in such a confused state that he was not in any condition even to write to Freud—but Freud, who subsequently referred him to Mack Brunswick for treatment, presumably didn't see Pankejeff again at this time (Wolf Man 1957, 456–57).

On reflection, however, it is perhaps unsurprising that Mack Brunswick adopts a position on the Wolf Man that comfortably and, one might even say, reassuringly endorses Freud's own earlier views that had been set out in his original 1918 case study (*SE*, 17), given that she consulted Freud over both the treatment and the drafting of her text. It might have been possible to paint a different picture from Freud's, but against the backdrop of the most detailed and complicated of Freud's case histories, to do so would have been a considerable theoretical, not to mention personal, achievement; for the theoretical and diagnostic presence of Freud is not, it should be observed, the only manner in which Freud is present in the case. He is there in other ways as well—in fact, he casts a shadow over the entire treatment and is a continuous presence in the transference, even to the point, one suspects, of being for Mack Brunswick an irritant, if an unacknowledged one, in the transference itself.

Mack Brunswick considers the Wolf Man's four months in analysis with her to be an analysis with Freud by proxy. She writes as if this circumstance were innocuously neutral, or even a virtue for the treatment, when she writes, "Throughout the present analysis . . . I acted purely as mediator between the patient and Freud" (Mack Brunswick 1928, 476). However, Freud's presence in the transference ultimately has the effect of transforming the relationship between Mack Brunswick and the Wolf Man into one of rivalry and imaginary competition between analyst and analysand. This at least is my contention. I think Freud's presence proves to be a serious difficulty that borders on being a disaster for the treatment, and I think it results in the serious exacerbation of the Wolf Man's symptoms, effectively compounding the grave condition of a man whose psychosis has been triggered in the years between his treatment with Freud and Mack Brunswick.

The transferential complexities in Pankejeff's analysis with Mack Brunswick were very considerable indeed: at the time of receiving him, Mack Brunswick was in analysis with Freud, as were her husband and husband's brother; and at this same period Freud referred Muriel Gardiner, a subsequent friend and confidant of Pankejeff, to Mack Brunswick for analysis as well. Moreover, Mack Brunswick is indebted to Freud because he has presented her with a golden opportunity to make a name for herself. Pankejeff is already famous. She knows, just as Pankejeff does, that being the analyst of Freud's "trophy" analysand will assure her a place in the history of the movement, and that, as Paul Roazen has justly written, "anything she published would become famous in the clinical literature." Moreover, she was, and presumably Pankejeff knew that she was, an intimate of the Freud family; Freud attended her wedding, she dined regularly with the Freuds, she visited him over summer and was on good terms with the Freud children. Again as Roazen notes, "In recognition of her special standing, Ruth became one of the few women who received a ring from Freud" (2005).

Now, this means that while Mack Brunswick observes that "throughout the present analysis . . . my own role was almost negligible; I acted purely as mediator between the patient and Freud" (1928, 476), she is in fact no simple conduit, like some foreign ambassador sending her dispatches from the Russian front, as it were, to headquarters, nor is she simply some place marker for Freud himself. In thinking of her role as negligible, she underestimates, to the point of *méconnaissance,* her role in Pankejeff's analysis with her, and, above all, as things develop she misses the emerging indications that the imaginary dimension of the transference is placing her in a persecutory role with respect to her patient.

One can speculate on Mack Brunswick's attitude toward Freud and Pankejeff in the transference, but what is clear is that Freud is never absent from the transference itself; but then neither is she. This triangle is the background against which we should view Mack Brunswick's strategic assault on what she refers to as Pankejeff's "megalomanic" resistance to the treatment. Whereas Freud had put the onus onto Pankejeff by setting a term to the analysis in the face of his unassailable attitude of "obliging apathy" (*SE,* 17:11), Mack Brunswick engages in a full-frontal attack; but it is one with drastic consequences.

Mack Brunswick appreciates that discussion of Pankejeff's delusional idea about the damage to his nose remained off-limits during the analysis. The topic was sheltered, she writes, behind an impregnable narcissism. Her response is to set herself the task of breaking through his "invulnerability" on this and other topics. As it happens, however, the two measures she adopts have major effects upon the transference and succeed in tipping Pankejeff over into a frankly paranoid position, effectively destabilizing a treatment that, at four months in duration, takes place over quite a short time period.

The first measure, one that has the effect of placing Mack Brunswick in a dangerous position of omnipotence, occurs one morning when she announces to an unsuspecting Pankejeff the news that Professor X, the dermatologist who occupies a mildly persecutory position for him, had died the previous day. She knows that Professor X's death will have been announced in the daily press, but because the newspaper had not hit the street by the time of Pankejeff's session, Mack Brunswick knows that she will surprise him with the news of the death of his persecutor. To her satisfaction, Pankejeff responds with an overt declaration of his previously silent murderous intent: "My God, now I can't kill him anymore!" (Mack Brunswick 1928, 456). Her satisfaction is misplaced, however, as we can recognize in his outburst that the murderous desire with respect to the small other, his *semblable,* his counterpart ("I will kill him because he wants to kill me"), has brought the relationship down to an essentially imaginary dimension. Such is the effect of this first step in her assault.

The second measure, which she explicitly undertakes in order to break through Pankejeff's "narcissism," which, again, is an assault addressed at the level of the imaginary, is to undermine his mistaken beliefs—but are they really mistaken?—about Freud's concerns for and interest in him. As Mack Brunswick remarks:

> He added that through me he was really getting all the benefit of Freud's knowledge and experience, without coming directly under his influence. When I asked how this was possible, he said he was sure that I discussed all the details of his case with Freud, so as to be advised by him! I remarked that this was not the case, that I had, at the beginning of his analysis, asked Professor Freud for an account of his former illness, and that since that time I had barely mentioned him nor had Freud inquired for him. This statement enraged and shocked the patient. He could not believe that Freud could show so little interest in his (famous) case. He had always thought Freud sincerely interested in him. Freud, in sending him to me, had even said—but here his recollection of what had been said became hazy. He left my office in a rage at Freud, which led to a dream in which his father was obviously castrated. (457)

Mack Brunswick's strategy, then, consists of making a concerted, even brutal attack on his narcissistic armor by undermining "the patient's idea of himself as the favourite son" (456), revealing to him his true position with Freud, and stressing the absence of any personal or familiar relationship between them: his is not the only published case, nor is it even the longest analysis. And when, at the end of his tether, Pankejeff stresses the nonprofessional nature of his relationship to Freud, Mack Brunswick archly enquires, "If such were the case," then why was he "never seen socially at the Freud's?" *[sic]* (456).

This relentless pursuit of an interpretative approach that reinforces the rivalrous dimension of the relationship with Freud effectively breaches the protective carapace that the psychotic Pankejeff has constructed around himself, brutally reducing it to an imaginary relationship with serious consequences in the analysis. As Mack Brunswick's own comments make clear, under her concerted attack Pankejeff begins to display a series of disturbingly psychotic reactions. Indeed, Mack Brunswick paints an alarming picture of a patient who has started to conduct himself

> in the most abnormal manner. He looked slovenly and harassed, and as if devils were at his heels, as he rushed from one shop window to another to inspect his nose. During the analytic hours he talked wildly in terms of his phantasies, completely cut off from reality. He threatened to shoot both Freud and me—now that X. was dead!—and somehow these threats sounded less empty than those which one is accustomed to hear. One felt him capable of anything because he was in such complete desperation. (462)

Not having the theoretical understanding—we owe this to Lacan—for drawing a clear distinction between the mechanisms of neurosis and psychosis, Frosch (1967) follows Mack Brunswick's own analysis of the development, and thereby fails, as does Mack Brunswick, to fully appreciate the Pandora's box she has opened. This failure leads him to state without further comment that the destruction of Pankejeff's grandiose ideas has brought his persecution to the fore and raised the question whether the megalomania was not part of a defense cloaking his homosexuality.

It is clear that by placing so much faith in the letter of Freud's own analysis of the Wolf Man, Mack Brunswick misses all the warning signs of a potential disaster. She misses the significance of Pankejeff's presenting hypochondria, which ought to have put her on her guard at the very least. There was at that point no reason to think that what Lacan says in relation to Schreber, namely, "What we see from the start are symptoms, initially hypochondriacal, which are psychotic symptoms" (1988, 313), should not apply equally to Pankejeff. And the two consequences of her attack on his megalomania—the falling away of the protective function of his carapace and the emergence of the murderous impulses arising from its demolition—are both futile and dangerous.

Moreover, Mack Brunswick's analysis of the Wolf Man has quite special features owing to the peculiar conjuncture of relations between Freud, Pankejeff, and herself, and although the Wolf Man's psychosis was triggered several months before she took him into treatment, which is a development Mack Brunswick failed to appreciate, this conjuncture was instrumental in provoking the psychotic episode that must have emerged quite quickly in the course of this brief analytic treatment of four to five months' duration.

Mack Brunswick's explanation, which is that Pankejeff's megalomania had provided him necessary protection that her attacks had deprived him of, is perhaps true but insufficient, because it leaves out any mention of the crucial relationship to Freud, which as she herself observes dominates the transference. Mack Brunswick thinks that symptomatic of Pankejeff's "megalomania" is the claim to a special relationship with Freud that is not a merely therapeutic one but a personal and even intimate one, hence her dreadful interpretation: "Why, then, are you never seen socially at the Freud's'?" She recognizes, then, that in Pankejeff's adherence to a special relationship with Freud it is a question of love; but as a result of her idealization of the figure of Freud she erroneously regards this attachment as an expression of megalomania when it is actually the mainstay of Pankejeff's insertion into the symbolic. Thus, what Mack Brunswick does not appreciate is that this is a special type of love, for it is transference love, which as we have come to understand it is love addressed to knowledge. And the addressee is Sigmund Freud, who plays the role of suppletion in the case of the Wolf Man.

As the fashion in psychoanalysis turned toward emphasizing the analysis of the transference, Freud came under the criticism that he had left Pankejeff in a situation of lifelong dependency on both himself and the psychoanalytic community by not having addressed the underlying transference issues in his work with this patient. In 1919 Pankejeff returned, destitute, to Vienna, where he underwent a further four months of analysis with Freud. There is a curious difference between Freud's and Jones's accounts of why. According to Jones, he suffers from "an obstinate hysterical constipation" (Jones 1974, 309), but as Freud tells it, at the time Pankejeff informed Freud that immediately following the termination of his analysis in 1914 he had, as Freud says, "been seized with a longing to tear himself free from my influence" (*SE*, 17:121–22*n*), and after a further four months of analysis "a piece of the transference which had not hitherto been overcome was successfully dealt with" (122*n*). Freud reiterates in "Analysis Terminable and Interminable" that he had helped "him to master a piece of the transference which had not been resolved" (*SE*, 23:218). And yet, as Ernest Jones comments, "Freud not only treated him without a fee but regularly collected from colleagues and pupils sums of money that sustained the patient and his invalid wife for the next six years, years when making a livelihood in stricken Vienna was a highly precarious undertaking" (1974, 309). The claim to have been Freud's "favourite son" not being without foundation, then, the transference to Freud dominates the analysis with Mack Brunswick, and, in fact, while we can agree with Mack Brunswick that it is the disruption to, and the imaginary dimension of the attack on, this transference that causes the serious deterioration in Pankejeff's condition, it is likely that, despite Mack Brunswick's efforts, the situation stabilizes with the reestablishment of his enduring belief in a special relationship with Freud—a belief he never relinquished for as long as he lived.

If it is the case that Mack Brunswick's strategy is effectively an assault on the role of suppletion that Freud plays for Pankejeff, then a different interpretation of the dream that Mack Brunswick welcomes as a dream of "good portent" is possible. Here is the dream:

> The patient and his mother are together in a room, one corner of whose walls is covered with holy pictures. His mother takes the pictures down and throws them to the floor. The pictures break and fall into bits. The patient wonders at this act on the part of his pious mother. (Mack Brunswick 1928, 462)

Mack Brunswick claims that in the dream it is she who is the mother, who, instead of giving the patient religion as the historical mother did, destroys religion and the accompanying Christ fantasy for him. But how can we fail to see instead a continuation of the aggressive assault on the image of Freud as the suppletion that holds Pankejeff's world in place and whose destruction unleashes the paranoid aggression of the relation's imaginary lining?

This attitude revolves around what we could call Pankejeff's position as Freud's "informant," or, as Pankejeff would express it quite some years later, in early 1957, in his analysis with Freud, "I felt myself less as a patient than as a co-worker, the younger comrade of an experienced explorer setting out to discover a new, recently discovered land" (Wolf Man 1973, 158). And, he adds, "this feeling of 'working together' was increased by Freud's recognition of my understanding of psychoanalysis, so that he even once said it would be good if all his pupils *[sic]* could grasp the nature of analysis as soundly as I" (158). What dominates Pankejeff's relationship to Freud, and does so across the entire history of their relationship, is that Pankejeff places himself as an object in the service of Freud's desire for knowledge. He is always there, and one wonders whether he considers it his due to be paid, effectively, for services rendered to Freud and the cause.

It should be noted that by placing himself at Freud's service, as if he were Freud's loyal servant in his noble quest, this desire for knowledge on Freud's part prevents Freud from occupying the position of omnipotence that would be a threat to the stability of the transference, even as it maintains Pankejeff in this curious position of trophy of the analytic movement. It is this relatively stable edifice that, when sapped by the interpretative approach of Mack Brunswick, risks coming crashing down around him.

I've gone into this treatment in some detail because of the role Mack Brunswick's interpretations play, as I have argued, in the sudden deterioration of Pankejeff's condition in his brief therapy with her. What I have stressed is not the fact of the interpretations per se but their nature, namely, that they emphasize the imaginary dimension of the transference relationship by the focus on the rivalry over Freud that marks Mack Brunswick's relationship with Pankejeff. Whatever the merits might have been of such an approach in the case of a neurotic subject, though even then one would still wonder about the role of Mack Brunswick's transferential relationship to Freud, she courts disaster in her treatment of Pankejeff. The Wolf Man's strong transference to Freud and, thereby, the place he occupied as a living psychoanalytic specimen, should be seen as a major component of his ordinary psychosis, where in its role as suppletion it provides stability to his ordinary psychosis with its schizophrenic tendencies. c/c

BIOGRAPHY

Russell Grigg is a philosopher at Deakin University and a psychoanalyst in private practice in Melbourne, Australia. He is a member of the French school of psychoanalysis, the École de la Cause Freudienne, the New Lacanian School, and the Lacan Circle of Melbourne. His recent publications include *Lacan, Language, and Philosophy* (2008).

NOTE

1. See the periodical of the London Society of the New Lacanian School 2009, *Psychoanalytical Notebooks*, 19, *Ordinary Psychosis*, for a collection of excellent articles on this topic.

BIBLIOGRAPHY

Blum, H. P. 1974. "The Borderline Childhood of the Wolf Man." *Journal of the American Psychoanalytic Association* 22: 721–42.

Brousse, Marie-Hélène. 2009. "Ordinary Psychosis in the Light of Lacan's Theory of Discourse." *Psychoanalytical Notebooks* 19: 7–19.

Freud, Sigmund. 1953–74. *The Standard Edition of the Complete Psychological Works of Sigmund Freud [SE]*. 24 vols. London: Hogarth Press.

Frosch, John. 1967. "Severe Regressive States during Analysis—Introduction." *Journal of the American Psychoanalytic Association* 15: 491–507.

Gardiner, Muriel. 1973. "The Wolf-Man in Later Life." In Muriel Gardiner, ed. *The Wolf-Man and Sigmund Freud*. Harmondsworth, U.K.: Penguin.

Grigg, Russell. 2002. "Enjoy-meant of Language and Jouissance of the Letter." *Psychoanalytic Notebooks* 8: 57–65.

Jones, Ernest. 1974. *Sigmund Freud: Life and Work. Vol. 2. Years of Maturity 1901–1919*. London: Hogarth Press.

Lacan, Jacques. 1988. *The Seminar of Jacques Lacan. Book I. Freud's Papers on Technique*, trans. John Forrester. Cambridge, U.K.: Cambridge University Press.

———. 1993. *The Seminar of Jacques Lacan. Book III. The Psychoses*, trans. Russell Grigg. New York: Norton.

Lysy-Stevens, Anne. 2002. "What One Calls 'Untriggered' Psychoses." In *Courtil Papers*. http://www.ch-freudien-be.org/Papers/index.html.

Mack, J. E. 1969. "Dreams and Psychosis." *Journal of the American Psychoanalytic Association* 17: 206–21.

Mack Brunswick, Ruth. 1928. "A Supplement to Freud's 'History of an Infantile Neurosis.'" *International Journal of Psycho-Analysis* 9: 439–76.

Mahony, Patrick J. 1984. *Cries of the Wolf Man*. New York: International Universities Press.

Maleval, Jean-Claude. 2000. "Why So Many Borderlines?" *Psychoanalytical Notebooks* 4. http://www.londonsociety-nls.org.uk/maleval_borderlines.htm.

Miller, Jacques-Alain. 1999. Ed. *La psychose ordinaire: la convention d'Antibes*. Paris: Le Paon.

Miller, Jacques-Alain. 2009. "Ordinary Psychosis Revisited." *Psychoanalytical Notebooks* 19: 139–67.

———. 2010. "The Wolf Man II." *Lacanian Ink* 36: 6–85.

Offenkrantz, W., and A. Tobin. 1973. "Problems of the Therapeutic Alliance: Freud and the Wolf-Man." *International Journal of Psychoanalysis* 54: 75–78.

Ordinary Psychosis. 2008. *Psychoanalytical Notebooks*, 19.

Roazen, Paul. 2005. "Brunswick, Ruth Mack (1897–1946)." *International Dictionary of Psychoanalysis*. Ed. Alain de Mijolla. Vol. 1. Gale Cengage. *eNotes.com*. October 6, 2012. http://www.enotes.com/ruth-mack-brunswick-reference/.

Wolf Man. 1957. "Letters Pertaining to Freud's 'History of an Infantile Neurosis.'" *Psychoanalytic Quarterly* 26: 449–60.

Wolf Man. 1973. "My Recollections of Sigmund Freud." In Muriel Gardiner, ed. *The Wolf-Man and Sigmund Freud*. Harmondsworth, U.K.: Penguin.

SOPHIE MARRET-MALEVAL

"And, as in uffish thought he stood"

"*Mar. 10 (Tu)*. Called at the Deanery to arrange about our expedition tonight,[1] and to borrow a Natural History to help in illustrating *Alice's Adventures*" (Green 1953), writes Lewis Carroll in his diary (Carroll [1865] 1965, 193). The illustrations for these famous stories were thus inspired from the sketchbooks of naturalists. The designs that Carroll produced for the first manuscript version of the work as well as the better-known engravings by Tenniel, which accompanied the edition of *Alice's Adventures in Wonderland* in 1865, allow us to think that the analogy concerned their use as much as their content, which is confirmed by the didactic address to the reader: "If you don't know what a Gryphon is, look at the picture" (Carroll [1872] 1965, 124). In the context of the century marked by Darwin (the *Origin of Species* appeared in 1859), the link established by Carroll between *Alice's Adventures* and natural history seems essential. Lacan underlined this: "It is not in vain that Alice appeared at the same time as the *Origin of Species* of which it is, if I can put it like this, the other side. Hence, the epic register which undoubtedly is expressed as an idyll in ideology" [from Lacan's comments on Lewis Carroll on France Culture on December 31, 1966 (Lacan 2002, 12)]. The *Alice* books are the product of the scientific era. They celebrate it through fiction and question it at the same time.

ILLUSTRATION AND PROOF

"And what is the use of a book . . . without pictures or conversations?" (Carroll [1865] 1965, 25) asks Alice on the threshold of her adventures. The little girl is bored; her sister's reading does not capture her imagination. Speaking of the uses of books (their demonstrative and didactic function are privileged over and above their recreational side), she teaches us that words, alone, are useless. Thus, Alice goes to sleep and dreams. The story of her dream will be full of illustrations. The work has the structure of a scientific treatise. The dream is already associated with the formalization of knowledge.

A SCIENTIFIC WRITING

A contemporary of Venn and De Morgan, with whom the origin of the application of mathematics to logic originated, Charles Lutwidge Dodgson, alias Lewis Carroll, professor of mathematics at Oxford, was the author of a dozen manuals on algebra, geometry, and above all logic. Anticipating Hilbert's axiomatization of logic, he set himself the task of organizing Euclid's propositions logically while conceiving a symbolic language with which it was possible to avoid, through the use of algebra and logic, the ambiguities of natural languages. This unsatisfactory work was pedagogical and in this respect modern. His attempt at translating Aristotelian syllogisms in diagrammatic form was related to this aim.[2] He presented his square diagrams in *Symbolic Logic* (Carroll [1896] 1958), along with an indexical method for solving syllogisms. Contemporary treaties on the history of logic also highlight the modern nature of his approach. He referred to this manual, to which he gave all his energy at the end of his life, as a "work for God" (Cohen 1979, 1100).

His nonsensical stories are from the same drawing board as his treaties on mathematics, to the point of serving them as a model since he presented his last work of geometry, entitled *Euclid and His Modern Rivals* (Dodgson 1879), in the form of a fictional dialogue. This pedagogical approach should not be seen as being merely an attempt to entertain the reader. Lewis Carroll's mathematical work is inscribed within the movement that led from the mathematization of logic to the logicization of mathematics brought about by Gottlob Frege. The triumph of science goes hand in hand with the refinement of its tools, of the elaboration of a method, hence the accent brought to bear upon what (in his homage to Lewis Carroll) Lacan referred to as "materialized dialectic": "illustration and proof" (Lacan [1966] 2002, 12). As Ernest Coumet has emphasized, Carroll learned a lot from his contemporaries:

> The personal merit of Venn lies in having seen in diagrams something other than an approximate illustration; arguing against "conceptualists" such as Mansel, who went so far as to assert the possibility of representing concepts by spatial figures, he suggested, by contrast, that there should be a structure of equivalence between schemas and relations expressed verbally by propositions. . . . Do we want something other than suggestive imagery? A clear analysis of one's use of diagrammatic representations is not superfluous. But this being done, one would be given, through the same means, a method which would be both intuitive and rigorous. It is in this spirit

> that Carroll also thought to combine, thanks to this double advantage, the useful and the enjoyable. (Coumet 1966, 261–62)

If there are affinities between Lewis Carroll's literary and mathematic work, the essential reason for this is due neither to the introduction of fantasy within the serious manuals of logic nor to the trace of "the mathematician's mind" in his nonsensical texts. It is rather due to the scientific approach that informs the writing of *Alice,* where intuitions about "logical impossibility" and the subject of the unconscious, excluded by science, are deployed at the same time.

The opposition between rational thought and the emergence of the unconscious runs throughout his work to the point that he conceived *The Pillow Problems* (Dodgson [1895] 1958) for "ordinary mathematicians" in order to occupy their minds with mathematical problems so as to free them from overinvasive obsessions that create obstacles to falling asleep. Logic set in opposition to emotion and even to desire (in his commentary, (Lacan [1966] 2002) laces the emphasis more on the division in Carroll between logic and his "love" of little girls, between logic and dream, his conservatism and the genius of his intuitions, than on that between his mathematical and literary work, which literary critics have focused on), such is the antinomy that informs the two faces of his literary work. Although he signed his stories with his pen name and his mathematical treaties with his surname (and kept his literary double at a distance), *Symbolic Logic* was published under the name Lewis Carroll, finally marking the point where the two fields of his work meet. The purely factual character of his diaries testifies to his wish to let nothing of what animated him appear there. Without doubt this contributed to Lacan's feeling that "one's curiosity [to know how Carroll managed to do what he did] remains unsatisfied, for the biography of this man who kept a meticulous diary gives nothing away." Thus if Lacan says that he speaks of Carroll "without emotion . . . according to the authentic order of the simmering of his work," (1966] 2002, 12) it is on condition of taking the fantasy seriously, of grasping what it owes to the development of logic, but also of understanding that it put a questioning of scientific rationality into play, from which the emergence of an other knowledge concerning the unconscious came.

SCIENCE AND MYTH

In this sense, Lacan can assert that "through his work, Lewis Carroll illustrates and even proves all sorts of truths." Deriving its support from science, does the craftsmanship of the work prove to be propitious for the emergence of "a knowledge that is not known"? (Lacan 2007, 33). Three years after his Homage to Lewis Carroll in *The Other Side of Psychoanalysis,*

Lacan underlines that the subject of the unconscious logically follows on from the advent of science:

> As stupid as this discourse of the unconscious is, it is responding to something that stems from the institution of the discourse of the master himself. This is what is called the unconscious. It imposes itself upon science as a fact. (Lacan 2007, 91)

This statement can be usefully related to a previous statement about the opposition between mathematics and mythic knowledge:

> This is how mathematics represents the master's knowledge insofar as it is constituted on the basis of other laws than those of mythical knowledge. In short, the master's knowledge is produced as knowledge that is entirely autonomous with respect to mythical knowledge, and this is what we call science. (Lacan 2007, 90)

After first identifying *Alice's Adventures* and also *Sylvie and Bruno* as belonging to the genre of the "Mythic Novel," Lacan adds:

> One must quickly qualify this with the precious discovery that Wonderland, the land through the looking glass and the anguishing couple of Sylvie and Bruno who have escaped from other lands, are neither myths, nor from myth, and that the imaginary is to be distinguished from myth. Neither story, nor plot appeal to any resonance of signification that could be called profound. Genesis and tragedy are not evoked in them, nor is destiny. (10)

This statement should be referred to an article by Paul Schilder (1938) quoted by Lacan and roundly criticized. Part of a tradition that conceives novels as a "neurotic's individual myth," Schilder seeks to grasp the subject's fantasies in literary works, while at the same time indicating Carroll's supposed schizophrenia. He was not the only one to have advanced such a hypothesis. Lacan refutes it, reminding us that one should not link the subject's division with schizophrenia.

> To come to the author himself, at this time of homage to him, as for anyone, one does him no justice, if one does not set out from the idea that the so-called discordances of his personality are only relevant if we recognize the necessity through which they arise. . . . Lewis Carroll is certainly divided, if that is what you're after, but the two are necessary for the production of the work. ([1966] 2000, 11)

Lacan lends himself to this type of approach, which was widespread in 1966, when he emphasizes that one should not take Carroll's stories for myths and search for so-called profound meanings in them. However, his remark goes further. He here links myth to the dimension of signification, in a way that corresponds to the expression "mythic knowledge" that he opposes to mathematics. Here again he is targeting the structural proximity between Carroll's literary works and logic.

PEDAGOGY AND SUBVERSION

We must recall the context for this homage to Lewis Carroll. It came in a radio interview broadcast on France Culture on December 31, 1966, in a program hosted by Jacques Brunius entitled "Lewis Carroll: Master in the School for Skivers" ("Lewis Carroll: maître d'école buissonnière") which probably marked the centenary of the publication of *Alice's Adventures in Wonderland*.[3] In 1998, when the centenary of Lewis Carroll's death was celebrated, France Culture repeated this broadcast on August 29 and 30 in an edited form, without Lacan's intervention. The psychoanalytic point of view was not represented. Instead, Denis de Rougemont underlined that *Alice's Adventures* are about "the child's most fundamental freedom," namely "whether to grow up or not" and emphasized "the anxiety provoked by learning the simplest mathematical operations in arithmetic." It is a bitter pill to swallow to have to admit that a simplistic psychology founded on the ego was the only one to be broadcast. The comparison serves to underline the scope of Lacan's intervention. The forgetting of this intervention, which is never mentioned by Carroll's main critics, deserves to be questioned.

SLIP

"In 1971, the French editors of these *Cahiers* were again a small group of specialists, partners in their affection and in their relative marginality," indicates Jean Gattégno in the preface that he wrote in 1987 for the reedition of the edition of *Cahiers de l'Herne* (1971) devoted to Lewis Carroll. Carroll can be counted among authors who are universally known and read, commented upon abundantly, but whose place in the canon of English literature remains uncertain. Moreover, the specificity of a text written as a dialogue, founded on nonsense, has without doubt contributed to the fact that relatively few university studies have been devoted to it. Jean Gattégno thus notes the continuing air of confidentiality that characterized Carrollian criticism in 1971, and it would have been all the more so in 1968, a context that should have proved favorable for noting Lacan's interest in it. Instead, retracing the development of Carrollian criticism through the 1970s, Jean Gattégno concludes in 1987, "On the other hand, the Freudian approach did not develop much, perhaps because the essential work had already been done by William Empson and Phyllis Greenacre, present in this volume" (10). Despite having written his university thesis on Lewis Carroll in 1970, then a biography, and finally overseeing the edition of Carroll's works in the Pléiade collection, was Jean Gattégno unaware of Lacan's intervention? It was not indicated in any of the works or bibliographies that I examined. The contributions of William Empson and Phyllis Greenacre, who are among those whom Lacan criticized, are cited everywhere. William Empson ([1971] 1987) discreetly appeals to the fantasies of the author in order to study the works' symbolism. His approach is to show that the *Alice* books constitute a pastoral of childhood. Phyllis Greenacre ([1971] 1987) sought to grasp the unconscious signification of the work on the basis of a psychological study of Carroll's biography. These approaches have nothing in common with the analysis that Lacan proposed. The radio format of his intervention no doubt contributed to the fact that it did not leave any trace in critical memory, but this in itself does not suffice to fully explain this act of forgetting on the part of Carrollians. No doubt their significance was not yet audible, notably because of the emphasis that he placed on the real. The exploration of the imaginary level of the fantasy (upon which the most fantastical and contradictory interpretations have been based) prove more reassuring in delivering a signification, while Lacan noted how the text breaks through beyond this dimension, which it interrogates, making the articulation among the three registers of the symbolic, imaginary, and real come to light: "The three registers through which I have introduced a teaching that does not pretend to innovate but merely to re-establish some rigour in psychoanalytic experience, play there in a pure state in their simplest relationship" ([1966] 2002, 10).

A SUBVERSIVE AUTHOR?

In 1966, Lacan was certainly not the only one to emphasize the place of logic in Carroll's work, but it must be emphasized that none of the other commentaries on the program rebroadcast in 1998 managed to go beyond the level of signification, with the exception, perhaps, of Philippe Sollers, who noted that nonsense is about the work of language and, through this fact, strikes a chord with Freud's work, without going any deeper than that. If most of the commentaries in the broadcast (for the most part coming from famous authors) sought to learn something from Carroll's texts, it was to the extent that they could deliver them a lesson. Thus Andre Maurois said of Alice that in "the art of saying the most profound and difficult things while masking them in the form of an improbable story," he saw "the most ferocious satire of Victorian society that ever was written." In his *Anthologie de l'humour noir,* quoted in the course of the broadcast, André Breton made Carroll "our most important master in the school for skivers." In nonsense he saw "the vital solution to a profound contradiction between the acceptance of faith and the exercise of reason, on the one hand and, on the other, between a sharp poetic consciousness and the rigours of professional duty." He adds, "The key to this subjective solution lies in doubling it in an objective solution of a poetic order." Lacan is most probably replying to him when he emphasizes Carroll's religious conservatism:

> One knows the case that the surrealists have made and will always make of it. This gives me the opportunity to extend the rigour of my method, no matter if it annoys the partisan spirit, Lewis Carroll, and I recall it, was religious, religious in the most naïve faith, in the most parochial of ways, should this word, which you have to consider in its crudest light provoke repulsion in you. ([1966] 2002, 11)

Breton could not account for what has its roots in the subject's division between knowledge and truth. However, Lacan refuses to take this effect of division for a contradiction solved through the absurd.

Others, like Breton, hold Carroll to be a master in the art of subversion. Raymond Queneau confesses that he experienced a vivid pleasure in reading Carroll that he situated on the side of the Marquis de Sade. Eugene Ionesco indicates, more subtly, that *Alice* is a "pure nightmare," but he also celebrates its power of subversion. For him, the work gets closest to the child's way of seeing things, which is "full of terror," while the logic of adults serves to hide "their fundamental fear." According to Marguerite Duras, who comments in the broadcast on Carroll's letters to little girls, "He used this logic and this morality to shed an ironical light upon them in a way that had never been done before. . . ." She holds on to the work's power of moral subversion, whereas Lacan underlines that, through the work of logic that governs it, it opens onto a knowledge about the impossible, in the same way that Marguerite Duras's work itself does. We understand why Lacan says that "he would have liked to hear her speak about this work as a novelist" ([1966] 2000, 12). Claude Roy, on the other hand, situates *Alice* among the three books that, for him, constitute "archetypes of British consciousness and unconscious," along with the Bible and the works of Shakespeare. He suggests that *Alice's Adventures* are a precious resource for heads of state, politicians, journalists, and theater directors. It is because the story contains wisdom—"mirroring universal absurdity"—he proposes a "liberating vision of the world." This book provides a veritable "practical guide." There Alice finds the most just attitude in life, for she "never gives way before what she considers to be stupid or bad." Here we find the continuous paradox of readings of *Alice,* celebrating edifying virtues alongside subversion.

This contradiction can also be found, in a more articulated way, in contemporary criticism, which still concludes on the resolution of the work in a given meaning. In *Lewis Carroll,* Jean Gattégno emphasizes the formative aspect of the work. His thesis is based on a Piagetian approach according to which Alice's acts of revolt give her access to self-discovery (1970, 211), contributing to a decline in her egocentricity thanks to the discovery that she has made of the world outside (223), and correspond to the passage of the child from the prelogical stage to the logical stage (222), in her journey toward adulthood. Donald Rackin (1991) prefers to insist on the subversive power of the work. For him, Alice's growing up consists in taking account of the disorder subjacent to an impression of the rational order in the world. He does not dismiss the pedagogical side of the work, but he is also called to put it in tension with its power of subversion. It is also what Kathleen Blake does in *Play Games and Sports* (1974), when she shows that the *Alice* books celebrate the rule, but that, through this, they pose the question of knowing what rules to respect, which brings a denunciation of Victorian conventions. In *Structures logiques et representations du désir* (1973), Henri Laporte insists on the limits of the subversive power of Carroll's work. According to him, the *Alice* books testify to a total impossibility of imagining the pleasure principle, in the same way as the structuralist formalizations that he opposes, for he believes that they are based on the social repression of pleasure that transforms desire into absence. In *Philosophy of Nonsense* (1994), Jean-Jacques Lecercle concludes for his part that nonsense is a fundamentally paradoxical genre that supports order and subverts it at the same time. He comes closest to the assertion Lacan formulated, according to which "Lewis Carroll is certainly divided, if that's what you're after, but the two are necessary for the realisation of the work" (Lecercle 1994, 11).

CONTRADICTION AND DIVISION

Resolving the ambiguity of the work proves to be necessary if one can see it only as a message, bearing a signification, as most of the commentators of the work try to do, apart from Jean-Jacques Lecercle, who can accommodate contradiction thanks to the thesis he adopts: "Language speaks." It is a vehicle for discourse independent of the speakers wanting to say *[vouloir dire].* In the context of 1966, the interviews broadcast on France Culture all remain prisoners of a quasi-allegorical approach to the work. Lacan's intervention breaks with this: "Neither the text, nor the plot," he says, "evoke any resonance of significations that one could call profound." The knowledge carried by the text always proves to be confused with that of the author as far as the other personalities of the broadcast are concerned. This is noticeable in Françoise Brocas's exposé and in Pierre Mabille's preface to André Bay's translation quoted during the broadcast. Mabille saw in Carroll a "prophet of the profound revolution which occurred a hundred years ago in the domain of logic, reason and more particularly in mathematical logistics," "expressing the same thought, sometimes in a poetic form, sometimes in a mathematical form." But Lacan reminds us that "in the very époque of the renaissance of logic and the inauguration of the mathematical form established since then, Lewis Carroll, however amusing his efforts are, remains a follower of Aristotle" ([1966] 2000, 11). Françoise Brocas lays emphasis on the mathematical knowledge lodged in the literary work in order to make this into a "demonstration by the absurd that the sense of time cannot be changed." For her, mathematics is about the inscription in the work of a scientific knowledge assimilated by the author and delivered through the text conceived as a demonstration.

In 1969, in *Logique du sens,* Gilles Deleuze took up Alice, in his turn, and held it as an exemplary text for putting the work of sense into perspective. The Carrollian neologism unveils the fact that meaning is founded on "an empty square," on the basis of which signifier and signified articulate on the surface of language and being. He contrasts Carroll with Antonin Artaud. For Artaud, language is only a surface. Artaud was in a way a kind of born revolutionary, an authentic practitioner of schizolinguistics lauded by philosophy. Besides the contestable character of Deleuze's approach to schizophrenia and the ideological substrate upon which it is founded, Deleuze paradoxically supports this thesis at the cost of neglecting Carroll's work on logic, which he considered a matter of signification and not of sense. Because of this, he separated the literary work's contradictions between its defense of conservative ideas in matters of logic and language and the semantic, even formalist intuitions, that inscribe themselves there. Again, he ignores the effects of division at the level of the structure of the subject as constitutive of the work. If Lacan advanced that "it is psychoanalysis which can best account for the effect of this work," ([1966] 2002, 9) one must already grasp how his intervention illustrates that only psychoanalysis can grasp the contradictions of the work, not as the inscription of a paradox but as an effect of the division of the subject between knowledge and truth, as he had defined it at the time in "Science and Truth": "This lead did not guide me in vain, for it led me, at the end of the year, to formulate our experienced division as subjects as a division between knowledge and truth" (2006c, 727). This division of the subject is precisely evacuated by the form of psychoanalysis to which Paul Schilder refers that reduces the inscription of unconscious knowledge in the text to a dangerous pedagogy of subversion. This book is not to be put in everyone's hands, he says, because it is founded on a "primary aggressivity" (Schilder 1938, 167). According to him, Carroll is a "particularly destructive writer." What horrifies him in the text is the unconscious that shows itself there. For him, what matters is saving the illusions of the ego.

MYTH AND STRUCTURE

"That's what myth is, the attempt to give an epic form to what is operative through the structure," Lacan later writes in *Television* (1990, 30). If Carroll's work is "the epic of the scientific era," it is also what gives access in its lines to a knowledge about the unconscious. The epic dimension refers essentially to the form of the story, to fiction (one could refer here to the definition given in *Littré*). Through its imaginary form, epic allows one to grasp a knowledge about the structure. Epic is also the imaginary reduced to its "real consistency" (Lacan 1975, 98), to its relation to the other two registers of the real and the symbolic. "Out of images, a pure play of combination is made, but what effects of vertigo cannot be obtained from them?" observes Lacan when he seeks to answer the question, "How has this work managed to obtain such a hold?" "History, certainly, is dominant in psychoanalytic treatment of the truth but this is not the only dimension: structure dominates" ([1966] 2002, 9), Lacan stresses in his intervention, targeting the individual history of the subject. In this sense, could not Lewis Carroll's text be qualified in terms of myth, if we refer to the definition Lacan gives it in *Television* that we cited previously? Elsewhere, in *The Other Side of Psychoanalysis,* Lacan says, "In short, half-saying is the internal law of every species of enunciation of the truth, and what embodies it best is myth"(2007, 110). The paradox is only surface; Carroll's text is oriented by science but, by playing on its limits, it lets us grasp, in the story, what it excludes.

Doesn't Lacan conceive the manifest contradictions of the text as a way of accessing the impossible of logic when he begins his intervention with a statement designed to bring out its effects of paradoxical appearance: "One can see here that without taking the form of any disorder one can produce uneasiness, but that from this uneasiness he derives a singular enjoyment"? The impossible of logic is targeted from the start. "This myth can have no other sense here than the one I have reduced it to, a statement of the impossible" says Lacan in *The Other Side of Psychoanalysis* (2007, 125). "I will emphasize this to start with," Lacan continues in his intervention, "in order to lay aside the confusion which threatens if I were to propose that it is psychoanalysis that could best account for the effect of this work" ([1966] 2002, 9). One observes that the other critical approaches of the period tended to evacuate the impossible that was already manifest in the contradictory effects of the work. Only psychoanalysis can account for the knowledge about the real brought by the work where other readings tend rather to mask it. Without doubt, this has remained sufficiently obscure for this intervention to be forgotten by them. "Through his work, Lewis Carroll illustrates and even proves all sorts of truths; truths which are certain although not obvious" (9). It is that the truths in question concern the truth of the unconscious (a few lines further down, Lacan returns to the term of truth, this time in the singular), that which Oedipus wanted to know (9)."For the analysand who is there, in the $, the content is his knowledge. We are there in order to get to the point where he knows everything that he does not know even as he knows it. That's what the unconscious is" (Lacan 2007, 113).

This is what Lacan indicates in *The Other Side of Psychoanalysis* (2007, 113) at a time when the concept of truth is still privileged. If truth can only be half-said, it is because it touches the real, as Lacan emphasizes again in *Television:* "I always speak the truth. Not the whole truth, because there's no way, to say it all. Saying it all is literally impossible: words fail. Yet it's through this very impossibility that the truth holds onto the real" (1990, 3). The unconscious knowledge contained in Carroll's text bears upon the real.

SOME TRUTHS

One cannot overstate the affinities between Lewis Carroll's nonsensical works and the formations of the unconscious, as what Carroll says of their origin in the preface to *Sylvie and Bruno* ([1889] 1983) bears out. All his writings sprang from ideas and fragments of dialogues that came to his mind and that he noted down in order not to forget them, without his being able to trace them to a precise cause:

> Sometimes one could trace to their source these random flashes of thought—as being suggested by the book one was reading, or struck out from the "flint" of one's own mind by the "steel" of a friend's chance remark—but they had also a way of their own, of occurring, *a propos* of nothing—specimens of that hopelessly illogical phenomenon, "an effect without a cause." Such, for example, was the last line of "The Hunting of the Snark," which came into my head (as I have already related in "The Theatre" for April, 1887) quite suddenly, during a solitary walk; and such, again, have been passages which occurred in dreams, and which I cannot trace to any antecedent cause whatever. ([1889] 1983, 255)

Nonsense is close to dream and consequently proves suitable for unveiling the truths of the unconscious. "An effect without cause" arises "out of nothing"; we would rather be tempted to say an effect of a cause that cannot be discerned by logic or circumscribed by the signifier, an effect of nothing, the writing of the work here finds itself linked to an origin qualified as "illogical." According to Carroll's own terms, it is thus closely related to his chosen discipline as a mathematician but concerns its other side: "Effect without a cause"—can we not see in this statement an intuition that the work originates in the impossible of logic?

OUTLINE

Let's remember that when Carroll wrote these lines, he had just completed his last story and was about to devote himself entirely to writing *Symbolic Logic*. Also, Carroll's texts are crammed full of neologisms that refer only to absent and even unimaginable referents. In fact, Carroll refused to allow the Snark to be represented with an illustration (Carroll 1867). Elsewhere, the neologisms of "Jabberwocky," a nonsensical poem inserted into *Alice through the Looking Glass,* do not refer to an image either, just as the explanation given Humpty Dumpty fails to allow one to form a representation of the creatures to which they refer: "a *'borogrove'* is a thin shabby-looking bird with its feathers sticking out all round—something like a live mop" (Carroll 1998, 189). Or again:

> "And what are *'toves'*?"
>
> "Well, *'toves'* are something like badgers—they're something like lizards—and they're something like corkscrews."
>
> "They must be very curious-looking creatures." (Carroll [1872] 1965, 271)

These hardly satisfying descriptions seem to serve the function of preventing the reader from forming an image of these creatures.

As Lacan indicates, in Carroll's work "one sees that without taking the form of any disorder one can produce uneasiness, but that from this uneasiness he derives a singular enjoyment" ([1966] 2002, 9). In fact, nonsense remains in the register of the marvelous and not in that of the fantastic. It is not based, like *Frankenstein* or *Dracula,* on the intuition that anxiety occurs when the object *a* appears in the real. When the Baker finally encounters the Snark, he fulfills his uncle's prophesy and disappears while exclaiming, "It is a boo. . . ." The object of anxiety encountered is here represented by an unpronounceable signifier. The narrator concludes, "For the Snark was a Boojum, you see" (Carroll 1867, 96). The reader sees precisely nothing, and is left with two signifiers that fail to represent any referent whatsoever. Uneasiness (*The Hunting of the Snark* is something of a nightmare) is transformed into jubilation.

"When I use a word . . . it means just what I choose it to mean—neither more nor less," Humpty Dumpty, the looking glass world's egg linguist, exclaims elsewhere (Carroll [1872] 1965, 169). If the rest of the chapter serves to undermine the claims of this character, Lacan underlines in "Function and the Field of Speak and Language" "that he is, after all, master of the signifier, even if he is not master of the signified from which his being derived its shape" (2006a, 242). Through his texts, Carroll's language mathematizes itself; the neologisms appear as so many letters that break with the author's own conceptions of language.

Profoundly attached to Aristotle, Lewis Carroll cannot stop trailing after him and assume the ontological cost implied by logic's break with natural languages. Also he adopts a conservative stance in relation to his contemporaries' contributions. In particular, he defends the idea that universals have an existential import against John Venn's interpretation that such propositions are hypothetical. Carroll could not break with the idea that words give access to the being of the thing; this is clear from his definition of the term definition in *Symbolic Logic*. In any case, for him it is a matter of seizing the thing itself:

> It is evident that every Member of a *Species* is also a *Member* of the *Genus* out of which that Species has been picked, and that it possesses the *Differentia* of that Species. Hence it may be represented by a Name consisting of two parts, one being a Name representing any Member of the *Genus*, and the other being the *Differentia* of that Species. Such a Name is called a "Definition" of any Member of that Species, and to give it such a Name is to "define" it. (1896, 6)

Moreover, the definition must obey the nature of the thing. The ontological significance of logic for Lewis Carroll can be clearly seen here: it is carried by the word that serves to present being.

> Contrary to this perspective, the neologisms of "Jabberwocky" as well as Humpty Dumpty's nominalist assertions put an intuition of the arbitrary nature of the sign into play, underlining the bar that separates the signifier from the signified. Signifiers reduced to their function, Carrollian neologisms confirm Lacan's analysis that outlines the combinatory mechanism of his texts in these terms: "Out of images, a pure play of combination is made," before insisting on "the power of word-play." ([1966] 2002, 10)

COMBINATIONS

However, we must remember the large part played by dialogues in Carroll's works, particularly in the *Alice* books. The nonsensical conversations, based on misunderstanding, are one of the factors that keep returning the text to a succession of language games that undermine Victorian conceptions, although they are supported and justified by the author. As Jean-Jacques Lecercle notes, "In its linguistic practice, Nonsense reflects the discourse upheld by language specialists," notably Horne Tooke, Trench, and Max Muller. "The implicit idea that guides this practice is that language is an instrument of communication, the imperfections of which must be corrected, while nevertheless celebrating its powers. These three *topoi* indicate the principle trend of the discourse on language throughout the English 18th century" (1995, 240).

Far from the abundant metaphorical productions engendered in criticism by Carroll's texts, the systematization of language games contributes, on the contrary, to making a "pure play of combination" out of these images. As an example, Lacan gives the term sylligism taken from *Sylvie and Bruno* (Carroll [1889] 1983, 388). We can again quote the conversation between Alice and the Mock Turtle about school:

> "I only took the regular course."
>
> "What was that?" inquired Alice.
>
> "Reeling and Writing, of course, and then the different branches of Arithmetic—Ambition, Distraction, Uglification and Derision." (Carroll [1865] 1965, 129)

"Word-play in Carroll is always without equivocation," as Lacan stresses ([1966] 2002, 10). It is a pure organization of signifiers without the creation of sense. Jean-Jacques Lecercle has shown how nonsense always derives its support from the literal in order to impede the production of metaphor (1994, 63–68). The proliferation of significations opened by the play on words (often willfully bad) finds itself reduced to a number of limited and strictly controlled possibilities. As Lecercle indicates, the Mock Turtle's puns are organized in a series, itself governed by paronomasia (playing on words that sound alike), permitting neither true confusion (there is no possible error in interpretation) nor the creation of meaning. With univocity as its ideal, nonsense thus holds the ambiguities of language under control. It prevents all unprecedented productions of sense, any vagueness of interpretation. This mode of functioning contributes to the mathematization of language, making language into "pure play of combination." Here again, nonsense is taking part in the scientific era, anticipating the Saussurian definition of language as a differential sign system.

FROM THE SEMANTIC TO SYNTAX

Moreover, nonsense shifts the emphasis from semantics to syntax. The structure of the first stanza of "Jabberwocky" is a striking example of this:

'Twas brillig, and the slithy toves
Did gyre and gimble in the wabe:
All mimsy were the borogroves,
And the mome raths outgrabe. (Carroll [1872] 1965, 270)

R. D. Sutherland has brought out the syntactical cogs of this sequence:

'Twas ____, and the ____y ____s
Did ____ and ____ in the ____:
All ____y were the ____s
And the ____ ____s ____. (Sutherland 1970, 208)

The plural marks and the y of adjectival endings allow the reader to assign a grammatical function to each of the terms used. Henri Parisot (1990) has preserved this principle in the French translation:

Il était reveneure: les slictueux toves
Sur l'allouinde gyraient et vriblaient;
Tout flivoreux vagueaient les borogroves;
Les verchons fourgus bourniflaient.

Observing a coherent syntactical structure contributes to the readability of the poem, which although deprived of signification nevertheless makes sense. When Alice gets to know this poem for the first time, she exclaims:

> "It seems very pretty," she said when she had finished it, "but it's rather hard to understand!" (You see she didn't like to confess even to herself, that she couldn't make it out at all.) "Somehow it seems to fill my head with ideas—only I don't exactly know what they are! However, somebody killed something: that's clear, at any rate." (Carroll [1872] 1965, 197)

Here the neologism appears like an empty form. At this moment, the *creation* of meaning does not take place. Moreover, by allowing semantics to be displaced by the centrality of syntax, Carroll anticipates the movement achieved by Frege, who made it possible for logic to become the underlying support of mathematics. The Cheshire Cat's syllogism is a striking example of these intuitions:

> "We're all mad here. I'm mad. You're mad."
> "How do you know I'm mad?" said Alice.
> "You must be," said the Cat, "or you wouldn't have come here."
> Alice didn't think that proved it at all: however, she went on: "And how do you know that you're mad?"

"To begin with," said the Cat, "a dog's not mad. You grant that?"

"I suppose so," said Alice.

"Well, then," the Cat went on, "you see, a dog growls when it's angry, and wags its tail when it's pleased. Now I growl when I'm pleased, and wag my tail when I'm angry. Therefore I'm mad."

"I call it purring, not growling," said Alice.

"Call it what you like," said the Cat. (Carroll [1865] 1965, 89)

While the Cat draws upon a syllogism to prove to Alice that he is mad, he is led to turn logic into a syntactical affair when he asserts that the fact that he growls or purrs doesn't affect the validity of his argument. Moreover, his main error is really of the order of syntax and not of semantics, as he ought not to be able to conclude anything other than "I am not a dog." Their conversation concludes with another misunderstanding, this time of a semantic order. Alice has just told him that the baby turned into a pig; the Cat disappears for a few minutes then returns and asks, "Did you say 'pig' or 'fig'?" (Carroll [1865] 1965, 90). Jean-Jacques Lecercle presents this example as an anticipation of the structuralist thesis concerning the differential value of phonemes: the test proposed by the Cat bears upon a minimal pair since the English words concerned are pig and fig (Lecercle 1994, 140). This example again reduces language to a pure play of combination, all the more since the response to the question (situated on the side of semantics) really seems to be unimportant. Thus, it seems that the knowledge that comes to lodge itself in nonsensical texts opposes the theses defended by Lewis Carroll that sought to preserve the privilege of the semantic dimension.

"Out of images a pure play of combination is made, but what effects of vertigo cannot be obtained from them? With combinations," Lacan continues, "all sorts of virtual dimensions can be fitted out, but these are those that deliver access to what, in the last analysis, is the most assured reality, that of the impossible become suddenly familiar ([1966] 2000, 10). Certain of the syllogisms proposed by Carroll in *Symbolic Logic* preserve the trace of this vertigo, in examples like this one: "Nothing intelligible ever puzzles me, logic puzzles me, logic is unintelligible" (1896, 102). The failure of this treatise testifies to the impasses that he encountered and that Carroll perhaps condensed in this neologism in the form of an admission: sylligism: syllogisms reduced to stupidity. Logic ends up stumbling against the subject and the real; Lewis Carroll's literary work testifies to this.

■ THE SUBJECT OF THE UNCONSCIOUS

The nonsensical word play fails to totally thwart metaphor; this is indicated by Alice when she dreams after having read "Jabberwocky": "Somehow it seems to fill my head with ideas." Even if she adds, "Only, I don't exactly know what they are!" (Carroll [1872] 1965, 197). Perhaps here a veiled knowledge is touched upon concerning the function of equivocation that nonsense aims particularly to avoid. Thus certain word play contributes instead to bringing to light what the commonest expressions owe to metaphor. Thus when, in the guise of an introduction, the Caterpillar asks Alice the banal question, "Who are *you?*," he asks her to specify her name and her social identity. She responds to him as follows: "I—I hardly know, Sir, just at present—at least I know who I *was* when I got up this morning, but I think I must have been changed several times since then" (67). She turns this common question into an existential interrogation related to what has been preoccupying her. The most ordinary statements come to be liable to diverse interpretations; the competences of the speaker are not put in question here but rather the subjective charge that this statement carries for Alice. She thus makes this question appear as a dead metaphor. From then on the conversation between the little girl and the Caterpillar becomes a form of verbal jousting (the principle upon which nonsensical dialogues are based, as Jean-Jacques Lecercle has shown) in which the desire of the Caterpillar, who attempts to remain in the register of common sense (metamorphoses awaits him, and it seems that this is what he wants to know nothing about), and the desire of Alice, who wants to find an answer to her question about being, confront each other. The misunderstanding is vertiginous and is what highlights the subject in that instance.

When the Caterpillar elsewhere asks Alice to explain her sense of no longer being herself, she responds, "I can't remember things as I used—and I don't keep the same size for ten minutes together!" (Carroll [1865] 1965, 69). Alice attributes this only secondarily to her changes in size. She rather insists on the fact that "it speaks." The Caterpillar asks her to explain: "Can't you remember what things?" "Well," replies Alice, "I tried to say *'How doth the little busy bee,'* but it all came different!" (69). In a way, Alice is experiencing subjective division: she is no longer the master of the statements she produces. Words that she has no intention of saying surge forth. Her experience recalls the experience that Lewis Carroll testified to in writing his stories. Nonsense lets an intuition of the subject of the unconscious emerge.

By turning things upside down in this way, Carroll's stories ruin all hope of making natural languages into the tool of logical rationality. Its ontological aims are reduced to nothing. The only response to the question of identity proves to be a tautology *"I'm I"* (Carroll [1865] 1965, 35). Furthermore, Alice produces this statement herself at the start of her adventures. She shows, on the one hand, the absence of identity with oneself (by virtue of the fact that a signifier cannot signify itself, the second *I* is different from the first), and, on the other hand, that the signifier, which designates the subject, is devoid of sense.

THE IMPOSSIBLE

Alice's experience and the nonsensical text certainly prove to be an apposite means of illustrating a statement Lacan makes in "The Object of Psychoanalysis" (the seminar that was running at the time of his intervention on France Culture), which aims precisely at defining the real as the impossible: "All that comes to us [from the subject] of the real, is inscribed first in the register of the impossible, of the impossible realised. The real in which the pattern of subjectivity is cut is the real we know so well because we find it on the other side, so to speak, of our language, each time that we want to grasp what there is of the real, the real is always the impossible" (1965–66, 19). Alice doesn't stop experiencing the impossible from the moment she is confronted with the limits of language.

"Each time we speak of something called the subject, we make a one of it," indicates Lacan a little further on.

> Thus what must be conceived is this, that the subject's name is as follows. He lacks one to name himself. What will come to function as this one? Certainly many, very different things, the object *a*, on the one hand, for example, and the proper name, on the other, fulfill the same function; it is clear that one cannot understand anything about what distinguishes them (for when they are seen to fulfill the same function they are thought to be the same thing) or about why they fulfill the same function. (1965–66, 31)

From the point of view of the reader this time, the character of Alice contributes to making these distinct dimensions that fulfill an equivalent function appear. Alice's proper name, but also the image, the illustration are the marks of the one, while Alice even teaches us about the function of the proper name as an approach to S_1.

In his "Homage to Lewis Carroll," Lacan underlines the phallic value of the little girl, another point where he situates the encounter with the impossible in Carroll's text:

> Only psychoanalysis can clarify the import of the absolute object that the little girl can become, it is because she incarnates a negative entity, which bears a name that I will not pronounce here, so as not to throw my listen-

> ers into the usual confusions. Lewis Carroll makes himself into the little girl's servant, she is the object that he designates, she is the ear he wants to reach; she is the one who he is aiming at among all of us. ([1966] 2000, 9)

It is not surprising that we find another reference to *Alice* in "The Object of Psychoanalysis" in relation to the commentary Lacan gives of Velasquez's painting *Las Meninas*. "Is this being, in this position of fixed life," he says about the child,

> in this death which makes her rise up for us across the centuries, almost alive, like a geological fly in amber, do we not, by having made her pass over to our side in order for her to say "let me see," evoke in her regard, the same image, the same fable of Alice's leap which would join our own by plunging, in accordance with an artifice which the literature of Lewis Carroll and others right up to Jean Cocteau, knew how to use and abuse: the passage through the mirror. (1965–66, 15)

Or again:

> Here, our little Alice, in her sphere, as a representative, is indeed in effect like Carroll's Alice, with at least one element which—I have already used this metaphor—presents itself like figures on a playing card. This king and this queen whose unbridled exclamations are limited to the decision: "Off with her head.'" (1965–66, 18)

The child, the slit,[4] is the sign that comes in the place of the lost object, of the painter's gaze; the character of Alice, constructed through her name and her image, figures the division of the subject and reveals "that the phallus itself is nothing but the site of lack it indicates in the subject" (Lacan, 2006b, 745). Alice in fact has no image in the mirror but would like to see what she cannot see that lies beyond:

> "First, there's the room you can see through the glass—that's just the same as our drawing-room, only the things go the other way. I can see all of it when I get upon a chair—all but the bit just behind the fireplace. Oh! I do so wish I could see that bit!" (Carroll [1872] 1965, 180–81)

Breaking through the frame of the mirror, she feels that she has become invisible: "I don't think they can hear me . . . and I'm nearly sure they can't see me. I feel somehow as if I was getting invisible . . ." (187). Alice is a name, hardly an image, over nothing. Tenniel's illustrations cover this fundamental lack with an image that topples into the register of a dull Victorian ideal.

Alice is a profoundly contradictory figure. She gives body to an ideal founded on the desire to abolish desire, while she is also an incarnation of the desiring subject. Her hybrid character and her contradictory desires contribute to indicating how the subject is correlated with the impossible (see Marret 1998). Alice's contradictions add themselves to those of the text, between joy and illness, between its defense of the author's conservative theses and its relentlessness assault upon their foundations, between a practice of writing that aims at scientificity and the unveiling of the real and of the subject of the unconscious toward which it proceeds.

The text is itself a paradigmatic evocation of the impossible of logic. One has to be a mathematician and a "dreamer, poet, lover if you like" (Lacan [1966] 2000, 11) for *Alice* to be born. Lacan notes, "It is really from the conjunction of these two positions that there arises this marvellous object, still indecipherable and still dazzling: his work." What of the work approaches the side of the real, "is a consequence of uneasiness," but also of this "singular joy," the sign that it is "an elected place to demonstrate the true nature of sublimation in the work of art." As Lacan says elsewhere, "The practice of the letter here converges with the use of the unconscious" (1965, 9). The text is constructed around a phallic image that veils and unveils "the indescribable object" (13), but its very writing constitutes a littoral: "And thus it came to pass that I found myself at last in possession of a huge unwieldy mass of *litterature*—if the reader will kindly excuse the spelling—which only needed stringing together, upon the thread of a consecutive story, to constitute the book I hoped to write" (Carroll 1889, 256) says Lewis Carroll, in his preface to *Sylvie and Bruno,* speaking of the composition of his works on the basis of statements arising from nobody knows where and from fragments of dreams. Through the word play that he shares with Joyce (see Lacan 2006c, 18; Lacan 1987, 26), he confirms how much his art proceeds toward the "recuperation of a certain object." C/C

BIOGRAPHY

Sophie Marret-Maleval is professor of psychoanalysis at the Department of Psychoanalysis, Paris VIII University. Her recent publications include *Lewis Carroll: de l'autre côté de la logique* (1995) and *L'inconscient aux sources du mythe moderne, les grands mythes de la littérature fantastique anglo-saxonne* (2010).

NOTES

Essay translated from the French by Philip Dravers. Title taken from Lewis Carroll's neological poem, "Jabberwocky" ([1872] 1965, 191).

1. He had to take Alice Liddell, Doyen's daughter, for whom he invented *Alice's Adventures* during a boating trip to see the lights at Oxford on the occasion of the Prince of Wales's marriage.

2. See Sophie Marret (1995), *Lewis Carroll: de l'autre côté de la logique.* Rennes: Presses Universitaires de Rennes.

3. The first edition was published in 1865, but Lewis Carroll withdrew the print run from sale, as he and Tenniel were not satisfied by the print quality of the illustrations. The work finally went on sale in 1866.

4. Here Lacan is playing on the phonetic proximity of the words *infante* and *fente.*

BIBLIOGRAPHY

Blake, Kathleen. 1974. *Play, Games and Sports: The Literary Works of Lewis Carroll.* Ithaca, N.Y., and London: Cornell University Press.

Carroll, Lewis. [1865] 1974. *Alice's Adventures in Wonderland.* In *The Annotated Alice,* ed. M. Gardner. Harmondsworth, U.K.: Penguin.

———. [1867] 1974. *The Hunting of the Snark, an Agony in Eight Fits.* In *The Annotated Snark,* ed. M. Gardner. Harmondsworth, U.K.: Penguin.

———. [1872] 1965. *Through the Looking Glass and What Alice Found There.* In *The Annotated Alice,* ed. M. Gardner. Harmondsworth, U.K.: Penguin.

———. [1872] 1990. *De l'autre côté du miroir,* in *Lewis Carroll, Œuvres,* édition publiée sous la direction de Jean Gattégno. Paris: Gallimard.

———. [1889] 1983. *Sylvie and Bruno.* In *The Penguin Complete Lewis Carroll.* London: Penguin.

———. [1896] 1958. *Symbolic Logic.* New York: Dover.

Cohen, M. N., ed. 1979. *The Letters of Lewis Carroll,* 2 vols. New York: Oxford University Press.

Coumet, Ernest. 1966. "Lewis Carroll logicien." In Lewis Carroll, *Logique sans peine.* Paris: Hermann.

Deleuze Gilles. 1969. *Logique du sens.* Paris: Minuit.

Dodgson, Charles Lutwidge. 1879. *Euclid and His Modern Rivals.* London: Macmillan.

———. [1895] 1958. *The Pillow Problems.* New York: Dover.

Empson, William. [1971] 1987. "Alice au pays des merveilles ou La pastorale de l'enfance." *Lewis Carroll: Cahers de l'Herne* 17.

Gattégno, Jean. 1970. *Lewis Carroll.* Paris: Corti.

———. [1971] 1987. "Preface." In *Lewis Carroll: Cahiers de l'Herne* 17.

Green, R. L., ed. 1953. *The Diaries of Lewis Carroll,* 2 vols. London: Cassell & Co.

Greenacre, Phyllis. [1971] 1987. "Charles Lutwidge Dodgson et Lewis Carroll: reconstitution et interprétation d'une evolution." *Lewis Carroll: Cahiers de l'Herne* 17.

Lacan, Jacques. 1965. "Hommage fait à Marguerite Duras, du ravissement de Lol V. Stein," *Ornicar?* 34. Also in 2001. *Autres Écrits.* Paris: Seuil.

———. [1966] 2002. *Homage to Lewis Carroll.*
———. 1965–66. *L'objet de la psychanalyse* (unpublished seminar).
———. 1975. RSI, *Ornicar?* 3.
———. 1987. "Joyce le symptôme I." In *Joyce avec Lacan,* ed. Jacques Aubert. Paris: Navarin.
———. 1990. *Television: A Challenge to the Psychoanalytic Establishment,* trans. Denis Hollier, Rosalind Kraus, and Annette Michelson. London: Norton.
———. 2002. "Hommage rendu à Lewis Carroll," *Ornicar?* 50: 9–12. Originally broadcast as part of the radio program: "Lewis Carroll: maître d'école buissonnière." France Culture. Paris, December 31, 1966.
———. 2006a. "The Function and the Field of Speech and Language in Psychoanalysis." In *Écrits,* trans. Bruce Fink, 237–68. London: Norton.
———. 2006b. "Science and Truth." In *Écrits,* trans. Bruce Fink, 726–45. London: Norton.
———. 2006c. "The Seminar on 'The Purloined Letter.'" In *Écrits,* trans. Bruce Fink, 6–48. London: Norton.
———. 2007. *The Other Side of Psychoanalysis,* trans. Russell Grigg. London and New York: Norton.
Laporte, Henri. 1973. *Structures logiques et représentations du désir.* Paris: Mame.
Lecercle, Jean-Jacques. 1994. *Philosophy of Nonsense*. London: Routledge.
———. 1995. *Le dictionnaire et le cri.* Paris: Presses Universitaires de Nancy.
Marret, Sophie. 1998. "Impossible Alice." In *Alice,* ed. Jean-Jacques Lecercle. Paris: Autrement.
Rackin, Donald. 1991. *Alice's Adventures in Wonderland and through the Looking Glass: Nonsense, Sense and Meaning.* New York: Twayne.
Schilder, Paul. 1938. "Psychoanalytical Remarks on Alice in Wonderland and Lewis Carroll." *Journal of Nervous and Mental Diseases* 87.
Sutherland, Ronald D. 1970. *Language and Lewis Carroll.* The Hague: Mouton.

JONATHAN D. REDMOND

Memento: Elementary Phenomena and the Delusion of Interpretation

> It is very difficult to understand what negation means. If you look at it a bit closely, you realize in particular that there is a wide variety of negations that it is quite impossible to cover with the same concept. The negation of existence, for example, is not at all the same as the negation of totality.
>
> —Lacan 1998, *The Seminar, Book XX, On Feminine Sexuality: The Limits of Love and Knowledge*

> Though this be madness, yet there is method in't.
>
> —Shakespeare, *Hamlet*

IN THIS ESSAY, I discuss how Lacanian accounts of psychosis can be developed through an analysis of the film *Memento* (2000) and, in particular, by a focus upon the character, Leonard. Lacan's classical statement on psychosis as that which is foreclosed in the symbolic returning in the real is developed in the context of elementary phenomena and the construction of a delusion. The notion that elementary phenomena are signifiers that appear in the real and that do not produce sense for the subject is discussed in the context of Leonard's relation with his bodily tattoos. Specifically, I argue that Leonard's perplexity, shown in the context of his encounter with enigmatic signifiers that he has inscribed upon his body, can be situated in relation to the mechanism of foreclosure rather than the neurological condition—anterograde amnesia—that Leonard provides as the mechanism underlying his memory loss. I highlight where perplexity and the enigmatic experience are shown throughout the film and develop how these themes can be theorized using a Lacanian account of elementary phenomena and the construction of a delusion. I begin with some general plot issues and then outline the notion of how mechanisms of projection and foreclosure, and the notion of elementary phenomena, can be conceptualized in the context of Leonard's delusion of interpretation.

MEMENTO AND NARRATIVE

The film *Memento* (2000), directed by Christopher Nolan, is a psychological thriller that revolves around the character Leonard Shelby, a former insurance claims assessor driven by murderous revenge after the rape and murder of his wife. The film quickly became a cult classic and was critically acclaimed, in part due to unique cinematography, narrative, and plot devices. *Memento* is unique inasmuch as it is shot in reverse chronological order; viewing begins at the end of the film's narrative; conversely, the final scenes of the film are the beginning of the narrative (Klein 2001). *Memento* is made more complex by the assembling of the scenes in a nonlinear temporal narrative sequence. Although most of *Memento* is shot in color, a series of black-and-white scenes interspersed throughout the film precede the color scenes in narrative position. Thus, the black-and-white scenes featuring Leonard alone in a hotel room speaking on a telephone with Teddy occur prior to the color scenes. Moreover, the black-and-white scenes are shown in chronological order, contrasting with the color scenes, which are shown in reverse chronological order. In short, *Memento* provides the viewer with a complex narrative form and plot line that demands multiple viewings in order to unpack and construct the story from this unique cinematic assemblage. Although the viewer has to do considerable work in order to construct the story by reassembling the temporal sequences of events as shown in *Memento*, another feature of the film that requires reflection concerns the central character, Leonard Shelby.

Memento is centered on the character Leonard Shelby, a former insurance agent who since the death of his wife has been driven by murderous revenge. That is, Leonard is driven by the motive to find and kill the man who allegedly raped and killed his wife. The problem that Leonard has to overcome, though, is his apparent neurological condition that emerged due to a traumatic brain injury—anterograde amnesia—sustained during his wife's assault. Leonard's "condition'" (a term that I return to in a discussion of how the signifier *condition* connects Leonard with the character Sammy Jankis and Leonard's delusional construction) entails that he is unable to make new long-term memories; although Leonard has memories of events preceding his wife's death, the traumatic brain injury that he allegedly suffered during the attack entails that *no new memories* have been made since these events. The only "memories" that Leonard has been able to create consist of an array of notes and bodily inscriptions that he makes in the course of his day—these inscriptions are attempts to organize his experience and, more important, create a "system" for collating evidence in Leonard's attempt to find and kill the man who he believes murdered his wife, referred to by Leonard as *John G.* Thus, the basic plotline of the film involves Leonard's attempts to find and kill John G. to avenge his wife's violent death. Information outlining clues to the real identity of John G. are provided to Leonard by various characters—Teddy and Natalie—who themselves are driven by vested interests in having Leonard find and kill John G. However, nearing the end of *Memento,* the viewer learns from Teddy that Leonard's condition may be more complex than a traumatic brain injury; other psychological mechanisms may lay behind Leonard's condition, and Leonard's account of his wife's death may be inaccurate.

At the end of the film, which is the first scene in the series of color shots in the film's temporal narrative sequence, the viewer learns about new information from Teddy that subverts Leonard's account of events. Teddy's disclosure calls into question both Leonard's motives and the spectator's position, which entails a revision of the plot and storyline. The crucial information that Teddy provides Leonard regarding his wife's death and condition contradicts many of the key elements of Leonard's self-report made throughout the film. On the one hand, Leonard's version of events concerning his condition and the circumstances surrounding his wife's death, a perspective congruent with the spectator's experience of the plot for most of the film, is as follows:

- Leonard reports that his wife was raped and murdered in the family home by two masked assailants who have some connection to drug use or drug dealing.
- During the rape and murder of Leonard's wife, Leonard manages to shoot dead one of the attackers; however, during the attack, he is struck on the head by a second attacker who subsequently escapes.
- Due to the head trauma received during the home invasion, Leonard incurs a brain injury that lies at the basis of his condition, referred to as "anterograde amnesia."
- Leonard's condition is *the same* condition that Sammy Jankis had. Sammy, a former client of Leonard's when he was an insurance worker, was assessed for neurological damage due to memory loss after a car accident. Leonard's report concluded that Sammy's condition was not neurological—the implication being that some unknown psychological mechanism was operative—because simple

conditioning experiments should have shown some behavior modification, when brain damage is evident, in response to a subject being exposed to aversive stimuli.

- Since the incident, Leonard has been unable to form new long-term memories. The last thing he remembers from his life as an insurance assessor is his wife dying in front of him; nothing since the time of the accident has been recorded in long-term memory.
- Leonard is able to keep focused only for approximately fifteen-minute intervals (shorter when he is stressed). When Leonard's memory is effaced, he suddenly finds himself in an alien situation, having no idea about what he is doing, whom he is with, and why he is there.
- Finally, Leonard's drive to avenge his wife's death is now solely focused upon the task of finding and killing John G. (the second attacker).

In contrast, Teddy's testimony to Leonard at the end of the film (though near the beginning of the narrative) discloses to Leonard that he is involved in a process of self-deception concerning both his wife's death and the nature of his condition. In hearing this disclosure to Leonard the viewer learns that, with Teddy's help, Leonard killed the real John G. more than a year ago, and that Leonard has *repeatedly found and killed individuals fitting the description of John G.* Moreover, Leonard's reference to "Sammy Jankis" is a massive self-deception that covers the traumatic truth of how Leonard's wife died, that is:

- She survived the initial assault but Leonard sustained a head injury and developed memory loss.
- It is she who does not believe in his condition—his inability to make new memories—and continually tests him. Consequently,
- It is he, Leonard, who accidently kills his wife by repeatedly injecting her with insulin; in her inability to cope with Leonard's condition, she tests his love for her by prompting him to continually inject her with insulin once his memory of the previous injection has been effaced with the resulting tragic outcome.

In *Memento* the viewer is positioned to identify with Leonard's point of view. It is not until the end of the film that the viewer learns of an alternative scenario, disclosed by Teddy, that Leonard is a serial killer who has negated the traumatic event of accidently killing his own wife. Consequently, Leonard's account of his wife's murder and the story of Sammy

Jankis are construed by Teddy as massive distortions of actual events. In this scene, Leonard's reaction is to deny Teddy's version of events; moreover, after learning that Teddy's real name is John Gammell (i.e., *another* John G.), Leonard then sets in motion a chain of events, through his use of tattoos and notes, that will lead to Teddy being targeted as another John G. for Leonard to find and kill. Leonard's murder of Teddy, shown at the beginning of the film, is thus a culmination of events that Leonard sets in motion at the end of the film, when Teddy discloses to Leonard that he repeatedly killed John G. However, despite an affirmation of part of Teddy's story (i.e., that Leonard is a serial killer), what remains unresolved for the viewer in *Memento* is Leonard's account of his wife's death and the mechanism underlying his "condition."

The first point to make in relation to the film's narrative—an issue that has been debated extensively in online blogs and by film critics—is that no determinate position has been reached as to the nature of Leonard's condition. Film critics and bloggers, who have yet to arrive at a clear understanding of Leonard's condition, have deliberated the uncertainty as to whether Leonard is brain damaged:

> Still, even after so many viewings, after reading the script and discussing the film for months, I haven't been able to come up with the "truth" about what transpired prior to the film's action. Every explanation seems to involve some breach of the apparent "rules" of Leonard's disability—not merely the rules as he explains them, but the rules as we witness them operating throughout most of the film. (Klein 2001)

For example, Leonard's inability to make new memories is contrasted with the last thing he remembers: his wife dying in front of him in their home. Although Leonard's case is a fairly accurate representation of anterograde amnesia, his capacity to remember the traumatic event that led to the neurological disorder is inconsistent with the neuroclinical phenomena encountered in brain injuries (Pendick 2002). Thus, a seemingly indeterminate plot line is one of the interesting features of *Memento;* the inability for the viewer to know whether Leonard has a neurological condition that developed from a traumatic brain injury, or, whether another mechanism is operative, has led commentators and theorists to speculate that Leonard is psychotic (Klein 2001) or suffering the effects of trauma (Little 2005, 67; Thomas 2003, 207).

Reference to the film script, written by Jonathan Nolan, provides the basis for a reading of the film relative to psychosis, as the protagonist Leonard is first introduced in a psychiatric hospital. Moreover, in the film itself, there are several brief shots, which appear as fragments of Leonard's introspection, showing both Sammy Jankis and Leonard in a psychiatric ward (Klein 2001). However, there is no explicit reference to psychosis in the film, and commentators who have made note of this connection in the original screenplay have not developed this point in detail. In the trauma literature on *Memento,* the contention that dissociative episodes underlie Leonard's condition has some merit—dissociation may explain Leonard's fragmentary experience and the memory gaps concerning his wife's death—however, this account has a limited explanatory capacity inasmuch as no attempt is made to contextualize the discussion of trauma in broader diagnostic terms concerning the psychoanalytic notions of neurosis or psychosis. In addition, Leonard's condition has not been conceptualized in the context of *repetition,* a central theme of *Memento;* thus, within literature engaging *Memento,* the broader contours of the function of repetition in psychosis has not been developed and is thus a significant gap in the literature on the film.

In my reading of *Memento,* I contend that Lacan's concept of foreclosure in psychosis provides a useful conceptual framework for elucidating Leonard's subjective position and the problems his condition raises for making sense of the plot. I suggest that the Lacanian concept of foreclosure articulated within psychosis provides a mechanism to account for a variety of phenomena that occur in *Memento,* which develops the notion, suggested by film critics (Klein 2001), that Leonard is mad. The inability of the spectator to determine a basic underlying premise regarding Leonard's condition, which has consequences for how the film is to be read in its totality, can be fruitfully developed by using the concept of foreclosure. Throughout the film, most obviously in the context of Leonard's relationship with bodily inscriptions, but also with "bits of the real" that are shown in the film, the return of the real in the form of elementary phenomena provides the basis for regarding Leonard's condition as psychosis. The key point that orients my discussion of Leonard's condition concerns the emergence of psychotic phenomena—the return of signifiers in the real—and the construction of a delusion of interpretation. Before examining foreclosure in *Memento,* we first examine some of Freud's theorization of paranoid psychosis; this will situate our subsequent discussion of the defensive function of projection in Leonard's delusion.

■ PROJECTION WITHIN PSYCHOSIS

Although Freud did not engage with psychosis in his clinical work on an extensive basis and was pessimistic as to the role that psychoanalysis could have in the treatment of psychosis, his comments regarding the psychical processes operative in psychotic disturbances are nevertheless enlightening. As early as 1892, in a letter to Wilhelm Fliess, Freud made the following astute remark concerning the mechanisms of defense in paranoia:

> In every instance the delusional idea is maintained with the same energy with which another, intolerably distressing, idea is fended off from the ego. Thus they love their delusions as they love themselves. That is the secret. . . . The delusional idea is either a copy of the idea fended off or its contrary. (Freud *SE*, 1:211–12)

The defense in paranoid psychosis that Freud isolates here is *projection*. The delusional idea that is projected into the outside world is either a direct copy of the psychotic subject's primary concern or its opposite. In addition, Freud notes the strong attachment to this defense; his comment "They love their delusion as they love themselves" emphasizes the unique narcissistic investment in the delusion. Moreover, Freud also argues that in paranoia "the content and affect of the incompatible idea are retained . . . but they are projected into the external world. Hallucinations, which arise in some forms of the illness, are hostile to the ego but support the defence" (212). The point is that the attachment to projection is so strong in psychosis because the delusion is a form of recovery (71); that is to say, the formation of a delusion in paranoia is a mode of recovery from more disorganized expressions of psychosis, such as schizophrenia. Thus, to give up the delusion risks a return to a more pervasive and disorganizing psychosis such as schizophrenia. However, Freud's point that hallucinations are hostile to the ego yet support the defensive function of projection in paranoia is worth considering because it highlights the complexity of how different psychotic phenomena in psychosis may stabilize or destabilize the ego. *Memento* returns to this issue of hallucinations in paranoia in the context of Leonard's auditory hallucination of the signifier *Sammy*.

Freud's thesis concerning paranoia—that an intolerable idea is fended off by the ego via the mechanism of projection; that is, that the idea is projected upon the Other—is a central feature of Leonard's psychosis. Leonard's delusion is constructed around two conflated scenarios: Leonard's story about Sammy Jankis—that Sammy Jankis accidently killed his wife through repeated injections of insulin due to his anterograde amnesia (the same condition as Leonard's)—is conflated with the home invasion when Leonard and his wife were attacked by John G., the junkie who raped, *but who did not kill*, his wife. Thus, the delusional idea that Leonard develops is the following: "John G. raped and murdered my wife and I have a neurological condition such that I cannot make new memories." The assumption that Leonard is psychotic entails that a triggering of psychosis is assumed to have occurred in connection with his wife's sexual assault. Psychotic phenomena that Leonard experiences subsequent to the triggering event concern the inability to make new memories, feelings of perplexity, subtle hallucinatory phenomena, and the construction of a delusion. Thus, Leonard's condition may be construed as the effects of a triggering of psychosis.

Thus, Leonard's central delusional idea concerning the murder of his wife and the story of Sammy Jankis is a defense against recognizing his own involvement in her death. According to the testimony of Teddy, it was Leonard's wife who was diabetic and *Leonard* was the one who killed her after repeatedly injecting her with insulin. The story of Sammy Jankis provides the locus for the delusional idea that is a *copy* of what actually happened to Leonard; thus, Leonard tells us that *Sammy's* wife was unable to cope with his memory loss, which was incurred after a car accident. She tested the limits of his condition by orchestrating Sammy to repeatedly inject her with insulin: if he "really loved her," then love would somehow "override" the automatic memory loss that Sammy experienced. However, as Sammy was unable to remember each successive injection, the continual shots of insulin resulted in his wife's overdose and death. It is this scenario that Teddy attributes to Leonard; however, instead of a car accident, the traumatic incident concerns the home invasion that resulted in Leonard's head injury and his wife's sexual assault. When Teddy confronts Leonard and discloses that he has already killed multiple people whom he believed to be John G. and that Leonard was responsible for his wife's death, Leonard chooses to negate this knowledge (he destroys any supporting notes and photos supporting Teddy's claims) and instead, preserves the status quo of his delusion. Consequently, I suggest that Leonard maintains a delusional construction in which the distressing idea (that of Leonard killing his wife) is fended off by combining features of his home invasion and the story of Sammy Jankis; however, in order to develop other features of Leonard's condition, such as his experience of perplexity and minor sensory disturbances, Lacan's concept of foreclosure and the return of signifiers in the real can further develop the motif of psychosis in *Memento*.

MEMENTO AND FORECLOSURE

The foreclosure of the Name-of-the-Father is the central mechanism in Lacan's approach to psychosis and is the mechanism that differentiates psychosis from neurosis (the latter being organized around repression). The mechanism of foreclosure, developed by Lacan from Freud's (1957 [1911]) reading of the Schreber case is a form of negation that is contrasted with repression; rather than signifiers being turned away from consciousness into the unconscious—as in repression—the negation of signifiers in foreclosure entails a more radical procedure. Instead of signifiers being denied entry into conscious, which presupposes an affirmation of the judgment of existence underlying the process of negation, foreclosure, in contrast, entails the negation of the signifier such that the signifier is never registered in the subject's symbolic register. Hence, foreclosure is a peculiar form of negation insomuch as the existence of a signifier is never registered in the symbolic order. Here Lacan states:

> Regarding castration, Freud tells us that this subject "did not want to know anything about it in the sense of repression.". . . And to designate this process he uses the term *Verwerfung*. . . . Its effect is a symbolic abolition. For, when Freud says . . . "he excises" castration . . . he continues: "thereby one cannot say that any judgment regarding its existence was properly made, but it was as if it had never existed." (Lacan 2006, 322–23)

In psychosis, it is the signifier, the Name-of-the-Father, a signifier that is pivotal in introducing castration in the subject's relation to jouissance, that is, foreclosed from symbolic yet returned in the real. In psychosis, the foreclosure of the signifier, the Name-of-the-Father, entails that the subject may encounter a hole in the symbolic and this encounter may result in the triggering of psychosis. Thus, what needs to be taken into consideration when examining foreclosure are the effects that this has upon the subject; unlike repression, where we speak of *the return of the repressed*—evident in slips of the tongue and other parapraxes—the repressed signifier remains in the symbolic order. In contrast to repression, the mechanism of foreclosure is characterized by return of the *signifier in the real and not the symbolic*. This is an important distinction that has thematic resonance in *Memento,* an issue that has not been considered in other commentary on the text (Little 2005, 207; Thomas 2003, 67).

Repetition is a recurrent theme throughout *Memento;* repetition is implicit in Leonard's condition, the use of needles to inscribe signifiers on the body, and finding and killing John G. Before exploring these themes in more detail, it is worth considering an important aspect of the film concerning Leonard's serial murders, an issue that refers to the significance of Leonard marking his body with tattoos. In the scene when Teddy discloses to Leonard that he has *already* killed John G., we also learn that Leonard was supposed to have inscribed his chest with a tattoo, "I've done it," after killing the first John G. However, for reasons unknown, Leonard decides *not to* inscribe these signifiers upon his body; the absence of these signifiers is significant and provides the context in which Teddy and Leonard debate whether Leonard will continue to find and kill other John G.s or whether Leonard will stop the killing by reaching a point of resolution and closure. Although the viewer does not know the reason why Leonard did not get the tattoo "I've done it" inscribed in his chest after the first killing, the implication is that this signifier would function as castration by placing a limit upon Leonard's jouissance and inscribing his act in the symbolic. I return to this point shortly. The second point to note concerns Teddy's position. Teddy concludes that Leonard will always continue to find and kill John G., while Leonard maintains that he "will remember," and killing the right John G. will result in the end of the killing. In *Memento* it is clear that Teddy is right—that Leonard has already killed John G. and that he will keep killing. Ironically, Teddy's confidence in maintaining this position is brought to bear on his own untimely death, as he becomes Leonard's next victim (this occurs after Leonard learns that Teddy's real name is John Edward Gammell . . . aka John G.). However, although it is clear that Teddy is correct concerning Leonard's repetitive murderous acts, he is right for the wrong reasons because his rationale for making this judgment is based upon *psychologism:*

> So you lie to yourself to be happy. We all do it. Who cares if there is a few little details you would rather not remember. . . . I guess you can only remember the things that you want to be true. . . . You're living a dream kid: a dead wife to pine for, a sense of purpose to your life, a romantic quest that you wouldn't end even if I wasn't in the picture. (Nolan 2000)

If we assume Leonard is psychotic, then Teddy's recourse to psychological factors as motivating behaviors is problematic, because psychological motivations do not constitute the mechanism of psychosis. Moreover, Teddy's position is akin to our discussion of Freud's analysis of paranoia; both accounts of psychosis remain in the domain of the ego and do not address the subject's position in the unconscious. This observation returns us to my first point concerning Leonard's failure to inscribe "I've done it" on his chest.

As indicated, the implication made in *Memento* is to say that Leonard no longer continues to kill once a "master signifier" has been tattooed on his body. The assumption here is that once Leonard inscribes "I've done it" upon his body his persecutory delusion and murderous acts will dissolve. The problem with this notion is that it does not take into consideration the fact the psychotic subject does not have access to the phallic function; consequently, although Leonard uses language, the symbolic register does not function in terms of castration and placing a limit upon jouissance. Without the Name-of-the-Father to function within the symbolic register, Leonard's relation with the signifier remains mediated by the real. The notion that Leonard could simply give up his delusion, which is what is at stake in avowing the death of John G., is naïve, because Leonard's persecutory delusion involving John G. is an essential component of his mode of stabilization. Here, the phenomena of repetition in the context of Leonard's serial murders shows the impossibility of accessing symbolic castration in psychosis; although Leonard attempts to reach "closure" on his wife's death through his own sense of retributive justice, he continually fails in this attempt because his actions are never realized in the symbolic but instead remain at the level of the real. The absence of the tattoo on Leonard's chest is merely a footnote indexing the impossibility of castration in psychosis. Leonard's quest for John G. is a Sisyphean task that will not stop being enacted; although repetition of the structure of his delusion can be assessed as an ego defense; because Leonard is projecting and defending against ideas incompatible with his ego, the mechanism of foreclosure entails that castration cannot be achieved through the symbolic.

ELEMENTARY PHENOMENON AND THE CONSTRUCTION OF A DELUSION IN *MEMENTO*

In Lacan's account of psychosis, his most important thesis concerning the emergence of psychotic phenomena concerns the foreclosure of the Name-of-the-Father. That is to say, when a signifier is foreclosed, there is something of its substance that remains intact: and in fact, returns to the subject in the order of the real. Lacan states, "It's the mechanism that makes what has got caught up in the *Verwerfung*—that is, what has been placed outside the general symbolization structuring the subject—return from without" (1993, 47). I suggest that the return of the signifiers in the real in *Memento* provides an important conceptual framework for situating Leonard's actions, his experience of perplexity, enigmas, and ultimately, the construction of a delusion. Moreover, the use of various cinematic techniques such as subliminal editing and flashbacks may be construed as showing the viewer "bits of the real" that emerge in Leonard's subjective universe. I now consider *Memento* in relation to the distinction between elementary phenomena and the formation of delusions that Lacan articulates in paranoid psychosis.

In Lacanian accounts of psychosis, the concept of elementary phenomena is important for several reasons; first, in forms of untriggered psychosis, elementary phenomena are minimal psychotic phenomena that may provide one of the few clues, from the point of view of signs and symptoms, that a psychotic disturbance is evident. Moreover, theorists suggest that elementary phenomena provide clues as to possible forms of stabilization in psychosis (Sauvagnat 2000, 95); this assertion is evident in paranoid psychosis as the notion that the delusion is a form of recovery that can be traced in relation to the emergence of elementary phenomenon and the construction of a paranoid delusion. To illustrate these concepts I first outline some of Lacan's general comments pertaining to elementary phenomenon and paranoid psychosis and then discuss how these tropisms are evident in *Memento*.

In Lacan's concept of elementary phenomena and the construction of a delusion the emergence of elementary phenomena may indicate a triggering of psychosis; that is to say, when the subject has a psychotic structure, various events will trigger psychotic phenomena of varying degrees of severity. At times of triggering, brief and transitory elementary phenomena may emerge and dissipate over time; conversely, the emergence of elementary phenomena may develop into a severe psychotic disturbance that can result in the construction of a delusion. However, the onset of psychotic phenomena is always the same; that is to say, the subject is drawn upon to use the Name-of-the-Father but instead encounters a hole in the symbolic.

When confronted with this hole in the symbolic, the psychotic subject is unable to defend against the real; in psychosis, this encounter with the real leads to perplexity and enigmatic experiences. Various forms of psychotic phenomena arise from the subject's encounter with the hole in the symbolic; "symptomatic" responses are essentially an attempt by the subject to defend against the real and regulate invasive jouissance. In the context of paranoid psychosis, the formation of a delusion is one response that may arise from the psychotic subject's encounter with the real. Here Lacan states:

> In the symbolic order, the empty spaces are as signifying as the full ones; in reading Freud today, it certainly seems that the first step of the whole of his dialectical movement is constituted by the gap of an emptiness. . . . This is what seems to explain the insistence with which the schizophrenic reiterates this step. In vain, however, since for him all the symbolic is real. He is very different in this respect from the paranoiac whose predominant imaginary structures . . . that is, the retroaction in a cyclical time that makes the anamnesis of his troubles so difficult, the anamnesis of his elementary phenomena which are merely presignifying and which only attain that ever partial universe we call a delusion after a discursive organization that is long and painful to establish and constitute. (2006, 327)

The issue that Lacan points out here is that the encounter with the gap in the symbolic is countered differently by the schizophrenic than the paranoiac; within paranoia, the construction of a delusion is a kind of discursive organization that stabilizes the subject and offers some possibility of defending against the real.

In the formation of a delusion, elementary phenomena provide what Lacan refers to as "elements of structure" that, even though they are "presignifying," may affect the composition, theme, and motivation underlying the formation of the delusion. The issue that Lacan points out here is that although elementary phenomena are "presignifying," in paranoia, the construction of a delusion is a signifying organization that stabilizes the subject. That is, according to Lacan, the relation between elementary phenomena and delusions is characterized, in one sense, by *continuity:*

> Elementary phenomena are no more elementary than what underlies the entire construction of a delusion. They are as elementary as a leaf in relation to the plant, in which a certain detail can be seen of the way in which the veins overlap and insert into one another—there is something common to the whole plant that is reproduced in certain of the forms that make it up. Similarly, analogous structures can be found at the level of the composition, motivation, and thematization of a delusion and at the level of the elementary phenomenon. . . . It's always the same structuring force, as it were, at work in a delusion, whether it's the whole or one of its parts that is under consideration. . . . This means that here the notion of element is to be taken in no other way that as structure, differentiated structure, irreducible to anything other than itself. (1993, 21)

Elementary phenomena may be considered as a kernel "identical to itself" that is operative in the overall composition, motivation, and theme of the delusion. A delusion recapitulates a structural element, namely, a signifier in the in real; in psychosis, the delusion is then a discursive elaboration of signifiers in the real. Miller suggests, "We ought to understand that the delusion is an elementary phenomenon given that delusion has the same structure as an elementary phenomenon" (2008, 7).

According to Miller, both the structure of elementary phenomena and their discursive elaboration can be contextualized in relation to language, specifically, the mechanisms of metaphor and metonymy. Elementary phenomena are characterized by a failure of signification and therefore of meaning—due to the absence of metaphor and metonymy—while the emergence of a delusion presupposes meaning, and hence, the unfolding of the signifying chain. A distinctive feature of psychosis, which is illuminated by the concept of elementary phenomena, is the subject's experience of enigma; elementary phenomena produce an enigmatic state as the subject is confronted by an *absence of meaning*. Miller suggests that the absence of meaning results when the normal substitutive unfolding of the signifying chain is disturbed. Thus, when signifiers do not unfold according to the substitutive mechanisms of language—as evident in the process of metaphor and metonymy (2008, 18)—then the subject is confronted with an absence of meaning, an event that is experienced as enigmatic. To say this another way, elementary phenomena are signifiers that appear in the real—not the symbolic—and although signifiers, they are not connected to the signifying chain but, rather, appear as bits and pieces of the real.

Returning now to *Memento,* we can see how Leonard's relation to the signifiers inscribed upon his body seem close to this notion of elementary phenomena—that is, signifiers in the real that are characterized by the *absence of meaning.* When Leonard loses his short-term memory he becomes perplexed, confused, and has to begin the reconstruction of meaning over again—that is, he has to figure out what he is doing in real time in order to orient himself to the situation at hand. He actively attempts to compensate for this "almost impossible" (Nolan 2000) condition by writing down facts and creating *mementos:* photos, notes, drawings, and tattoos orient him again once his short-term memory is effaced. Particularly important facts are inscribed directly upon his body. Thus, it is through the condition of writing, and in particular, of marking his body with signifiers, that Leonard is able to "archive" information that can be used in the future. This is the key point, because the perplexity of "memory loss" runs parallel with an encounter with signifiers in the real. That is, the overall result of these bodily inscriptions is to create an array of nonsensical signifiers that, in essence, signify nothing.

In *Memento,* it is Leonard's experience of reading these bodily inscriptions that elicit a state of perplexity—he knows that they signify something but because of his inability to make new memories the signifiers are not located in a signifying chain and, as such, do not produce sense. For Leonard, signifiers appear "outside" of the signifying chain; tattoos mark his body, yet they are essentially enigmatic—they do not signify meaning. The signifiers exist materially yet are not integrated in any signifying chain that would allow Leonard to make sense of how and why these signifiers are important for him. In addition, although the tattoos upon his body are a kind of enigmatic encounter, these bodily inscriptions are the first step in Leonard's process of constructing meaning. Leonard's perplexity in reading these material signifiers becomes the first step in a construction of meaning, which is highly suggestive of a paranoid delusion. *Memento* stages the psychotic subject's encounter with enigmatic signifiers; moreover, it is the materiality of the signifier—these letters—that are both a fixation to a mode of jouissance and the basis for constructing a delusion. Thus, I suggest that Leonard's relation with bodily inscriptions lends itself to a description of elementary phenomena in psychosis, both at the level of the enigma and in the subsequent construction of a paranoid delusion.

ELEMENTARY PHENOMENA, KNOWLEDGE IN THE REAL, AND THE CONSTRUCTION OF A DELUSION

If elementary phenomena are signifiers that stand in isolation cut off from the signifying chain, then a delusion, conversely, occurs when elementary phenomena are integrated in a signifying chain to produce meaning. That is to say, the binary signifier of knowledge, written S_1-S_2, is the matheme for the formation of a delusion (Miller 2008, 21). The distinction between elementary phenomena and a delusion is outlined in the context of the master signifier (S_1) and knowledge (S_1-S_2). Here Miller states:

> The One signifier, S_1, the lone signifier, is always elementary, that is to say it doesn't know what it signifies. Only when signifier Two appears, S_2, can the signification of S_1 emerge. We translate therefore what role the signifier has in interpretation. And I conclude by approximation that what we have called the elementary phenomenon puts us in the presence of an S_1, and for this reason the signification does not unfold. In contrast, the delusion is equivalent to the S_2. That is, the meaning happens as a result of the delusion. (2008, 21)

It is important to note that the relation between elementary phenomena and delusions is marked by both discontinuity and continuity; the discontinuity is evident in the signifier in isolation, while continuity is evident in the elaboration of this "signifier in the real" in the form of a delusional construction. That is to say, elementary phenomena are traceable in a specific delusional construction, a notion explicit to Lacan's assertion that delusions are a discursive organization containing themes, motivations, and compositional elements that are derivative of elementary phenomena (Lacan, 1993).

The thematic component of delusions emphasized in Lacan's account of paranoia highlights the importance of meaning within a delusional system. Miller, suggesting that delusions constitute a form of knowledge, has developed the discursive organization underlying Lacan's conception of delusions. Here he states:

> Consequently, upon placing the delusion in the place of the S_2—that is, of knowledge—it shows us that all knowledge is delusion and delusion is a type of knowledge. Listening repeatedly, what Lacan affirms is interest-

ing about the invention of knowledge, the psychotic would present as a delusional that does not retreat in the face of the elaboration of knowledge with the element of delusion that is always part of the invention. (2008, 22)

The invention of knowledge is central to the delusional construction, but this knowledge is derived from an elaboration of a signifier in the real, an elementary phenomenon.

In *Memento,* continuity between elementary phenomena and the delusional construction is evident through an examination of the signifiers "Remember Sammy Jankis"—these signifiers tattooed upon Leonard's hand are central to the conceptualization of Leonard's delusional construction. On the one hand, the "contents" regarding his wife's death are projected onto the other in a delusional construction. On the other hand, the centrality of the signifier "Sammy Jankis" in Leonard's psychosis is evident in an *auditory hallucination* that he experiences near the end of the film; in the final scene the return of signifiers in the real appear when Leonard "hears" the dead John G. say, "Sammy." This intrusion of the real, in the form of an auditory hallucination, occurs after Leonard has just killed John G.; as Leonard pulls the body down the stairs, the corpse appears to utter the word *Sammy.* This signifying fragment occurs in the context of Leonard's subjective awareness—both the spectator and Leonard are privy to these signifiers—moreover, upon hearing this signifier Leonard is beset with persecutory anxiety and confusion. Leonard's response—his anger and violence toward Teddy—appears to support Freud's claim that in paranoia, hallucinations—when they do appear—*are hostile to the ego yet support the defense* (Freud *SE,* 1:212). Although the auditory hallucination induces anxiety and aggression, destabilizing the ego, the overall delusional construction is not threatened, because Leonard is able to integrate this contingency in his delusional construction. In this case, persecutory anxiety and confusion are induced when Leonard finds out that "John G." knows about Sammy Jankis. When Leonard questions Teddy concerning this issue, Leonard is asking the Other how it knows that it was he who killed his wife. It is not by accident that Leonard decides to kill Teddy after he discloses that Leonard— and not John G.— was the one who killed his wife. In this sense, Leonard's new victim—Teddy—is chosen specifically in relation to the preservation of the defense, as this knowledge will be "taken to the grave."

Finally, other elementary phenomena in *Memento* that I discuss revolve around Leonard's use of needles and the syringe. In *Memento,* the needle is a recurring motif: it is shown in short subliminal fragments, such as Leonard injecting his wife with insulin; it is the central theme underlying the Sammy Jankis narrative that Leonard invents (that Sammy Jankis accidently killed his wife through repeated injections); and finally, the recurrence of the needle is evident in Leonard's tattooing. Thus, the needle motif is present in an array of phenomena—most obviously, in the delusion involving Sammy Jankis and the act of tattooing. I suggest that tattooing be considered as a form of psychotic acting out that recapitulates, through the use of needles, the object that Leonard used to originally kill his wife. Although the delusion is one form in which knowledge in the real can be articulated, it is also the case that other psychotic phenomena, such as hallucinations and acting out, are attempts to elaborate knowledge in the real. The thesis here is that the delusion, hallucination, and acting out are all equivalent, in the sense that all three are an interpretation that is the psychotic's elaboration of an element of knowledge in the real. Hence, different psychotic phenomena provide different forms of an elaboration of knowledge. Here Miller states:

> Yet, in what terms does Lacan speak of the phenomenon of *acting out?* He refers to it as interpretation. He shows that *acting out* is structured like a hallucination, and that in the case of the Wolf Man the lack of a signifier in the structure of the subject makes it such that what is foreclosed, returns in the real. . . . *Acting out* is equivalent to a hallucinatory phenomenon of the delusional type. (2008, 13–14)

In this sense, Leonard's self-knowledge concerning the reasons underlying his wife's death are not enunciated in the symbolic register but remain in the real. In this sense, the question of whether there is knowledge in the real raised by Lacan in his later seminars (1973–74) and developed by Miller (2006, 1998) are issues especially pertinent to psychosis and that appear staged throughout *Memento;* that is, if what is foreclosed returns in the real, then the real becomes the locus for a kind of knowledge that is inaccessible to the subject, in the sense of signifiers articulated in a signifying chain. This knowledge appears in the context of psychosis as real, yet it has effects in relation to the subject. The construction of a delusion is essentially the testimony of knowledge in the real; the elemental signifiers that are excluded from the signifying chain yet remain in the real. Leonard's repetitive tattooing may be considered as acting out in psychosis, an interpretation of knowledge in the real. If we assume that the original act of killing his wife is foreclosed, then Leonard's delusions and acting out are all elaborations of an element of knowledge in the real. The elaboration of knowledge, of the element that returns in the real, is based around distortions and inversions of a traumatic experience that Leonard has not registered in the symbolic. The tattoo upon Leonard's hand—"Remember Sammy Jankis," which features prominently in the film—is an elementary signifier marking the part of the body that was directly involved in his wife's death. Moreover, with every act of tattooing (he does many of them himself) and with every note that he writes to himself, Leonard is confronted with his own truth that remains inaccessible to symbolization, but that is elaborated in a delusional construction where what has been foreclosed returns in the real.

The focus upon the subject's encounter with the real in *Memento* entails an engaging narrative and complex cinematography. *Memento* provides an array of narrative tensions and inconsistencies that have been extensively examined by film critics and theorists. By examining Leonard's actions using the concept of projection and foreclosure, the viewer may begin to piece together how Lacanian tropes on paranoid psychosis can illuminate features of plot and narrative through approaching the problem of Leonard's condition from the vantage point of paranoid psychosis. C/C

BIOGRAPHY

Jonathan D. Redmond received his PhD in psychoanalytic studies from Deakin University in Melbourne, Australia, and is a member of the Lacan Circle of Melbourne. He teaches clinical theory at the Australian College of Applied Psychology.

NOTE

I thank Russell Grigg for editorial assistance and critical feedback in the drafting of this article.

BIBLIOGRAPHY

Freud, Sigmund. 1953–74. *The Standard Edition of the Complete Psychological Works of Sigmund Freud* [*SE*]. 24 vols. London: Hogarth Press.

Klein, Andy. 2001. "Everything You Wanted to Know about *Memento*." *Salon.com.* http://www.salon.com/entertainment/movies/feature/2001/06/28/memento_analysis/index.html.

Lacan, Jacques. 1973–74. *The Seminar. Book XXI, The Non-dupes Err/The Names of the Father,* trans. Cormac Gallagher. Unpublished.

———. 1993. *The Seminar. Book III. The Psychoses,* trans. Russell Grigg. London: Norton.

———. 1998. *The Seminar. Book XX. On Feminine Sexuality: The Limits of Love and Knowledge,* trans. Bruce Fink. New York: Norton.

———. 2006. "Response to Jean Hyppolite's Commentary on Freud's *Verneinung*." In J.-A. Miller, ed. *Ecrits: The First Complete Edition in English,* 318–33. New York: Norton.

Little, William. 2005. "Surviving *Memento*." *Narrative* 13, no. 1: 67–83.

Miller, Jacques-Alain. 1998. "The Seminar of Barcelona: On *Die Wege der Symptombildung*." *Psychoanalytic Notebooks* 1: 11–65.

———. 2006. "The Symptom: Knowledge, Meaning and the Real." *The Symptom* (Spring): 7.

———. 2008. "The Invention of Delusion." *International Lacanian Review* 5: 1–29.

Nolan, Christopher, dir. 2000. *Memento*. New Market.

Pendick, Daniel. 2002. "Memory Loss at the Movies." http://www.memorylossonline.com/spring2002/memlossatmovies.htm.

Sauvagnat, François. 2000. "On the Specificity of Psychotic Elementary Phenomena." *Psychoanalytic Notebooks* 1: 95–110.

Thomas, Peter. 2003. "Victimage and Violence: *Memento* and Trauma Theory." *Screen* 44, no. 2: 200–207.

THE ANALYTIC EXPERIENCE

HEATHER CHAMBERLAIN

Entering Analysis

I MADE A NUMBER OF ATTEMPTS to enter analysis starting in my twenties, with an attempt to get help from someone at the Tavistock about the misery around my first marriage, but she began interpreting almost before I had sat down. Her supposition of knowledge about me left me completely bereft and hopeless. That encounter almost put me off psychoanalysis forever. In fact I gave no thought to it at all until I came face to face with death some twenty years later. A surgeon had said to me, "Breast cancer. . . . You have only a 40 percent chance of surviving for five years!" Those words had come down like a guillotine and chopped off my future, and without a future I would have to say good-bye to all that gratification I had been deferring until later for so long. I was forced to recognize that "later" now meant "never" and that my life was a pretty unsatisfactory affair.

On hearing the news my aunt asked me what I wanted to do with the time remaining to me. Much to my astonishment the word *psychoanalysis* popped out of my mouth, so I suppose that a powerful, quite desperate desire to speak coupled with a belief that a mythical someone existed somewhere who would listen to me had survived, even though I didn't know anything more about psychoanalysis than that. I set about finding out. I met a lot of therapists and analysts, object-relations and Jungians as well as Lacanians, but none of them seemed an attractive proposition. I have forgotten the details but now suspect that they all offered me something and I didn't want anything.

Then I gate-crashed a dinner party given by a Centre for Freudian Analysis and Research (CFAR) analyst to celebrate his being made a member. At the time I thought it was my impression of his generosity that made him The One, but it was the fact that he was just out of training that appealed to me. Not realizing that he had worked in Australia for many years before coming to the United Kingdom, I imagined he needed to practice on someone. I would be that someone.

When he replied to my question about whether he could help me with my academic difficulties with "I don't know," I rejoiced. He was perfect! My ridiculous hysterical desire to displace castration onto the other became a really passionate force in the transference. Over the next year I gave him all the details of the cancer treatment I was undergoing, knowledge that I thought would be useful for him when he came across other sufferers. I don't think I mentioned my own suffering.

Even though my speech must have been quite empty, being listened to seriously for the first time ever was deeply touching. Feeling that I was suddenly no longer alone brought out how absolutely alone I had always been, alone because I had always felt completely and hopelessly uninteresting. Now at least I had something for this analyst—this knowledge that I could give him, and he seemed to be interested in me. Entering into analysis was a lifeline for me. In fact the analyst also took on a ferocious aspect in the transference from the beginning; the two aspects existed side by side.

I had not noticed the ferocious one, and nothing much seemed to be happening until one day on leaving the session after having sat face to face with the analyst for about six weeks. I suddenly realized that his moustache was not the narrow Hitler one I had distinctly seen from the moment I met him, but a big bushy one! I had hallucinated a Hitler moustache onto what I could clearly see at the same time was a kind and gentle face. For years I had made a habit of observing minute facial details in order to make portraits. This encounter shattered my belief in my powers of observation, quickly replacing it with a profound awe before the power of the unconscious, and a new desire to know. I was completely hooked. The Bishopsgate bomb, which reduced the analyst's building in the city of London to rubble minutes after we had left it, made little impression on me by comparison.

Two years after I left the first analyst, I was asked to present a paper at Lacan's centenary celebration in Armenia because of my family ties with that country. It was a very important moment for me, but the paper I presented came out as disconnected bits and pieces. I was utterly humiliated. It was a repetition of the symptom that I had taken to the first analyst. Clearly I was urgently in need of a second analysis.

The transference to my second analyst had been established long before I made my demand to her for analysis, but I had lacked the courage to ask her for analysis, asking for supervision instead. When the desire for analysis became unavoidable I made a last feeble attempt to escape this transference by making my demand to another eminent analyst, but the fact that my desire was elsewhere had been abundantly clear to both of us when he asked, "Why me?," and I had answered, "Because you're a man!"

So eventually I made my demand to the right analyst, but I went to her like a lamb to the slaughter, knowing that the experience of analysis with her would be profoundly disruptive and change everything. I struggled desperately to cling to my fantasy of having, dreaming that she had a large hole in her tooth. For me *Penisneid* took the form of giving up everything, absolutely everything, a position of ravage that had always reduced me to bits and pieces (my paper) and that had nearly cost me my life, as I was to discover later. So entering into analysis with this analyst was quite overwhelming and had immediate traumatic effects: I got lost, misplaced and forgot things, and felt generally disorientated, until we switched from French to English, which she didn't speak very well at the time and that allowed me to imagine for a while that I was teaching her English!

That was the last time I entered analysis, a true bid for life and an experience utterly, radically different from any other. C/C

BIOGRAPHY

Heather Chamberlain is a practicing psychoanalyst in London and Lewes and a member of the New Lacanian School and World Association of Psychoanalysis.

DAVID HAFNER

The Art of Skipping Sessions and the Gift of Anxiety

When I was a baby, I used to sleep twenty-three hours of the day, or so my parents say. I continued to hone the art of excessive sleeping at the University of Chicago. After obtaining my bachelor's degree I moved back to Hawaii for a year. The plan was to earn experience in the mental health field by working in a suicide shelter and to augment my grade point average with part-time psychology classes at the University of Hawaii. During this year break from higher education, I started psychoanalysis. There was—and, so far as I know, is—no Lacanian psychoanalytic presence in Hawaii. So I researched who were the most prominent English translators of Lacan's works and chose Bruce Fink. Since he lives in Pittsburgh and I was in Honolulu, sessions had to be on the telephone. Psychoanalysis moved along at the leisurely pace of two sessions a week, when I didn't miss the sessions.

The days when I worked in the afternoon, I would sometimes wake up at the appointment time, stumble down into the teaching studio and call him, still half-asleep. In this waking state, my dreams and nightmares were clearer, and always persecutory. I dreamt I was in some ghastly carpentry butcher's shop, with blood-soaked cadavers lying out on tables under tarps. The artisan was cutting up the phallus of Bruce Lee, which was enormous. Mr. Fink reminded me that his name is also Bruce. In another dream I would find myself in an underground staircase of some cavern, fleeing a two-headed bull demon. I later described the minotauresque beast as the demon of wisdom.

My dreams tend to hide themselves behind the curtain of repression very quickly, and this half-asleep state assured their lucidity. My comatose state, however, insulated me from the effects of interpretation. Also since these calls were being made in my parents' house, in my mother's violin studio, specifically, there was an extreme, paranoid reluctance to say everything on my mind.

When the appointment was during my wandering working hours, I would take my lunch break in the car, with the windows rolled up, on the phone with Mr. Fink. The analytic studio was comically mobile: either my mother's teaching studio or my parents' car, parked outside a house with eight "clients" not quite acute enough for a hospital sojourn. Yet, I continued in this manner until I moved to Paris to continue my learning. There, at the Fondation des États-Unis, after many dropped Skype calls, I stopped international psychoanalysis and asked my teacher Mr. Guéguen to refer me to an English-speaking psychoanalyst residing in Paris.

Here psychoanalysis began again. The three questions I can remember from my first séance are as follows: Do you like boys or girls?, Are you a man or a woman?, and Why are you here? My responses were, respectively: I like girls; I have a penis so logically I must be a man; and I am both bored and boring. He pointed rather to my excessive sleeping, which I had mentioned in passing, as a symptom and suggested five sessions a week.

With my new analyst, psychoanalysis began in English, seeing as my French was still inadequate. During the first year, the same symptoms persisted. I slept an inordinate amount of time, missed sessions regularly, and generally had nothing to say beyond lamenting my boredom as my sleep cycle slowly but obstinately drifted later around the day, leading me toward nocturnality. I brought to one of my earliest sessions the following dream: I am in a foreign country, sightseeing. I wander among the many monuments and wonder how long it will take to see them all. The interpretation was "It's a dream about analysis. You are wondering how long you will dedicate to it."

After half a year, I noticed that French flowed more smoothly from my mouth, so I began to speak exclusively in French during analysis. The response was an astounded "Soudain, tu parles français?" However, using French seemed to only cover up the play of the signifiers. My countless grammatical and syntactical errors concealed the parapraxes, and so I started anew with English. It was during this time that I noticed the polylingual wordplay present in my dreams. I dreamt that my lover had found the ideal apartment for us. "The brick building looks run down, but inside it is beautiful and spacious. Plus it is cheap. The address is on rue chautigo." The neologism stems from *contigo*. However the *mot d'esprit* from the dream has the phoneme *(sho)*, as in "to show," *il fait chaud*, or even the name Parc des Buttes Chaumont.

After a year and a half of face-to-face sessions I was fed up and asked my analyst when "will I be able to lie down on the divan?" He promptly ended the session with the response "Next time." My speech immediately flowed more smoothly and with less hesitation.

In the waiting room, I often found myself becoming exhausted and falling asleep as I used to see my father fall asleep in front of the television. Sometimes I would even miss my turn because of these naps. When I joined the seminar of my analyst, I received the written interpretation "David qui fait semblant d'être endormi" (David who is pretending to be asleep). Since then I do not sleep in the waiting room but bring my laptop and write my thesis instead.

As the sleepiness diminished, a new symptom came to light, that of provoking anxiety in the other. As with any good cynic, the traditions and expectations of civilized people fall to the wayside in favor of anxiety. Once, I was asked to translate transcripts for a student free of charge. I started to, but did not finish the work, instead leaving her without enough time to find another translator. Moreover, I referred her to my friends who had given me a grade equivalence rubric to translate her transcripts in the first place. I lied to them, saying that I needed it for my own applications only to later send them my student, obliging them to discover my lie. This drive to illuminate anxiety in the other has crystallized into a three-person play, which repeats ad infinitum, including me, my lover, and a second woman who is a stranger to us both. I deceive the woman into thinking that I am available and then mention my partner at an inopportune time. The play centers on informing the third party of her place as desired yet forbidden. This oft-repeated act aims to evoke anxiety in the other. Perhaps it is a response to my analyst's demand from two years ago to get me out of my feigned autistic coma. He told me to go out and meet a girl or girls and to talk to them. I chose all of them.

Psychoanalysis has begun for me numerous times. Each of these changes—of analyst, of language, of furniture—entails a beginning of a new phase of analysis. And yet, it is not a continuous progression without backsliding, for just last week I missed two sessions. After having waited in the waiting room for two hours, I left without seeing my analyst. I do this frequently. Then, on Monday, I returned to the consulting room with the following dream:

> I am in my analyst's waiting room; he enters and asks us who really needs a session today since he doesn't have much time. I say everything is going fairly well. Then it is nighttime and I am in his apartment, which seems more like a museum. He has a cello, a chess table, a poker table; all are interests that I share with him. He puts his hand on my shoulder and I feel as though I am his son.

The dream of shared possessions with my analyst is new and seemingly pertains to identification at the level of a doppelgänger, of semblance. To not have much time or to run out of time could be read as maliciousness directed toward the analyst, which would resonate with the imaginary identification through possessions. Once he is gone I would inherit.

The question in my case is not, When did analysis truly begin? The answer to that question is "Continuously since the rupture." The question is, How long can the desire be sustained, and can backsliding be avoided during the periods when sleeping beauty pricks himself again? C/C

BIOGRAPHY

David Hafner is completing a doctoral thesis on the theory of resistances and the impact of language choice on psychoanalytic treatment at the University of Paris VIII, Department of Psychoanalysis.

FRANCE JAIGU

Two Layers of Time: Experiencing the First Session

■ ALL THAT DAVID COPPERFIELD KIND OF CRAP

My first psychoanalytical session had long been rehearsed. For the months I spent wondering whether I would contact the analyst whose phone number I had been given, I did more than imagine what I was going to say. I was set on summarizing the first twenty-five years I had spent on this earth. Everything in the nutshell of a few heartfelt, to-the-point sentences. A short yet clearly chronological account highlighting the drama of my life.

I knew very little about psychoanalysis. I hadn't read the slightest book, been to any conferences. All I knew is that I wanted to go to this place where I could discover the truth about myself, uncover the mechanisms that had been operating without my being aware of them. My conception of life was one of causes and effects, hence the idea that a chronological account of the years leading up to this moment was the required opening to psychoanalytical treatment. Psychoanalysis would be about hunting down the first cause, the one on which all events followed. "Start from the beginning": Isn't that what our parents tell us when we come to them, as children, with an argument, a problem, that we don't know how to solve?

Therefore, given this structured conception of life, a first session with a psychoanalyst was clearly something that I had to make the most of. Considering the solemnity of the moment, it is hardly surprising. Years later, I read Pierre Rey's *Une Saison chez Lacan:* Rey, a French novelist, describes how he dressed up for his first session, made polite conversation with Jacques Lacan, name dropping and smoking away. But my rehearsal was prompted less by the desire to make an impression. I was obsessing on the beginning of psychoanalysis.

Thankfully, however, nothing went as planned. I don't remember the impression the analyst made upon me. I don't remember thinking anything of her study. I don't remember walking there. I'm not even certain I remember what I said. But I distinctly remember feeling that my carefully rehearsed words had escaped me for good. Not that I had nothing to say. Quite the opposite, in fact. It all came to me like a long slip of the tongue: I had masses to say, but none of it had seemed important before that precise moment when I was sitting in front of this absolute stranger. And I had never imagined I would start the way I did: referring to the present rather than the beginnings of my life. . . .

Reflecting on this experience nearly twenty years later, the opening paragraph of J. D. Salinger's famous novel, *The Catcher in the Rye,* came back to me. As you may well remember, the book tells the story of a teenager from an affluent family who decides to leave school before being expelled. Rather than going straight back home, he embarks on a kind of soul-searching journey that takes him from a cheesy room in a New York hotel to the Natural History Museum, Central Park, and lands him in hospital probably recovering from depression. Holden Caulfield reflects on the dramatic events that shaped his life, especially the death of his younger brother. He speaks of his parents, his older brother, his sister whom he loves. But the narrative doesn't follow a coherent pattern. It is full of gaps, holes, and mysteries that all point to an event, an opening (Holden tells us he became sick) we are aware of but know nothing about. Despite the obvious reference to psychological pain, the protagonist, Holden Caulfield, is one determined storyteller. The fact is quite apparent from the very start with the opening lines of the book:

> If you really want to hear about it, the first thing you'll probably want to know is where I was born, and what my lousy childhood was like, and how my parents were occupied and all before they had me, and all that David Copperfield kind of crap, but I don't feel like going into it, if you want to know the truth. In the first place, that stuff bores me, and in the second place, my parents would have about two haemorrhages apiece if I told anything pretty personal about them. They're quite touchy about anything like that, especially my father. They're nice and all—I'm not saying that—but they're also touchy as hell. Besides, I'm not going to tell you my whole goddam autobiography or anything. I'll just tell you about this madman stuff that happened to me around last Christmas just before I got pretty rundown and had to come out here and take it easy. (Salinger 1951, 1)

Sitting in the small study facing the person who was going to become my analyst, it became obvious, the moment I opened my mouth, that my "goddam autobiography" was a load of "David Copperfield kind of crap," to quote Holden Caulfield.

What had just happened? I had kicked the *biography* out of *autobiography*. I had shed the linearity of academia, of culture, the tongue in which I had been schooled. But like Holden Caulfield, who refers to a major novel of English literature, I had needed the references of cultural or historical discourse to react against. Unfortunately, old habits die hard, and it would come back to me, often. But each time, the seductive reassurance of culture would prove a pure waste of time: linearity or chronology, paradoxically, would land me in the dark. In what the French have a pretty expression for, the *temps mort*.

BUTTONHOLING ONESELF

But on that day, a voice that was my own had escaped me within the walls of the psychoanalyst's study. I had shed the biography but kept the *auto* of *autobiography*. The language that I was hearing was taking form before me. It was not a language of the past, reflecting on what had been. Something "true" was emerging.

This leads me to another cultural "digression" that I hope will not be a *temps mort*. Actually, it's not really a digression, more a play on words resting on the French word for session, *séance*. A *première séance* in French is a film matinee. This is a pun Gérard Miller referred to in his documentary that was broadcast on French television on November 11, 2009. But I am thinking of a film that was shot in 1951 by a German photographer called Hans Namuth. Namuth had taken very beautiful photographs of Jackson Pollock painting and also made a black-and-white silent movie of Pollock the year before. The 1951 film shows us Jackson Pollock painting one of his famous "drippings" on a pane of glass. And this second movie isn't any good compared to the silent one. Why not? This probably has to do with the fact that all the while Pollock is painting, we hear him reciting a small autobiographical text in a deliberate yet hesitant tone: "My name is Jackson Pollock, I was born in Cody, Wyoming, thirty-nine years ago. . . . I like to paint on the ground etc. . . ." After the last day of shooting the movie, Pollock starting drinking again (he had been sober for over a year) and picked a fight with Namuth, to whom he repeated over and over again, "I'm not the phony, you're the phony."

Interestingly, *phony* is the adjective that the young Holden Caulfield uses time and time again in *The Catcher in the Rye* to describe the adult world that he rejects. And to wrap up these two references with my experience of the first psychoanalytical session, I would say that all goddam autobiographies are fictions and that Jackson Pollock, Holden Caulfield, and myself are phonies when we indulge in all that David Copperfield kind of crap.

One of my professors in English literature had an expression that she was fond of and used often when analyzing the opening chapter of a novel. She evoked the necessity for the writer to "buttonhole" his reader, catch him by the collar and make him want to read on. J. D. Salinger is very effective at "buttonholing" us with the opening lines of *The Catcher in the Rye:* we are hooked on Holden Caulfield's voice, his personality and authenticity. My experience of the first session was that I buttonholed myself. I got caught up in my own words and wanted to go on talking and reading.

Yet strangely, although I was aware of this, I still worried about buttonholing the analyst: if I failed to do so, she might not agree to see me again and refer me to someone else. I knew that the first few sessions were mere preliminary interviews and that I could end up with an altogether different analyst. The impulse to rehearse and give a near-perfect chronological performance had also come from the fear of being rejected by my analyst and failing the test of psychoanalysis. After a few times, I asked if she was willing to treat me. . . . Oh yes, she replied, almost flippantly. I got the impression I had missed the point and that psychoanalysis had started a while ago. But when had the last preliminary interview been? Which session had truly been the first? It was impossible for me to say. I had embarked on a journey that defeated all the traditional notions of construction, culture that I had been taught in school. . . . A journey made of gaps and holes, nooks and crannies.

It was therefore fitting that I should have missed the end of the preliminary interviews.

BEGINNING AT LONG LAST . . .

But could it be that psychoanalysis had not started yet? Wasn't that the simple reason why I was so puzzled? If I was still burdened by issues of chronological exactitude, the preliminary interviews, wasn't it because I was still standing outside, in the waiting-room in front of a half-opened door?

A while later, when I had been dutifully turning up for two sessions a week, I felt dissatisfied with the leisurely pace that had settled in. As I stepped out from the elevator on the landing in front of my analyst's practice one day, I almost caught my hand in the old-fashioned door. Lying down on the couch, moments later, I complained, "This is going nowhere. Also, I almost chopped off my fingers in the sliding door of your elevator!" This outburst failed to provoke the sympathetic response I had hoped for. So I picked up where I had left things the previous session. It all evolved around my disgust with food when I was a child. "The only person who understood I simply couldn't swallow my food was Mrs. Crawley (the lady who looked after me when I was a child)," I said. "She used to put out her hand in front of my mouth and tell me to 'spit it out' and throw it away." And then it clicked: the hand that Mrs. Crawley held outstretched before me had three missing fingers (she had had an accident at work when she was young). The poetry of free association had linked the elevator and Mrs. Crawley's hands.

At that moment, psychoanalysis started for me. The first session, the real one, isn't necessarily the first one in time. That much I could have guessed. But I needed that perfect moment disconnected from chronological time. The perfect moment took place that day when words from the past were given a new life in the present. When it became meaningful once again to "spit it out." C/C

BIOGRAPHY

France Jaigu is a practicing psychoanalyst in Paris and a member of L'Envers de Paris. She was associate professor in American civilization at Paris III-Sorbonne Nouvelle until 2009. She has published on Anaïs Nin, Edgar Allan Poe, Julian Schnabel, Jackson Pollock, Chuck Close, Hans Namuth, and Bill Viola.

BIBLIOGRAPHY

Miller, Gérard. 2009. *La Première séance.* France 3 Télévision, November.

Namuth, Hans, and Paul Falkenberg. 1951. *Jackson Pollock.* New York: Museum at Large.

Rey, Pierre. 1999. *Une Saison chez Lacan.* Paris: Seuil.

Salinger, J. D. 1951. *The Catcher in the Rye.* London: Penguin Books.

CULTURAL FICTIONS

Let whoever cannot meet at its horizon the subjectivity of his time give it up then. For how could he who knows nothing of the dialectic that engages him in a symbolic movement with so many lives possibly make his being the axis of those lives? Let [the analyst] be well acquainted with the whorl into which his era draws him in the ongoing enterprise of Babel, and let him be aware of his function as an interpreter in the strife of languages.

JACQUES LACAN

GÉRARD WAJCMAN

Three Notes to Introduce the Form of the Series

■ PSYCHOANALYSIS IS CONCERNED WITH THE UNIVERSE OF FORMS

FROM THE OUTSET, psychoanalysis appeared intimately linked to certain forms: in particular, the different forms of narrative. For Freud, two forms hold a place in the very architecture of psychoanalysis: the myth and the romance. Psychoanalysis colonized myths, for all, and Freud almost became the author of the myth of Oedipus, or its coauthor, perhaps, with Sophocles—and, of course, with Greek imagination. As for the romance, the neurotic, each neurotic, even when he suffers from inhibition, is by his or her very nature an author, at once the author and the hero of a "family romance" of which, it might be added, he or she is the only reader. It can be noted that it is in a book by Otto Rank on *The Myth of the Birth of the Hero* (2004), that Freud published in 1909 his text "Family Romances" (Freud *SE*, 9:235). At the same time, this little private romance in which the subject tells himself tales of kings and queens, with gala daddies and mummies, constitutes for subjects a general condition necessary for life in society.

This gives psychoanalysts good reason to examine the nature of the romance and its social function beyond any literary consideration or aesthetic value. As such, someone like Marthe Robert (1972) sees in the neurotic's romance, in what is a romance on the origins (of a subject's life), the very origin of the romance. Thus from the neurotic's romance we move on to the idea of a neurotic romance. A historical literary form surged forth from the subject's intimate structure. This is in conformity with Freud.

As for Jacques-Alain Miller and François Regnault, taking their bearings from Georges Dumézil, they refer these two forms, myth and romance, to their structural lines, revealing the way one replies to the other.

As such, "the mythical narrative can be distinguished by the functioning of a cause within it that is without reason" (Miller and Regnault 1967, 3). (Dumézil [1967] speaks of *furore* as a principle of "irrational determinism"); the romance is the opposite, meaning that it "rationalizes" the cause, by providing it with motivation. "Whence a definition of the romance as an introduction in the scenario of the myth of "psychological and judicial calculations of interest." The romance is born from an injection of the subject into the myth. In this way, various equations can be obtained: the romance is "the myth plus the subject," which as a result leads to the myth as "the romance minus the subject," a desubjectivized romance. In a way, this is the thread Lacan follows.

We know that in 1953, Lacan gave the counterpart of an "individual myth" ("The Neurotic's Individual Myth") to Freud's "family romance" (Lacan [1953] 1979). It is a new episode in the history of the two forms of the narrative that concern psychoanalysis. From a certain stance, the mechanism of the myth seems to be the reverse of that of the romance: whereas the romance would be what gives a social form to a private narrative, the myth would be a "social manifestation" of which "we can trace its function in the actual experience of a neurotic." However, Lacan specifies, "We proceed from the definition of myth as a certain objectified representation of an epos or as a chronicle expressing in an imaginary way the fundamental relationships characteristic of a certain mode of being human at a specific period" ([1953] 1979, 408). Finally, this is to say that, like the romance, the myth is held as being a *manifestation,* a certain expression of the human being. In this way, it seems we stick to the "Freudian but far from being a specifically Freudian" idea that it is not simply that any human creation draws upon the greatest depths of the human soul, but that, to a greater or lesser degree, each work *expresses* this greatest depth of the human soul.

The opposition of the myth and the romance is situated elsewhere. The romance is an *expression* of the fantasy, while the myth is a *manifestation* of the "fundamental relationships characteristic of a certain mode of being human" ([1953] 1979, 408). Lacan sharpened his idea of the myth by giving, in 1973, a clear definition of his own: "the attempt to give an epic form to what is operative through the structure" ([1973] 1990, 30). At last, we have a sort of complementary distribution: the romance, which is the romance of the subject; the myth, which is the structure of the Other. Romance-fantasy versus myth-structure? It is not so simple. It is clear that, according to Lacan, Joyce gently dynamites the form of the romance as the Freudian family romance. Faced with the romance-fantasy, he invents the romance-symptom. As for the myth, Lacan had already reduced it to structure, by a head-shrinking operation that condenses it in a tiny piece of writing, the matheme. In short, Lacan invented a new form, but a form without form. The matheme is like a freeze-dried myth, squeezed out of any "epic form," the narrative reduced to its core. In any case, there is with Lacan a commendation of the haiku. In a way, the matheme is the stock cube of psychoanalysis. As a result of this movement, the myth appears with Freud as an attempt at a matheme, as standing in for a quasi-matheme, a rather chubby matheme.

The forms of the narrative are not, of course, limited to the Freudian forms. Narratives are countless, present at all times, in all places, in all societies, emphasizes Roland Barthes. "Narrative starts with the very history of mankind; there is not, there has never been anywhere, any people without narrative." And Barthes sets up a typology of the narrative in its prodigious variety: "Among the vehicles of narrative are articulated language, whether oral or written, pictures, still or moving, gestures, and an ordered mixture of all those substances; narrative is present in myth, legend, fables, tales, short stories, epics, history, tragedy, drame [suspense drama], comedy, pantomime, paintings (in Santa Ursula by Carpaccio, for instance), stained-glass windows, movies, local news, conversation" (Barthes, 237).

Here I make two comments.

On the one hand, if we find in Lacan references to each of these forms; among those listed by Barthes, it seems that, beyond the Freudian forms, Lacan unfolded another that was new to psychoanalysis: the painting. With seminar 11, where it received a specific definition—"the function in which the subject has to map himself as such" ([1964] 1977, 100)—it could be said that the painting is raised to the dignity of the analytic form. The painting adds a Lacanian form to the Freudian forms of the myth and the romance.

On the other hand, a question arises concerning the universality of the permanence of the narrative supposed by Barthes. [The narrative is there], "international, transhistorical, transcultural" he says, "like life itself" (1957, 237). The expression is striking, knotting narrative and life, the uninterrupted narrative with the permanence of life. But what of the possibility of the narrative being suddenly interrupted? Walter Benjamin (2006) evoked this. He spoke about what would happen in the twentieth century. Born in the trenches of the First World War, this century, differing from all the others, would be born in silence. The response to the war, to which narratives have always been attached, epics and legends, was the mutism of men, back from the war, incapable of telling anything about what they had seen. Benjamin turned this impossibility of telling into a symptom of modern times. Here, the subject's silence carries the silence of the world, a silence filled with the noise and furore of the first inhuman war. The loss of the narrative became a suspension of life itself. A question arises: What form has transmitted this silence of death? We know that the path of the twentieth century was to be crossed once again by another silence.

Now, in Barthes's universal narrative, we come across another form of narrative than the Freudian one. In short, the narrative is not envisaged as the narrative of the subject, but as a "narrative of the world." Aloïs Riegl, the Austrian historian of art, who died in 1905, suggested that we see the expression of a *Kunstwollen* in forms, an *artistic will* that, beyond the personality of the artist, manifested the spirit of the times, of a people at a given moment in its history. It would be necessary, in any case, to conceive of there being narratives expressing not the human soul, but the soul of the world, of the spirit of the times, or civilization's discontents.

The series would be the form that expresses the spirit of the times.

Not only does the form *series* designate the television series, but it centers around the "American series." The American series founds a new grammar that singularizes it and breaks it away from other forms of narrative, such as cinema, the novel, or the painting, setting it up as a new genre. As a form, the American series can of course be produced elsewhere than in the United States, but what is called, for example, the French series, is not a variation on the American series, insofar as it can be reduced to other forms already in existence, like the French novel or the telefilm that is divided into episodes.

The American series is the "narrative of the world" of our times. We could even find reasons to say that our world is structured like an American series.

The series is characterized by a certain number of particular traits that are knotted together, or not. I do not deal with all of them here, although they are interesting, like the subject of production. I just say that the series marks the power of the producer and the scriptwriters, who are always working in a pool. The producer is usually himself or herself the creator of the series and the head of the pool of scriptwriters. This is to say that the series corresponds with placing the director in a secondary position, which differs from cinema.

What matters in the form of the series concerns the structure of the narrative and is held in a few recurrent elements that can be lined up in disorder and that, for the most part, are knotted together.

The triumph of the object: from the piece of wool to the cadaver, *CSI:*

Crime Scene Investigation raises the object-death to the rank of the recurrent hero. Or, take *Weeds* by Jenji Kohan in 2005, with the charming Mary-Louise Parker, where the whole story turns around the domestic production of cannabis. The framework and development of the story are not determined by the characters but by the objects.

Triumph of the fragment: The series form supposes by its nature a fragmentation of the narrative. It remains that the fragment is the very principle of the narrative that is marked by the constant presence of a multiplicity of characters, which goes as far as making it impossible to designate a main character, by exploded views, or still by the overlapping of stories, becoming labyrinth-like at times. The series is marked by an absence of hero, of a unique viewpoint or story: there is neither thread nor fixed point. It describes and sketches a universe in which the subjects and stories are at once multiple and dispersed. Nothing nor no one is connected. In this sense, it has to be said that it is not the series that implies the fragmentation, but that the fragmentation, which is the regime of today's subjects and world (as can be seen in the network of the Web), finds its form, its adequate expression, in the series.

Triumph of the city: We know that America is a fragmented nation, in states, cities, but primarily in its people, who are less united in a melting pot than fragmented in a salad bowl of communities. Of course, all the great American series speak about America. But more than just believing that the diversity of cities in these series restores an image of this America of peoples, of citizens and states that are difficult to unite, it would be necessary here again to conceive of it as an image of the fragmentation that characterizes the times. The multiplicity of cities, scattered like stars in the sky, more than militarily lined up on the Star-Spangled Banner. But there again, the importance of the city, which sometimes becomes the subject of a series, like *The Wire*, responds to the fact that what fundamentally animates the series, is the staging of jouissance, of jouissances (whence the central place taken up by drugs). In the series, the city is the locus of jouissance.

The defeat of psychology: Even if there is a sketch of the psychology of each character, indicating their division, it is not their psychological calculations, no more than those of their interests, that engender and generate the narrative's dynamic or the multiple narratives. We are far from the novel.

We could attach still more elements and see how they are all knotted together so as to make of the series a "narrative of the world," the very form of these hypermodern times.

Finally, opposing the series as narrative of the world to works that I would qualify as "Freudian," which would be the narrative of subjects, could be said differently: by opposing, to works of the sublime, the series as a work of the discontents of civilization, as the series-symptom. c/c

BIOGRAPHY

Gérard Wajcman is a writer, psychoanalyst, curator, and art critic. He teaches at the Department of Psychoanalysis of Paris VIII University and is a member of the École de la Cause Freudienne and the World Association of Psychoanalysis. He directs the Research Centre on the History and Theory of the Gaze. Recent publications include *Fenêtre, chroniques du regard et de l'intime* (2004) and *Les animaux nous traitent mal, photographies de Tania Mouraud* (2008).

NOTE

Translated from the French by Victoria Woollard.

BIBLIOGRAPHY

Barthes, Roland, translated by Lionel Duisit. 1975. "An Introduction to the Structural Analysis of Narrative." *New Literary History 6 (2), On Narrative and Narratives*: 237–72.

Benjamin, Walter. 2006. "The Storyteller: Observations on the Works of Nikolai Leskov." In *Walter Benjamin: Selected Writings, Vol. 3: 1935–1938*, eds. Howard Eiland and Michael W. Jennings, 143–66. Cambridge, Mass.: Harvard University Press/Belknap Press.

Dumézil, Georges. 1967. "Horace, une lecture de Tite-Live, suivi de Les Transformations du troisième du triple." *Cahiers pour l'analyse 7, Du mythe au roman*: 9.

Freud, Sigmund. 1953–74. *The Standard Edition of the Complete Psychological Works of Sigmund Freud* [*SE*]. 24 vols. London: Hogarth Press.

Lacan, Jacques. [1953] 1979. "The Neurotic's Individual Myth," trans. Martha Noel Evans. *Psychoanalytic Quarterly* 48(3): 405–25.

———. [1964] 1977. *The Seminar XI: The Four Fundamental Concepts of Psychoanalysis*, ed. Jacques-Alain Miller, trans. Alan Sheridan. New York: Norton.

———. [1973] 1990. *Television: A Challenge to the Psychoanalytic Establishment*, ed. Joan Copjec, trans. Jeffrey Mehlman. New York: Norton, 1990.

Miller, Jacques-Alain, and François Regnault. 1967. "Avertissement: L'orientation du roman." *Cahiers pour l'analyse 7. Du mythe au roman:* 3.

Rank, Otto. 2004. *The Myth of the Birth of the Hero*. Baltimore: Johns Hopkins University Press.

Robert, Marthe. 1972. *Roman des origines et origines du roman*. Paris: Grasset.

LAURENT GOUMARRE

Quit Laughing!
A Sofa Gets Tossed Out!

AFTER A FEW YEARS SPENT ON A COUCH, you can't look at a sofa the way you used to: you don't lie down on one the same way, even if a sofa and a couch are two different things—I know, I'm taking a short cut although I can't quite grasp what it implies yet.

What I do know is that the sofa I have in mind is the one we have been stuck in front of for the past decades watching *Friends, Married . . . with Children, The Nanny, Who's the Boss, . . .* a whole bunch of American TV series (in France, we tend to go for a *bistrot* chair in Marseille against an ochre sponge-painted wall) for a *Plus belle la vie*[1] version of life that had us glued to [TV Channel M6]. Those were the '90s—okay, the very end of the '80s if you want to be picky, the decade we were led to believe would go on forever thanks to the miracle of reruns. The decade we spent with Joey Tribbiani, Tony Micelli, and a whole team of nice-enough dumboes who you guessed (if you were capable of going beyond the awkward clothing) had been working out at the gym.

So here we were, two sofas, two families face to face, sharing the same frame of mind: Stay put! You're in for a laugh! And laugh we did. The family on the screen had its ups and downs, but the Barbara Cartlandish script saw to the happy ending: the male housekeeper married his boss—a beanpole mother of two with padded shoulders who looked like Fernandel[2] *(Who's the Boss)*, while Fran in *The Nanny*, despite the big hair and smarties' attire, swept an almost–Richard Gere look-alike off his feet.

But I wondered, Hadn't this type of laughter kept us in the right place? On the sofa, precisely? For this laughter was a far cry from the burlesque, the type of laughter that moves everything around, the laughter you find in American movies, where the bums and the beggars can cause scaffolding to come crashing down on the heads of New York cops. In the movies, cities literally fell flat on their faces, it was all out in the open air—and so was the laughter—and if anything was going on inside—inside a gentlemen's club or a well-decorated apartment with a matching sofa—things still came happily apart. There was always something that needed moving, that could be broken. In the movies and in society: you could always get the sack because the burlesque forbade you to settle in, nice and cozy. That was what the movies were aiming at.

TV, on the other hand, was a whole different ball game: a few years later, it was in its best interest to sit us down comfortably on the sofa laughing our heads off. For television had confiscated laughter: it had literally recorded and analyzed it, had skillfully modified its texture and taken away its soul.

That's exactly what went through our minds when we were watching the reruns of the '90s, listening to the canned laughter. That's when it all started, I thought, when we first heard people laughing about almost nothing, when we were shown that it was possible to laugh about almost nothing, which means, in fact, that *anything* can make you laugh. Because nothing and anything are part and parcel. That was the message television was sending us.

But once more I pondered, How can I define this canned laughter? What is its nature? It's anonymous and ghostlike, a soulless laughter, one you can't see, a reflex beyond the screen, a laughter without any*body* laughing: canned the way a body is put in a box, that barges in with mathematical regularity. In short, a mechanism that is disconnected from the living, whatever Bergson has to say. The horror of canned laughter lies in the fact that it points toward the disappearance of the human body. A body has simply vanished.

Then suddenly: enough! The sofa, the family, the friends, no one could stand them anymore, television itself was fed up. It all happened in 2002. Something to do with September 11? Whatever: in 2002, the HBO series *The Wire* chucked the sofa of laughter out the window. Literally. The way you get rid of a politician or a sink. The old sofa got dumped in a Baltimore neighborhood. Not a green but a rundown area. It landed up outside. The city's drug dealers roam around it, occasionally take a seat (preferably cowboy-style) in one of the most conceptual series of all times. To summarize the plot in a nutshell: the series gives us a version of the American nightmare made in Baltimore; on the one hand, a gang of drug dealers (with all the coming and going such an activity implies) bound by a common language, and on the other, the city police, who place a wiretap, put the gang under surveillance in an effort to "break the code." . . .

And at the center of all five seasons: a sofa. Outside, in the open, signaling the end of it all: of the family, of its friends, of the laughter *made in television,* of love—a casualty. No one will ever be able to sit down again. The situation has changed. But maybe this means it's time to come back to the couch to lie down on it or to break down. It's up to you. C/C

BIOGRAPHY

Laurent Goumarre is an art critic and writes for *Artpress* magazine. He is the assistant director for the International Dance Biennial in Lyons, the artistic director for the Gennevilliers Theatre Festival, and a producer for France Culture radio.

NOTES

Translated from the French by France Jaigu.

1. Currently in its fifth season, *Plus belle la vie* is a successful French TV series programmed on France 3 channel. It opened in August 2004 and is set in Marseille.

2. Fernand Joseph Désiré Contadin (aka Fernandel) (1903–71) was a huge star of French cinema.

SPEAKER'S CORNER

LAURA SOKOLOWSKY

The First Center for Psychoanalytic Consultation

C/C THIS ESSAY DERIVES from my doctoral research on the policy implemented by Freud and his students during the Weimar Republic. As I discuss the first psychoanalytic institution in history, I refer to some passages in the *Écrits* in which Lacan comments on the teaching delivered by the International Psychoanalytic Association (IPA) Institutes.

In the *Écrits*, in "Psychoanalysis and Its Teaching," Lacan points out that "the teaching in these institutes is merely professional teaching and, as such, fails to demonstrate in its programs either a plan or an aim that goes beyond those of a dental school, which are no doubt praiseworthy" (2006, 382). The study of the Berlin Institute enables us to grasp, beyond its undeniably caustic side, the nature and the deep import of Lacan's criticism as well as the way the IPA proceeded to include psychoanalysis in medical discourse—something Freud dreaded so much. How, by what means, was this inclusion made possible, in spite of Freud and yet under his very eyes? In order to answer this question, we must go back to the origins of this institute and more precisely to the consultation center that served as its matrix and had opened its doors three years earlier.

WAR NEUROSES

As Freud specified in 1925, the First World War hardly had any impact on the International Psychoanalytic Association. The war even had the effect of increasing interest in psychoanalysis in Western countries and particularly Germany (*SE*, 20). The creation of a psychoanalytic institution was to continue the progressive impregnation of popular conscience that Freud had hoped for to be able to insert psychoanalysis into culture.

One must remember that during the war, some of Freud's students, trained as psychiatrists, had been mobilized. The posts they held in the Army not only enabled them to study war neuroses very closely but also to treat them according to a method that combined both the deciphering of dreams and cathartic hypnosis. Freud was not unaware of the fact that the enigma of the recurring traumatic dream was still to be elucidated and that one also lacked the benefit of hindsight regarding long-term therapeutic results. However, war neuroses could help to fight medical resistance to psychoanalysis by diffusing the main notions of the Freudian theory of neuroses. It was an opportunity not to be missed. If the Army resorted to analytic therapy, the representatives of official psychiatry could no longer condemn psychoanalysis, as they had done at the time of the German Psychiatric Association Congress in 1913.

In a tactical step, the Fifth Congress of Psychoanalysis, which was held in Hungary under the patronage of the Budapest City Hall at the end of September 1918, was purposely dedicated to war neuroses. Army medical officers had come all the way from Germany and Austria-Hungary. The increasing powerlessness of psychiatrists to deal with the continuous flow of soldiers traumatized in the course of duty accounted for this sudden interest. Indeed, this congress was held in the immediate aftermath of the failure of the offensive launched by the German Army on the Western front in July and August 1918.

In front of a uniformed audience, Freud delivered his speech about the new ways of analytical therapy. At the end of his speech, he put forward the idea of creating consultation centers run by psychoanalysts that would provide neurotic patients who could not finance their analysis with free treatment. In appealing to the responsibility of public authorities, Freud was of course aiming at the government representatives who were present in the room.

At the end of September 1918, psychoanalysts were ready to set up treatment centers in the Army. In October, pioneer Hungarian psychoanalyst Sándor Ferenczi was contacted by the chief medical officer of the Health Department of the Budapest Military Command. In the report he had just delivered to the War Ministry, the latter recommended that a psychoanalytic *ward* be opened in the capital. Ferenczi thought it preferable to start with a "smaller experimental ward for about thirty patients" (Ferenczi and Freud 1996, letter 761, October 8, 1918). He also considered asking a colleague to come and work there. Things were looking very good.

But the prospect of creating psychoanalytic services in the Army was brought to a premature end. Before any consultation centers ever saw the light of day, the Armistice was signed on November 11 and war neuroses stopped being topical. Freud complained about it to Ferenczi:

> Our analysis has actually also had trouble. No sooner does it begin to interest the world on account of the war neuroses than the war ends, and once we find a source that affords us monetary resources, it had to dry up immediately. (Ferenczi and Freud 1996, letter 772, November 17, 1918)

With the fall of the central empires, the prospect of relying on the support of states to prove the public usefulness of psychoanalysis changed. Freud quickly revised his position, thinking that the lack of public funding should not hinder the creation of psychoanalytic institutions.

From March 1919 onward, and for 103 days, the Béla Kun's Soviet Republic gave hope that Hungary might be the first country in which psychoanalysis would enjoy official approval. The State Health Insurance office had plans for the opening of a psychoanalytic dispensary for workers as well as a clinic that would have been run by Ferenczi. Medical students wanted to found a psychoanalytic association under his patronage. Freud wrote his text on the teaching of psychoanalysis at the university as an answer to the students' petition.

Could the influence of the Bolshevik Revolution play a part in the development of psychoanalysis in Hungary? This is what Ferenczi very optimistically wanted to believe. He thought that in the new era, the practice of medicine would be nationalized and that psychoanalysis would only be practiced in hospitals. Since Ferenczi was appointed to hold the first chair of psychoanalysis at Budapest University, the insertion of psychoanalysis into the university discourse can be dated back to this period. Faced with such an encouraging prospect, Freud nevertheless held back. According to him, psychoanalysis had to keep its independence at all costs. Besides, Freud did not set much hope on the Soviet Republic. Very quickly, one had to yield to the evidence that the events would not lead to state psychoanalysis. Back in August 1919 an unprecedented wave of reactionary and anti-Semitic terror swept through Hungary with Rear Admiral Miklós Horthy's takeover. A number of Hungarian psychoanalysts joined the group Karl Abraham had founded in Berlin.

These events in Hungary show that the creation of a consultation center depended on different factors. First, its insertion into society could suffer directly from a failing in democratic functioning. The possibility of setting up an institution could not be abstracted from the political context. Second, it was also a matter of people and contingencies. In the postwar period the psychoanalysts of the first generation were seized by the urgency to work on the "propagation of the psycho-analytic species" (Eitingon 1923, 266), to use the expression favored at the time. Without the existence of an analytic society sufficiently organized to give its members guarantees in their professional practice, and, above all, without the appropriate material means, such an institution could not see the light of day. These are the three conditions that were to converge in Berlin.

THE CREATION OF THE BERLIN POLICLINIC

On July 21, 1919, the psychiatrist and psychoanalyst Max Eitingon informed Freud of his decision to open a Policlinic in Berlin the following winter. To get up and running without waiting for aid from a state in the course of construction and practically ruined, a policlinic, "in its modesty and feasibility" (Eitingon and Freud 2009, July 21, 1919), would be the preliminary stage to the subsequent creation of a research institute for psychoanalysis, he wrote. A few days later, on July 31, the Constitution of Weimar established a parliamentary democracy in Germany.

Freud went to Berlin in September. He visited Karl Abraham. Max Eitingon introduced him to his parents. Eitingon's father, who was of Russian origin, was extremely well off. He had made his fortune in the fur trade and was a great patron of the Leipzig Jewish community, where he had had a synagogue and a hospital built. After the recent death of his younger brother, who had run the branch of the family business in New York, Max Eitingon wanted to prove to his father that he was also capable of enterprising. The creation of the policlinic would help him fend off the heavy shadow of his dead brother while enabling him to hold a managerial position and to become a patron too. After being assured that the elder son of the family would occupy an important position in the association, Eitingon's parents agreed to finance the Freudian movement without asking too many questions.

The policlinic for the psychoanalytic treatment of nervous diseases was inaugurated on February 14, 1920. The institution occupied the fourth floor of a rather modest building near the city center, in the area that now corresponds to the former East Berlin. The premises fitted out by Ernst Freud, Freud's youngest son, who was an architect, had five consulting rooms. The largest room was also used as a conference and reading room. The rooms were soundproof and the furniture was simple and functional: a wicker couch, a lamp, a table, and a few portraits on the wall. There were about forty chairs in the waiting room.

In autumn 1919, the first capital outlay fronted by Eitingon amounted to 20,000 marks, the approximate equivalent of 5,000 American dollars of the time. This budget covered wages, rental fees, as well as the upkeep of the building and the running costs. Instead of asking a large number of analysts for a short time of practice, Eitingon had opted for the opposite. The idea was to incite a small number of analysts to devote the maximum amount of time to the policlinic, regularly and daily, not on a voluntary basis but on a contractual one. He derived his idea from the notion of "real time." With this expression, he was referring to the duration of effort, the time necessary to achieve good work, the unremitting time spent on the organization of service provisions as well as the time devoted to the policlinic by psychoanalysts: "One thing was clear to us from the very beginning: one of the most important factors in analytic practice is the element of time—the strength of our position lies in being prepared for the length of the fight," he emphasized (Eitingon 1923, 255). One of the characteristics of this set-up was the great flexibility of the setting. The analysts could receive policlinic patients either on the institution premises or in their private consulting rooms. Furthermore, at the same period, training analyses were sometimes directed free of charge in private practices. The policlinic had the same policy, until Eitingon decided to put an end to it after a few years of operation.

In spring 1920, twenty or so analysts were seeing patients, but only three of them were on the full-time payroll. In spite of the help from the members of the Berlin Psychoanalytic Society, the patients' waiting list lengthened quickly. After two and a half years of activity, about six hundred patients had gone to the policlinic. Some had seen the doorplate in the street; others had come by word of mouth; others had been sent by their physicians. The advertisements in newspapers had also attracted people to the extent that it was decided to limit the ads for fear of overcrowding. In 1921, between fifty and sixty analyses were in progress.

To solve the problem of the management of the flow of patients, Eitingon deemed it necessary to wait for demand to regulate itself until it reduced, while remaining constant: "Making analysis possible for a larger number of people was by no means synonymous to our minds with carrying on 'mass-therapy'" (1923, 256), he explained. This assertion enabled him to justify that the alloy of suggestion and analysis was not used as a therapeutic method at the policlinic, contrary to what Freud had imagined in the different context of the Budapest Congress. The analysts of the policlinic rather relied on the effects of indirect suggestion, that is, on the phenomenon of the impregnation of society by word of mouth. Besides, the presence in the waiting room of a multitude of patients acquired a new signification insofar as in "the crowded waiting-room reality impresses upon the neurotic that he is not the only one to whom the physician is a Father" (264). Be that as it may, the analysts had noticed that the concentration of patients produced in itself beneficial effects. They got the idea that the transference was directed more to the institution than to the person of the analyst as such. This did not prevent them from considering that the analyst could be perceived by the patient as a representative of the paternal function from whom they hoped to curry favor. Not being alone in the waiting room thus assumed a particular significance; it thwarted the fantasy of being loved by the father.

In 1922 it was noticed that the patients who contacted the policlinic were often suffering from "chronic [and] inveterate neuroses, . . . long-standing organic illnesses and . . . psychogenic formations engrafted onto the remains of organic diseases" (Eitingon 1923, 258). An improvement of the symptoms could lead to the termination of the analysis. Treatments were often "fractionary" (266); patients would resume stretches of successive analyses. The therapeutic results were noted on a graduated scale that went from stationary state to recovery.

To begin with, the length of sessions at the policlinic had been set at half an hour, but [Eitingon] added that this length

> could be managed only in the case of a small class of persons who were still, in spite of their neuroses, amenable to discipline, cases such as are not seldom to be found in Prussian Germany among civil servants and others. Generally we give three quarters of an hour or the classical full hour. (1923, 263)

An hour was the period of time devoted daily by Freud to each of his patients. Patients went to the policlinic three or four times a week, sometimes more, depending on how serious the case was.

Did the desire for orthodoxy prevent the Berliners from limiting the length of the treatments? Eitingon explained that they had tried to change the time parameter, and he added that

> the question of speeding up or shortening the analysis has been our chief endeavour at the Policlinic and is a subject to which we devote constant attention; but so far on the whole without result, though we eagerly make use of every favourable factor. Psycho-analysis is simply that process to which Freud gave this name and which Freud created. Anything else is no true analysis and cannot be counted a success for it. (1923, 264)

A majority of treatments had lasted between three and six months. A few treatments had lasted between twelve and eighteen months. Most treatments had led to significant improvement.

In Berlin, the principle of free treatment was not exclusive. Patients could contribute financially according to their means. If they could not pay at all, their analysis was free. But other patients who could afford it could pay quite a lot for their sessions. In 1922 the payment of sessions represented about 10 percent of the total policlinic budget. To justify this choice Eitingon relied on a remark Freud had once made to him concerning the drawbacks of free treatment without adding any more details.

These arguments are most likely related to the arguments Freud had developed in his study on the beginning of the treatment, dating from 1913, and in which the question of the payment or nonpayment of fees had been discussed. In this study Freud had noted that patients had a tendency to deal with money matters and sexual questions alike. He would then advise his practitioners to broach either question without false shame and with as much frankness as was necessary. The patient had to be told that the analyst would charge him in proportion to the difficulty of his work; it was a way of signifying that his work was at least as indispensable and worthy as a surgeon's. Freud laid the stress on the high store the analyst set on his practice. For this reason Freud estimated that if the analyst gave two free treatments a week for a month, his loss of earnings could correspond to the effects of a traumatizing accident. That is why a patient could be refused free analytical treatment; the beneficial effects for him would not compensate for the sacrifice consented to by the analyst. Freud explained:

> I may venture to form a judgment about this, since for ten years or so I set aside one hour a day, and sometimes two, for gratuitous treatments, because I wanted, in order to find my way about in the neuroses, to work in the face of as little resistance as possible. The advantages I sought by this means were not forthcoming. (SE, 22)

On the contrary, the patients' resistances had been increased by free treatment. Women interpreted it as a sign of love; men got bogged down in the debt to the father figure. So Freud presented the payment for the session as a value liable to rectify certain transferential effects. According to this reasoning, free treatment would be an obstacle to the concluding of the treatment insofar as it would make the analytic situation all the more unreal.

In contradiction with this, we know that Freud gave free analytic treatment to some patients. It must also be noted that if he decided to do so it was not necessarily linked to his patients' financial means; for example, he directed Marianne Kris's treatment from 1931 to 1938 free of charge.[1] Yet she was under no financial difficulties. Marianne Kris later confided that Freud did not let her pay for her treatment because her father, Doctor Oscar Rie, had not asked the Freud family for any fees (Grayson 1972). According to her, Freud was acting out of pure courtesy. It must also be recalled that in the 1920s nonpaying and paying patients sat together in the policlinic waiting room as well as in private consulting rooms. In 1922 Eitingon mentioned that no difference could be noted at the policlinic between free and paying treatments in therapeutic results, without giving any further details.

In the preface he wrote in 1923 for the publication of the first activity report of the policlinic, Freud laid the stress on the treatment of the intellectual classes that had been impoverished by the postwar crisis. He no longer evoked, as he had in 1918, poor people given over to drinking, women who succumbed to the weight of their frustrations, and children who could only choose between depravation and neurosis. Although it might seem insignificant, this detail is not without its importance given Freud's very reserved opinion on the subject expressed before the war. In fact, Freud doubted that poor people could be cured of their symptoms by psychoanalysis. Intellectuals impoverished by the crisis definitely could. But Freud did not have much hope for the poor, the poor people who were born poor, the kind of poor people Wilhelm Reich visited in their slums. He reasserted it in one of the few interviews he agreed to give to the press in the early '30s in which he explained that it was not in the interest of the poor to recover because their symptoms have an autodefensive function that allows them better to put up with the difficult conditions of their existence.[2]

The social diversity of the types of patients taken on in the first phase—ranging from "factory-girls and domestic servants to a daughter of a general, a niece of the Chief Minister of State . . . and a very influential politician" (Eitingon 1923, 257)—had evolved over the first two years. Gradually a public consisting mainly of people from the lower middle class and the intelligentsia was substituted for the initial diversity. This might appear contradictory with the only criterion that had been retained, that of subjective urgency at the time of the consultation (with the added precaution of staying as often as possible within the framework of neurosis). In order to justify the progressive rarefaction of the most indigent patients at the policlinic, Eitingon specified that "we were not willing to embark on the task of improving the general condition of the nation while our numbers were still so small" (257).

In the end, for Eitingon a simple arithmetic truth accounted for this evolution. As there were very few analysts, treating masses of people was just impossible. At first sight it made sense: analysts do not have the mission of changing society. What they did was to offer treatment to people who requested it, which, we may note, does not exactly coincide with Freud's initial project to offer the means to access psychoanalytic treatment to the masses.

Not embarking on the task of improving the situation of the nation: Did this mean that analysts should stay away from politics and confine themselves to the field of therapy? In Berlin another way might have consisted in admitting the political dimension of the wish to make psychoanalysis accessible to everyone, in return for which the consequences had to be faced without resorting to the false argument that there were not enough analysts to change society.

AN ELUSIVE ALLOY BETWEEN ANALYSIS AND SUGGESTION

At the beginning the consultations were given by Drs. Eitingon and Ernst Simmel for one hour a day, except on Sundays. Wednesdays were devoted to training. The patients had to go through a medical examination. When the symptoms necessitated referring the patient to a physician or when there was some doubt as to the symptoms' psychical origin, a certain number of patients were reoriented to the medical service of the charity hospital. This meant that the policlinic consultation was to be entrusted to a medical team.

Very quickly however, Eitingon took charge of the consultations on his own on the grounds that it was "easily possible to make a survey of the whole material" (1923, 262). Are these reasons connected to the other analysts' lack of experience on the subject of diagnosis? That seems out of the question insofar as from the very beginning of the policlinic, important figures of the analytic movement had joined the Berlin group. Most likely, as Eitingon suggests, it was more of an administrative decision necessary to control the whole set-up. In fact this tendency only became more pronounced over the years. That is why at the policlinic the administrative organization progressively overrode the "purely democratic constitution of the medical Staff" (256).

At the treatment level, the pure gold of analysis was not alloyed to the copper of suggestion for the simple reason that it is hardly possible to find "metals suitable for any such alloy," Eitingon (1923, 264) said.[3] Had no convincing results in this direction ever been reached? Was Freud's prognosis about the use of a mixed method back in 1918 already obsolete? The assertion that it was hardly possible to modify the traditionally used analytical technique conveyed the influence of the medical model. It is true that ideally the quality of care dispensed in a public service should not be inferior to that offered in private practice. It was not so much a matter of inner necessities connected to the evolution of psychoanalysis as the respect for an implicit deontology that accounted for Eitingon's attachment to "true analysis" as opposed to mass therapy as Freud had conceived of it just four years before.

Somehow, surprisingly, the policlinic liked to think it was even more Freudian than Freud himself. Freud's purpose had been to treat a large number of people, to develop a popular therapy and apply analytic therapy on a mass scale, which meant adapting the technique according to this extension. But the board of the policlinic thought that it should not lead to a degradation of the method perfected by the creator of psychoanalysis: the principles of the standard treatment had to remain unchanged. For this reason Eitingon defended the orientation according to which the rule of free association was the only one to be used in Berlin. He made it clear that suggestion should not be employed.

The choice of the immutability of the technique could be summed up as follows: to remain true to itself, to be "genuine," psychoanalytical practice must not vary. No technical rule should be employed but that of free association insofar as no discrimination must be exerted on a poor patient. The right to psychoanalysis for all implied the respect of this implicit deontology. The problem was that the inventor of psychoanalysis had considered things differently. The invention of new therapeutic ways was not only desirable, it was inevitable: when dealing with cases other than hysterical neuroses, an evolution in technique is necessary, as Freud insisted in 1918.

Besides, it is not difficult to find examples of Freud's freedom with regard to technique in his practice. He could purposefully choose to refrain from using the fundamental rule in order to treat a symptom without going through the deciphering of the unconscious. Freud's treatment, in a few sessions, of the conductor Bruno Walter, who suffered from a paralyzed arm, reveals how Freud could make use of the strong transference he provoked. Of course, Eitingon could have replied that Freud's prestige was such that it was hardly possible to imitate him.

To justify the discrepancy between the operations of the policlinic and the Budapest program, Eitingon sheltered behind good will put off by experience: we did try to find a new alloy, we failed to find one, we have not changed anything. Such was, in substance, the argument he put forward to explain that the proposition that consisted in modifying the technique to adapt it to new forms of demand could not be applied on a large scale. By assuming the lack, and admitting he had failed to find the new alloy, Eitingon subtly distinguished himself from Freud's position without questioning his authority. "True" analysis was here defined by the orthodoxy of the technique.

Karl Abraham had been giving introductory lectures to psychoanalysis at the policlinic since 1920. Later on he was in charge of advanced students, with an average of about twenty to thirty students per class. Hanns Sachs, who was not a doctor and who had been sent for from Switzerland, was the first to occupy the function of training analyst. Sachs's lectures were about how psychoanalysis could be applied to human sciences and to the interpretation of dreams. Karen Horney and Ernst Simmel lectured on the psychoanalytic attitude of the medically trained practitioner. Simmel also gave a course on psychoanalytic technique. At this time, students had to have been analyzed to become analysts. Through Eitingon's voice, the Berliners would impose this clause on the rest of the analytic community at the 1925 Bad Hamburg Congress by defending the conception according to which didactic analysis had to be considered as an independent branch of psychoanalysis. Berlin was thus serving as the field of experimentation for the break between pure psychoanalysis and psychoanalysis applied to therapeutics among associations affiliated to the International Psychoanalytic Association. The institution that was to materialize the Budapest vision was also the place from which the standardization of training—criticized by Michael Balint, Siegfried Bernfeld, and above all Lacan—was elaborated.

The initial wish expressed by Karl Abraham, that one of the requisite conditions to the practice of psychoanalysis at the policlinic should be "sufficient neurological and psychiatric training," was not granted (Abraham and Freud 1966, June 26, 1920). Likewise, the first didactician from Berlin, Hanns Sachs, was not a doctor. Yet most of the training students were physicians. There were people from Austria, Hungary, the Netherlands, the United States, and the United Kingdom. Once their personal analyses were over, students could become members of the analytic society and start receiving policlinic patients. The passage to practice was duly controlled, and they only received cases deemed suitable for beginners. Sometimes Eitingon would take a patient away from a student to carry on the treatment himself. The spirit of discipline and the organization founded on the respect of hierarchy were already present in 1922. Eitingon put it bluntly: "With the growth of the Institute, the purely democratic constitution of the medical Staff had to be exchanged for a rather stricter organization. . . . The control is now in my hands. . ." (1923, 257).

THE MODEL OF THE UNIVERSITY DISCOURSE

In spite of its original character, the organization of the university education inspired the way psychoanalysis was to be taught at the training institute founded in 1923 with its years of compulsory courses, the selection of its candidates, as well as the establishment of strict instructions for their training. Eitingon himself called the organization of the analytic training he had got on its feet in Berlin "Prussian-style" regulation. The students, mainly physicians who wished to complete their analytic training, had to submit to a whole raft of drastic measures:

- The Teaching Committee of the Institute could admit or refuse a candidate irrevocably after three preliminary interviews.

- An at least six-month analysis was compulsory.
- The training analyst of the candidate was appointed by the committee.
- According to the opinion of the training analyst, the committee could decide whether the candidate had gone far enough in his or her analysis to participate in the stages of more advanced training.
- The same committee imposed supervision with an analyst who had to be different from the candidate's.
- The supervisor had the right to take the patient away from the candidate if the candidate were incompetent.
- Finally, the candidate had to promise in writing that he would wait for a favorable opinion before calling himself an analyst.

Back in the mid-1920s Berliners recruited medically trained candidates preferentially, against Freud's recommendations, who had to bring down the full weight of his authority to tip the scales in favor of preserving a space for the training of lay analysts. Of course Freud by no means despised his medial colleagues. On the contrary, psychiatrists who approached him to start an analysis had a special place for him. From a strategic point of view, the psychiatrists who practiced psychoanalysis could make use of their influence within the medical profession. The insertion of psychoanalysis into society could but benefit from their position. What Freud refused was the subjection of psychoanalysis to a science or a therapeutic method of healing. One must consider that in the mid-1920s he took up a fight for nonmedically trained analysts against the American branch of IPA; he went as far as threatening to leave the international association if he did not win in a case that was of crucial importance in his eyes. His influence on Eitingon was such that the latter had to limit, without doing away with it, the preference given to the training of medically trained candidates in Berlin.

The invention that was to allow for the extension of the field of application of psychoanalysis turned in fewer than ten years into a rigid set-up framed by a hierarchical organization. The setting-up of the regulation on didactic analysis constituted a real turning point insofar as it led to differentiate a didactic analysis from a therapy-oriented one. Berlin thus served as the experimental field for the break between pure psychoanalysis and psychoanalysis applied to therapeutics within IPA-affiliated associations. The teaching of psychoanalysis set up in the Berlin Institute organized the profession of psychoanalyst through a curriculum that gave access to it rather than through the constituting object of one's own experience.

c/c

BIOGRAPHY

Laura Sokolowsky is a practicing psychoanalyst, member of the École de la Cause Freudienne, and a clinical psychologist. She has a PhD in clinical psychopathology from Rennes II University.

NOTES

Translated from the French by Catherine Massol.

This paper was delivered at the Diva Seminar, Université populaire de psychanalyse Jacques-Lacan, on September 25, 2010. Many thanks to Jacques-Alain Miller for inviting me to speak.

1. Freud did not make Eva Rosenfeld and Bruno Goetz pay either, nor Serguï Pankejeff (the Wolf Man) during his second stretch of analysis.

2. "For poor people—it is very sad to say, and I hope my remark will not be interpreted as cynicism—for poor people . . . neuroses do not simply mean an illness, but also one of the elements of self-defence in the struggle for existence. Very often, when we treated them free of charge, we experienced the fact that poor people did not want to allow themselves to be freed of their suffering before a change in their material situation had come about" (Freud 1932).

3. In the original German text of the Budapest Lecture, Freud spoke of the copper *(Kupfer)* of direct suggestion, not the lead. In Europe, copper was the alloy that could be mixed with gold to form currencies up until the second half of the nineteenth century. Freud's metaphor was monetary and not alchemical.

BIBLIOGRAPHY

Abraham, Karl, and Sigmund Freud. 1966. *A Psychoanalytic Dialogue: The Letters of Sigmund Freud and Karl Abraham 1907–27*. New York: Basic Books.

Eitingon, Max. 1923. "Report of the Berlin Psycho-Analytical Policlinic (March 1920–June 1922)." *International Journal of Psycho-Analysis* 4: 254–69.

Eitingon, Max, and Sigmund Freud. 2009. *Sigmund Freud–Max Eitingon, Correspondence.* Paris: Hachette.

Ferenczi, Sándor, and Sigmund Freud. 1996. *The Correspondence of Sigmund Freud and Sándor Ferenczi,* Vol. 20: 1914–1919. Cambridge, Mass.: Harvard University Press.

Freud, Sigmund. 1932. "Neurosen als Zeitkrankheit. Welche Heilerfolge hat die Psychoanalyse?" *Neue Freie Press* 24397 (August 14).

———. 1953–74. *The Standard Edition of the Complete Psychological Works of Sigmund Freud* [*SE*]. 24 vols. London: Hogarth Press.

Grayson, Robert. 1972. "Unpublished interview with Dr Marianne Kris, Nov. 15, 1972." In *A. A. Brill Archives and Special Collections of the New York Psychoanalytical Society and Institute.*

Lacan, Jacques. 2006. "Psychoanalysis and Its Teaching." In *Écrits: The First Complete Edition in English,* 364–83. New York: Norton.

An Interview with Ethan Watters, Author of *Crazy Like Us*

C/C: *Culture/Clinic* is a journal of Lacanian psychoanalysis, so it may strike you as odd that we decided to interview you, since you attacked psychoanalysis in one of your previous works. However, there are different psychoanalytic traditions, and the ideas you are defending in *Crazy Like Us* are almost Lacanian. For example, your definition of the symptom as a response to social structures and your idea that symptoms bind people together are consonant with the principles of our practice. Could you elaborate on your conception of the symptom and its relation to the social bond? How did you form your opinion on these matters?

ETHAN WATTERS: It is nice of you to invite me even though I have indeed questioned various tenets of psychoanalysis (although now that my wife seems intent on becoming an analyst herself, I've declared a cease fire on the topic for the good of the children). As to how I formed my ideas: it was twenty years ago that I began writing about recovered memory therapy and the attendant rise of what was then called multiple personality disorder and is now called dissociative identity disorder (DID). The articles and books I wrote on that topic were a remarkable lesson in the idea that the therapist–patient relationship can amplify cultural beliefs of which the patient and the healer might only be vaguely aware. The therapy session is like a lightning rod for the electricity in the Zeitgeist. This observation parallels Edward Shorter's contention that patients are drawn to "symptom pools." The patients in a given time and place are prone to expressing their distress in a manner that corresponds to the cultural beliefs about the mind—beliefs that are in no small part formed by the mental health community. So there is something of a feedback loop by which therapy can often manifest in the symptoms and experiences of the patient the preconceived beliefs of the healers. With the lessons I learned from studying the recovered memory movement, I asked the obvious next questions: What other mental illnesses besides DID are to significant degrees shaped by cultural beliefs of mental health and healing? The brief answer, I believe, is, All of them. Then, if American beliefs are a globalizing force in this regard, to what extent are we homogenizing experiences of mental illness and health in other cultures around the world? Those are the questions I tried to tackle in *Crazy Like Us*.

C/C: The field known as that of "mental health" has always been the site of heated controversies: broadly speaking, and in distinct guises at different times, the proponents of the biomedical model oppose the supporters of the talking cure, itself articulated to a belief in psychical causality. In *Crazy Like Us* you adopted a perspective distinct from the biomedical model: your perspective is respectful of cultural singularities and subjective solutions. Can we ask you to elaborate on your position in this respect?

EW: My take is entirely practical. I believe that a study of the history of mental illness and a cross-cultural perspective on the subject prove conclusively that cultural beliefs about the mind shape the experience of those who suffer from mental illness. Another way to say this is that to understand any illness experience it is necessary to understand how our fungible cultural beliefs interact with our biology. There has been a trend to claim the "realness" of mental illnesses by pointing to biological markers (with the underlying argument that all "real" treatments and interventions will also be biologically based). This is reductionist thinking, which illustrates an insecurity on the part of the mental health professionals operating under the skeptical gaze of medical doctors. Culture, at the end of the day, is every bit as "real" as biology. Why is it that anorexia, to take an example, will be in the symptom pool for one generation of women and bypass the next? There is no way to understand this illness without comprehending its psychosomatic nature, its potential to spread by group contagion, its connection with modernity and societal change, and the myriad cultural cues and habits that put the disease in motion. Yes, there is biology at play, but such illnesses will never be understood or mitigated on that level alone.

What is remarkable to me is that every generation of mental health healers can clearly see how the tides and currents of culture affected the *previous* generations of practitioners and patients. At the same time you can find general agreement that such cultural influence is now safely in the past. It is very easy to see culture at play when one looks back at epidemics of hysterical leg paralysis and the like, but devilishly difficult to see in one's own time. We can become psychologically unhinged for many reasons, such as personal trauma, social upheaval, or a chemical imbalance in our brain. Whatever the cause, we invariably rely on cultural beliefs and stories to understand what is happening. Those stories, whether they tell of spirit possession or serotonin depletion, shape the experience of the illness in surprisingly dramatic and often counterintuitive ways. In the end, all current mental illnesses, including depression, PTSD, and even schizophrenia, are every bit as shaped and influenced by cultural beliefs and expectations as hysterical leg paralysis, or the vapors, or any other mental illness ever experienced in the history of human madness. Mental health providers don't need to get beyond or away from culture. They need to embrace it and understand it.

C/C: Your book is a strong political statement indicting the American approach to "mental health" outside its borders. In what could almost be considered a postcolonial intervention, you highlight, through four highly convincing case studies, the U.S.'s export of a discursive structure for the translation of subjective and cultural singularities into the terms of an apparently neutral, because scientific, discourse. On the basis of your observations, do you think it may be possible to draw broader conclusions on the research culture in academic circles? On the production of knowledge with a "scientific" status?

EW: Yes, I think whole libraries full of research have to be reevaluated given what is coming to light about how deeply culture shapes human psychology. I'm not the only one who believes this. There was a recent blockbuster paper in the journal *Behavioral and Brain Sciences* [Henrich, Heine, and Norenzayan, 2010] which calls into question fundamental research from the fields of cognitive, behavioral, and social psychology. The authors of the paper argued that the population of humans most often studied in these fields is just too "weird" a group to draw larger conclusions from. By "weird" they mean both unusual and Western, Educated, Industrialized, Rich, and Democratic. The evidence is now in, they contend, that "WEIRD societies" produce individuals with perceptions, behaviors, and motivations that are almost always sliding down one far end of the bell curve. Basically, these researchers suggest that psychologists have been doing the equivalent of studying penguins while believing that they were learning insights applicable to all birds. We are the penguins.

Many of these differences arise from the unusual way we in the West conceive of the human self. Westerners, particularly Americans, tend to view the human psyche as independent rather than interdependent. We think of ourselves in terms of our personality traits and attitudes while much of the rest of the world tends to think of themselves in terms of their roles and relationships within the group. That general difference has many psychological consequences that go very deep, including the findings that Americans are much more likely to have a positively skewed view of themselves, a heightened valuation of personal choice, and an increased motivation to stand out rather than fit in. This difference in self-conception influences the very way we reason. Unlike the vast majority of the world, we tend to reason analytically as opposed to holistically. Put another way, our American minds tend to separate out people and objects from the situation or context they exist in. We try to figure out the world by taking it apart and examining its component pieces. Minds more prone to holistic thinking keep the person or object within its given context and try to understand it through its relationship to the world around it.

We'll know little about what is universally human until we take our psychological tests across cultures. Of course that endeavor raises a whole raft of epistemological questions beginning with: Are the very questions we're asking relevant in other cultures?

C/C: Critics of the *DSM [Diagnostic and Statistical Manual of Mental Disorders]* are increasingly frequent these days, as with Edward Shorter's book *Before Prozac* (2008), for example. You reach similar conclusions to Shorter in underlining the responsibility of pharmaceutical companies for exporting symptoms that fit their medication. But there is more to your approach than the sheer denunciation of the excesses of a capitalist culture. You also argue for the importance of listening to the particularity of each symptom without fitting it into a ready-made, one-size-fits-all framework. Can you say more about this aspect of your reflection?

EW: Cultures not only have their own unique expressions of mental illnesses, but those illnesses are always tied to local modes of healing. So our interventions are often problematic on two levels: (1) we are exporting our expectations about symptomatology and (2) we are disconnecting that local population from indigenous modes of healing or finding solace. The most egregious example of this happens when Western trauma counselors rush into far off disaster zones on a few days' notice brandishing their PTSD checklists as if the local population would have no understanding of negative psychological reactions to tragic life events. One psychologist asked me to imagine the scenario reversed. What if, he asked, shamans from Africa flew to New York in the days after 9/11 and began knocking on the doors of the survivors to instruct them on the proper rituals to sever their connections from the dead? Would that make sense? Of course it would not, but we in the West seem to have no problem doing what is basically the reverse of this scenario. Again, we have failed to comprehend how our own culture has informed and shaped notions like PTSD. We in the West often think it is an enlightened notion to say that under the surface humans are fundamentally the same. Unfortunately, I think what we often mean when we say this is that under the surface, everyone must be like us. C/C

NOTE

Véronique Voruz conducted this interview for *Culture/Clinic*. Ethan Watters is the author of *Crazy Like Us: The Globalization of the American Psyche* (2010) and *Urban Tribes* (2004) and is the coauthor of *Making Monsters* (1995). A frequent contributor to the *New York Times Magazine, Discover, Men's Journal, Details, Wired,* and PRI's *This American Life*, he has appeared on CNN and such national programs as *Good Morning America* and *Talk of the Nation*. His work has been featured in the *Best American Science and Nature Writing* series.

BIBLIOGRAPHY

Henrich, Joseph, Steven J. Heine, and Ara Norenzayan. 2010. *Behavioral and Brain Sciences* 33 (2/3): 61–83.

Shorter, Edward. 2008. *Before Prozac: The Troubled History of Mood Disorders in Psychiatry*. New York: Oxford University Press.

Article Submission and Editorial Inquiries

Articles submitted to *Culture/Clinic* will be assessed using a double-blind peer review process; manuscripts should not be submitted for publication elsewhere while under review by *Culture/Clinic*. Please send electronic copies of completed articles (6,000–8,000 words) with endnotes and a bibliography as a .doc or .docx file by e-mail to veronique.voruz@le.ac.uk and mjaanus@barnard.edu. Direct requests foreformatting and style guidelines to veronique.voruz@le.ac.uk. You may send any inquiries to either editor via e-mail. Themes for forthcoming special issues will be announced on the *Culture/Clinic* webpage at http://www.upress.umn.edu/.